DATE DUE

MY 11 04			
MY 12 04			

Horror

THE GREENHAVEN PRESS COMPANION TO
Literary Movements and Genres

Horror

Michael Stuprich, *Book Editor*

Bonnie Szumski, *Editorial Director*

Scott Barbour, *Managing Editor*

David M. Haugen, *Series Editor*

Greenhaven Press, Inc., San Diego, CA

Every effort has been made to trace the owners of copy-righted material. The articles in this volume may have been edited for content, length, and/or reading level. The titles have been changed to enhance the editorial purpose. Those interested in locating the original source will find the complete citation on the first page of each article.

Library of Congress Cataloging-in-Publication Data

Horror / Michael Stuprich, book editor.
     p.   cm. — (The Greenhaven Press companion to literary movements and genres)
     Includes bibliographical references and index.
     ISBN 0-7377-0666-X (alk. paper) —
ISBN 0-7377-0667-8 (lib. bdg. : alk. paper)
     1. Horror tales, English—History and criticism.
     2. Horror tales, American—History and criticism.
     3. Gothic revival (Literature). 4. Grotesque in literature.
I. Stuprich, Michael. II. Series.

PR830.T3 H67   2001
823'.0873809—dc21   00-053573
                                        CIP

Cover photo: SuperStock
Hollywood Book and Poster, 22
Library of Congress, 107

Copyright © 2001 by Greenhaven Press, Inc.
PO Box 289009
San Diego, CA 92198-9009
Printed in the U.S.A.

CONTENTS

Chapter 1: Understanding Horror and Its Attractions

The oldest and strongest of human emotions is fear, especially fear of the unknown. When the unknown involves a sense of dark and malevolent powers operating somewhere beyond everyday human reality, it can generate a sense of "cosmic fear." This is the fear that the true weird tale generates.

As a genre, horror exists on three levels, each one defined by the emotion it aims to produce. The highest level aims for terror, the finest emotion; the second level aims for horror, more of a visceral response; and the third level aims for revulsion and disgust. The horror tale is by its very nature symbolic, and this capacity for symbolism—which allows for the expression of normally forbidden emotions—helps explain horror's appeal.

The paradox of horror lies in the fact that people obviously enjoy the negative emotions horror creates, emotions that they would avoid in "real" life. What people find pleasurable about horror is the confrontation with horrific beings—monsters—that defy normal cultural categories. The disclosure of such unknown and impossible beings calls for processes of proof, discovery, and confirmation that provide naturally curious human beings with cognitive pleasures.

The postmodern period in horror films began during the social unrest of the 1960s. The postmodern horror film exhibits five characteristics that operate together to define it: 1) the everyday world is violently disrupted; 2) boundaries are transgressed and violated; 3) the validity of rationality is questioned; 4) narrative closure is repudiated; and 5) a bounded experience of fear is produced. Horror literature often operates in a similar fashion.

Chapter 2: The Gothic and the Grotesque

nalize and psychologize the Gothic, thus proving his contention that "terror is not of Germany but of the soul."

Chapter 3: Three Classic Horror Novels

but not because he is monstrous; rather, he is monstrous because he is kept repressed.

Chapter 4: Modern Masters of Horror

FOREWORD

The study of literature most often involves focusing on an individual work and uncovering its themes, stylistic conventions, and historical relevance. It is also enlightening to examine multiple works by a single author, identifying similarities and differences among texts and tracing the author's development as an artist.

While the study of individual works and authors is instructive, however, examining groups of authors who shared certain cultural or historical experiences adds a further richness to the study of literature. By focusing on literary movements and genres, readers gain a greater appreciation of influence of historical events and social circumstances on the development of particular literary forms and themes. For example, in the early twentieth century, rapid technological and industrial advances, mass urban migration, World War I, and other events contributed to the emergence of a movement known as American modernism. The dramatic social changes, and the uncertainty they created, were reflected in an increased use of free verse in poetry, the stream-of-consciousness technique in fiction, and a general sense of historical discontinuity and crisis of faith in most of the literature of the era. By focusing on these commonalities, readers attain a more comprehensive picture of the complex interplay of social, economic, political, aesthetic, and philosophical forces and ideas that create the tenor of any era. In the nineteenth-century American romanticism movement, for example, authors shared many ideas concerning the preeminence of the self-reliant individual, the infusion of nature with spiritual significance, and the potential of persons to achieve transcendence via communion with nature. However, despite their commonalities, American romantics often differed significantly in their thematic and stylistic approaches. Walt Whitman celebrated the communal nature of America's open democratic society, while Ralph Waldo

Emerson expressed the need for individuals to pursue their own fulfillment regardless of their fellow citizens. Herman Melville wrote novels in a largely naturalistic style whereas Nathaniel Hawthorne's novels were gothic and allegorical.

Another valuable reason to investigate literary movements and genres lies in their potential to clarify the process of literary evolution. By examining groups of authors, literary trends across time become evident. The reader learns, for instance, how English romanticism was transformed as it crossed the Atlantic to America. The poetry of Lord Byron, William Wordsworth, and John Keats celebrated the restorative potential of rural scenes. The American romantics, writing later in the century, shared their English counterparts' faith in nature; but American authors were more likely to present an ambiguous view of nature as a source of liberation as well as the dwelling place of personal demons. The whale in Melville's *Moby-Dick* and the forests in Hawthorne's novels and stories bear little resemblance to the benign pastoral scenes in Wordsworth's lyric poems.

Each volume in Greenhaven Press's Companions to Literary Movements and Genres series begins with an introductory essay that places the topic in a historical and literary context. The essays that follow are carefully chosen and edited for ease of comprehension. These essays are arranged into clearly defined chapters that are outlined in a concise annotated table of contents. Finally, a thorough chronology maps out crucial literary milestones of the movement or genre as well as significant social and historical events. Readers will benefit from the structure and coherence that these features lend to material that is often challenging. With Greenhaven's Literary Movements and Genres in hand, readers will be better able to comprehend and appreciate the major literary works and their impact on society.

INTRODUCTION: THE ART OF HORROR

The subject of this collection is horror. Or, more specifically, horror art: works of the imagination that have been purposefully designed to evoke fearful responses. The focus here will be primarily on horror literature, and especially on horror fiction produced in England and the United States since the eighteenth century. But horror has never been respectful of boundaries—generic or otherwise—and any discussion of horror literature must open itself to other media as well, especially film, which from its very beginning recognized and embraced horror's cinematic potential, and the popular theater, which played an early, vital role in bringing many of horror fiction's best-known works, including *Frankenstein, Dr. Jekyll and Mr. Hyde,* and *Dracula,* to the public's attention. In fact, when television, radio, comic books, and board, video, and role-playing games are also thrown into the mix, it becomes clear that horror simply cannot be explained in purely literary terms, as, that is, a form of pleasure unique to literature. Horror undeniably has its pleasures—what one scholar calls its "dreadful" pleasures. How else can horror's widespread and enduring popularity be explained? But what are those pleasures? And how can they best be understood?

FEAR AND THE HORROR STORY

As a way of answering these questions, it might be best to begin with a relatively simple proposition: Horror art is ultimately defined not in terms of any particular form or content, but by the emotion it produces—and that emotion is fear.

Although horror art can certainly have its cognitive pleasures—*Frankenstein,* for instance, is on several levels a very thoughtful novel—the unique and identifying pleasure it offers is fearful pleasure. Humans, quite simply, enjoy being frightened, and so long as the thrills offered by any particular example of horror art are more or less "safe" thrills, it will likely find an audience.

As any competent horror artist understands, however, producing fear in a truly effective, "artful" fashion is a good deal more difficult than these general observations may suggest. For one thing, there are both different kinds and different degrees of fear, and the horror artist must recognize that between a simple gasp of shock and the more refined fearful emotions lies an enormous psychological space. A child in a Halloween mask can produce the first, but a truly hair-raising experience (horror comes from the Latin word *horrere*, meaning "to bristle") requires a great deal more than a timely "boo." What it requires is a story . . . a horror story.

EVOLUTION OF THE HORROR STORY

Horror art has always depended on stories: some event or sequence of events involving characters. Plays, films, computer games, and certainly long and short fiction—all are predicated in some way on stories, and even the frightful Stone Age images found on the walls of European caves generally suggest a story. Why? Because the production of fearful responses requires a certain emotional/psychological "commitment" from the reader/viewer. To experience fear in any genuine (if "artificial") sense, the reader/viewer must, to some extent, choose to believe—or, as the English poet Samuel Taylor Coleridge put it, choose not to disbelieve. Stories construct an imaginative vehicle—a fiction—through which this belief (or Coleridge's famous "suspension of disbelief") can be made possible.

Taken within this context, the issue of belief is theoretically complex, but on a simpler level it remains clear that a reader of a horror novel, for example, can become caught up in the text to a striking degree without ever coming to accept the fictional text as literally true. What catches the reader's imagination and makes possible the fearful pleasures of horror art is the novel's story—or, more precisely, the story's power to compel the reader to share the fear it generates. This can be a function of what is popularly known as identification, such as when the reader imagines himself or herself as the next victim of the novel's madman or monster. Or it may be that fear, even fictional fear, is somehow contagious. In any case, experience suggests that genuine fear is seldom produced in the abstract, in a vacuum. What the horror story does is to make fear effective by making it concrete. The horror story gives fear a face.

Understanding the fundamental relationship between horror art and the horror story establishes solid ground for

general discussion. A useful next step is to consider in more
specific terms how horror stories work—how they go about
evoking fearful responses.

Theories abound, of course, all concerned with locating
and explaining the common denominators of horror art,
such as recurring themes, character types, and narrative situations: what might be called a horror artist's basic tool kit.
Horror has certainly always identified and exploited the
deepest and most abiding of human fears, fears that many if
not all human beings share: the fear of entrapment or en-
tombment, for example, so common in the works of Edgar
Allan Poe; or the fear of losing one's sense of self or personal
identity, perhaps through insanity, or through being transformed into something totally alien and other, a common
experience in stories of vampires and werewolves, who typically transform their victims into monsters like themselves;
or what are possibly the most common fears of all, the fear
of death and the fear of the unknown.

These are not, strictly speaking, themes. They are instead
what horror novelist Stephen King calls "phobic pressure
points"—sensitive areas in the human psyche where "pressure," properly applied, can produce the fearful responses
elicited by horror art.

More particularly, however, what most horror stories
seem to share is a fascination with transgression. In manifold
ways, horror stories almost always travel beyond the limits of
everyday social and psychological reality, in the process challenging the basic perceptual models most human beings depend on to make sense out of their experiences.

Horror stories often begin in "normal" situations, but they
soon introduce forces of discontinuity and disintegration
that work to invert the normal. Horror stories typically go to
extremes; they delight in recounting acts of violence and violation, in breaking established rules, and in entering the
world of the forbidden, the taboo. In doing so, they tend to
blur, reconfigure, sometimes even erase those psychological
and cultural boundaries that separate—and thereby work to
define and protect—the all-important categories of self and
other, male and female, human and animal, sanity and madness, the real and the imagined, the living and the dead.

The fear evoked within such transgressive contexts often
moves beyond the purely visceral, taking on intellectual,
even metaphysical dimensions. Fundamental questions are

raised. Doubts creep in and linger. Does the vampire's "kiss" destroy or create? Is the werewolf a man who becomes a wolf or a wolf that becomes a man? Do demons really exist, and if they do, is their existence proof of angels? At this advanced level in horror art, the transgressive can easily become the subversive: When the initially normal world of the horror story is inverted, turned upside down or inside out, new perspectives are created that allow for a radical questioning of the way things are. Social and moral "givens" can appear in a new light, more open than usual to critical examination. Most horror stories do end conservatively, with social and especially moral order restored, but between the first word and the last exists an imaginatively rich space within which the fearful pleasures of horror can be enjoyed.

THE BEGINNINGS OF MODERN HORROR

The 1764 publication of Horace Walpole's *The Castle of Otranto: A Gothic Story*—the first Gothic novel—provides a convenient date for the birth of modern horror. Before 1764 horror had manifested itself in an extraordinary variety of forms, ranging from the monstrous elements in the epic of Gilgamesh, Western culture's earliest recorded story, and Homer's seventh-century B.C. *Odyssey,* to the gruesome events in Greek and Roman tragedy, to the spectacularly bloody scenes of torture, murder, and mayhem in the revenge tragedies of William Shakespeare's day. Such evidence suggests that the human delight in horror is essentially timeless and universal. Practically every human culture, in every historical era, has displayed some interest in horror, and that interest has been expressed in its art. But horror art is in many ways a distinctly modern phenomenon, created by many of the same forces that shaped modern culture. Following the great popularity of *Otranto,* horror art quickly became a thriving industry, and by the end of the nineteenth century horror's principal icons—the vampire, the Frankenstein creature, the werewolf, and the mad scientist—had been set firmly in place, ready to fuel the explosion of horror art in the twentieth century.

The story of modern horror's explosive success can probably be best understood in economic and technological terms—in terms of horror as a business. The emergence of the novel in the early eighteenth century, for example, doubtless provided horror with a powerful medium of expression, but it was only in the mid–nineteenth century, with improvements in printing technology and the discovery of much cheaper ways to produce paper, that horror literature could become a mass-market enterprise. And, of course, in the case of twentieth-century horror art, the single-most important event was not artistic but technological: the invention of the movie camera.

GOTHIC AND THE GOTHIC NOVEL

The importance of the Gothic novel to the evolution of modern horror art cannot be overestimated. Some scholars have even argued, in fact, that Gothic, considered as a certain set of attitudes rather than as a genre, was the creative force that shaped and defined modern horror—that the terms *Gothic* and *horror* should be seen as essentially synonymous. That may be putting it too strongly, but certainly the first two generations of Gothic novelists provided English literature with a basic blueprint for horror that for over two centuries proved to be enormously influential. Any story featuring gloomy castles, graveyards, haunted houses, or darkly menacing, aristocratic villains can be said to have Gothic antecedents, and that includes a great many of horror art's best-known works, from *Frankenstein* and *Dracula* to television's Gothic soap opera *Dark Shadows*.

Although Walpole more or less invented the Gothic novel, by 1764 the Gothic phenomenon was well underway in England and was finding expression not only in art and literature but in architecture as well. Wealthy English landowners of the period even had new Gothic "ruins" constructed on their property when an interest in all things Gothic was at its height. From a modern perspective, Gothic might seem little more than a popular eighteenth-century fad, more a case of style than substance, but it was much more than that. Gothic did involve a kind of hazily defined yearning for the past (in architectural terminology, *Gothic* suggests the medieval), but more importantly it involved a celebration of imagination over reason and, more important still, of feeling over thought. Gothic, in fact, can be seen as the first clearly defined literature of feeling, a literature in which the engagement and elevation of the reader's emotions came to be an end in itself. Since Gothic typically aimed to produce emotions of fear, dread, awe, and a kind of deeply reflective spiritual anxiety, calling Gothic literature the first literature of horror hardly seems unreasonable. Early Gothic novelists like Walpole, Ann Radcliffe, and Matthew Lewis marked out an imaginative terrain that future writers—writers whose primary intention was to horrify their readers—could productively work.

In the decades following the publication of *Otranto*, in novel after novel, some good, some bad, a recognizable and highly influential Gothic formula was hammered out in English literature. Typically, according to the demands of this formula, the story's action is located in the past, often in some European country rather than in England. Characters are portrayed more as types than as individuals: the virtuous young heroines, for example, together with the sensitive young heroes who are their spiritual counterparts; the weak, ineffectual paternal figures; and the brutal churchmen and nobles who threaten one and all in the name of autocratic power. Certain plot patterns and themes recur, frequently involving issues of family and marriage complicated by dark secrets from the past and hinting at forbidden sexual longings. And, of course, there are the many Gothic "accessories," the ghosts, tombs, secret passageways, and hidden chambers that work to create the proper Gothic atmosphere. Thus defined, writes David Punter, "'Gothic' fiction is the fiction of the haunted castle, of heroines preyed on by unspeakable terrors, of the blackly lowering villains, of ghosts, vampires, monsters and werewolves."[1]

The 1790s saw the heyday of the Gothic novel and the publication of the two most famous entries in the genre: Ann Radcliffe's *The Mysteries of Udolpho* (1794), probably the single-most popular and influential of all Gothic novels, and Matthew G. Lewis's *The Monk* (1796), a wild, violent, and overtly horrifying work featuring demons, murders, torture, seductions, rape, and incest. The undeniably great, two-prong influence of both writers on the next generation of Gothic novelists has been characterized by some scholars in terms of gender: a case of "male" vs. "female" Gothic. But the distinction, at least in its simplistic form, may be misleading. Both works, although through admittedly different strategies and for different purposes, are nonetheless alike in privileging subjectivity—feeling—in ways that would have struck many eighteenth-century readers as markedly feminine.

Gothic and Romanticism

Because many of the same factors—cultural and artistic—that made the Gothic novel possible also contributed to the rise of Romanticism, it is hardly surprising to find Gothic elements in the works of all of the major Romantic poets. What may be surprising, however, is the degree to which these poets were fascinated by such horrific figures from myth and legend as the lamia and the Wandering Jew, and especially by the key figure in horror literature since the nineteenth century: the vampire. Vampiric characters, male and female, can be found in any number of major Romantic poems, beginning with Coleridge's "Christabel" (1798) and including Byron's "The Giaour" (1816), Shelley's closet drama *The Cenci* (1818), and Keats's "La Belle Dame sans Merci" (1819).

Although from a Romantic perspective vampirism may have seemed a convenient metaphor for the exchange of energy in human and artistic relationships, it was no doubt the vampire's transgressive nature that appealed to the notorious Lord Byron, whose typical "Byronic Hero" is a proud, demonic outcast who shares "with the vampire a love of darkness, hypnotic eyes, an obsession with the destructive side of love, sneering smiles, and quivering lips."[2] Byron's most famous protagonist, Count Manfred, actually imagines himself drinking blood at one point, and Byron himself served as the model for Lord Ruthven, the title character in English literature's first vampire story, John Polidori's "The Vampyre" (1819), and was a key influence in the creation of the most famous vampire of all, Count Dracula.

Later Gothic Influences

By 1818, the date of Jane Austen's posthumously published satire of Gothic fiction, *Northanger Abbey*, what some contemporary critics derisively called "the Gothic craze" had essentially run its course, although Mary Shelley's celebrated *Frankenstein* appeared in the same year and was followed in 1820 by Charles Maturin's classic treatment of the Wandering Jew legend, *Melmoth the Wanderer*. The Gothic impulse, however, though subsided, continued to influence novelists through the middle of the nineteenth century, especially the Brontë sisters, who advanced the tradition as far as possible toward the realm of the genuinely tragic. Anne's *The Tenant of Wildfell Hall* (1848) can hardly be understood outside the Gothic tradition while Emily's *Wuthering Heights* and Charlotte's *Jane Eyre* (both 1847), dominated by their dark, brooding hero-villains Heathcliffe and Rochester, and telling stories of secrecy, madness, and obsession, can lay legitimate claim to being the greatest of all Gothic fictions.

Gothic influences are also evident in some of the best-known novels of the second half of the nineteenth century, from George Eliot's *Silas Marner* (1861) to Oscar Wilde's *The Portrait of Dorian Gray* (1891), as well as in the "sensation novels" of the 1860s, which included Wilkie Collins's *The Moonstone* (1868), part Gothic thriller, part detective novel. But about the same time Gothic also went "underground," inspiring a series of sensationalistic, lurid, and much more purposefully horrifying works sold on the streets in weekly and biweekly installments, usually for a penny per installment, and thus known as Penny Dreadfuls. Aimed primarily at lower-class readers and marketed under such titles as *Wagner, the Wehr-Wolf* and *Sawny Bean, the Man Eater of Midlothian*, the authors specializing in the Penny Dreadful made no pretense at literary excellence. Their goal, clear and simple, was to sell as many copies as possible. The result, in nearly every case, was the literary equivalent of junk food. But in terms of modern horror, their work had the important function of acting as a conduit through which many of the figures of horror traveled on their way to twentieth-century incarnations. This was especially the case for the vampire: Thomas Rymer's immensely popular *Varney the Vampire; or The Feast of Blood*, published serially in the 1840s and later collected in novel form, helped establish the vampire and his myth in the public imagination; and the character of Varney—like Polidori's Lord Ruthven, a mysterious and ruthless aristocrat—served Bram Stoker as one of the models for Count Dracula.

AMERICAN GOTHIC

If the impact of Gothic literature in England was great, in nineteenth-century America it can only be termed staggering, profoundly influencing the work of four of the century's most outstanding writers: Edgar Allan Poe, Nathaniel Hawthorne, Herman Melville, and Henry James. In fact, the American literary imagination seems always to have had a distinctly Gothic cast, and as a consequence American literature has always been, in the words of critic Leslie Fiedler, "bewilderingly and embarrassingly, a gothic fiction, nonrealistic and negative, sadistic and melodramatic—a literature of darkness and the grotesque . . . a literature of horror."[5] However radical Fiedler's words may sound, the evidence seems to bear him out—at least in part. Poe's reputation has had its ups and downs over the years, but there can be no doubt that many of his tales of psychological terror—"The Tell-Tale Heart," for example, and "The Black Cat"—are among the monuments of American literature, as are Hawthorne's *The Scarlet Letter* and *The House of the Seven Gables*, both of them Gothic, in various ways, but most noticeably in their shared concern with the suffering occasioned in the present by past transgressions. The Gothic influences in Melville's *Moby Dick*, one of the greatest of all American novels, are also clear, particularly Captain Ahab's darkly obsessive, "haunted" quest for the white whale, suggesting an earlier incarnation as a villain in one of Radcliffe's novels, and the Pequod, Ahab's ship, serving, symbolically at least, as a stand-in for the traditional Gothic castle. James's *The Turn of the Screw* (1897), arguably the finest ghost story ever written, contains so many traditional Gothic elements (though often transformed by typically Jamesian irony) that it is difficult not to label it a Gothic novel.

Gothic influences on American literature extended as well into the twentieth century, in the works, among others, of H.P. Lovecraft, Flannery O'Connor, Joyce Carol Oates, and, interestingly, William Faulkner, whose genuinely Gothic story "A Rose for Emily" is often included in anthologies of Gothic and horror literature.

From these examples, what American Gothic seems to have in common with its English counterpart is an interest in the past that can border on the pathological, an interest complicated in the American strain by the fact that America itself has a relatively limited past to draw on and not a single medieval castle to serve as a source of Gothic inspiration. They differ, however, in exactly what the past evokes, in how its psychological/emotional effects are figured. When the English Gothic looks to the past, the effect more often than not is one of a general, atmospheric awe, potentially but not necessarily sinister; when the American Gothic—deeply connected to a heritage of Puritanism and its doctrine of innate depravity—looks to the past, the effect is one of darkness, gloom, and guilt. In English Gothic the past *is* past; it's dead, recoverable only in a limited sense and only temporarily. In

American Gothic, to paraphrase William Faulkner, the past isn't dead; it isn't even past.

TWENTIETH-CENTURY HORROR

The immediate roots of twentieth-century horror can be found in late Victorian England. There, in the brief span of some thirteen years, appeared a collection of works that, with the help of Hollywood several decades later, charted the direction of horror throughout the following century. These include R.L. Stevenson's *The Strange Case of Dr. Jekyll and Mr. Hyde* (1886), Oscar Wilde's *The Picture of Dorian Gray* (1891), H.G. Wells's *The Island of Dr. Moreau* (1896), and Bram Stoker's *Dracula* (1897). The latter, in terms of modern horror, is probably the most influential novel ever written. *Dracula* fixed the myth and image of the vampire so thoroughly in the public imagination that no writer of vampire fiction since has been able to entirely evade its influence. *Jekyll and Hyde* is a classic treatment of the "transformation beast" (of which the werewolf is another incarnation) as well as a distinctly modern view of humankind's potentially tragic dual nature. *Dorian Gray* explores the theme of the *dopplegänger* (the double), and *Dr. Moreau* is an updating of the mad-scientist theme originated in *Frankenstein.*

In England the first decades of the twentieth century also comprised the golden age of the ghost story. M.R. James and Walter de la Mare are among the best-known names from this period, but the list of writers who tried their hand at this popular genre is long and includes H.G. Wells, Henry James, and Algernon Blackwood. Outstanding examples of the genre include W.W. Jacobs's "The Monkey's Paw" (1902), M.R. James's "Oh, Whistle, and I'll Come to You, My Lad" (1904), and Oliver Onions's "The Beckoning Fair One" (1911).

The major figure in American horror in the first part of the century was H.P. Lovecraft, although, ironically, up until the time of his death in 1937 he was virtually unknown. During the 1920s and 1930s, Lovecraft published a handful of "cosmic" horror stories (based on what came to be known as "the Cthulhu Mythos") in the popular horror magazine *Weird Tales.* By nature shy and reclusive, Lovecraft wrote literally thousands of letters during his lifetime, in the process creating many long-distance friendships, particularly with young admirers of his work. In the years after his death, a number of his former correspondents, now calling themselves "the

Lovecraft circle," were involved in founding Arkham House, a press devoted to publishing Lovecraft's work in collected form. In this way, during the 1940s and 1950s, Lovecraft's work was introduced to the general public and came to influence a new generation of horror writers, among them, by their own admission, Richard Matheson, Ray Bradbury, Robert Bloch, and Stephen King.

The story of horror in America from the 1930s through the 1950s can only be told through the perspective of Hollywood, the Universal Studios horror films of

Boris Karloff as the monster in Frankenstein

the 1930s in particular. Here, in film after popular, money-making film, a pantheon of horror icons—"Hollywood monsters" in the popular imagination—was established that quickly became part of the shared cultural experience and forever changed the way the public looked at horror. The "classic" horror films appeared from 1930 until 1940 and included *Dracula* (1931), *Frankenstein* (1931), *The Island of Lost Souls* (1931), *The Invisible Man* (1933), *Bride of Frankenstein* (1935), and *The Wolfman* (1940). The 1940s brought World War II, and with it came an altogether different set of horrors. As a result, the horror film dipped in popularity, only to be revived in the 1950s, under the pressure of Cold War anxieties, in films such as *The Thing* (1951) and *Invasion of the Body Snatchers* (1956), which combined elements of horror and science fiction in frightening packages. Two more important revivals should be noted: the films produced by England's Hammer studios during the late 1950s and early 1960s, including colorful—and intentionally sexy—remakes of *Frankenstein, Dracula,* and *The Wolfman*; and the low-budget but popular Roger Corman films of the early 1960s based on several classic Edgar Allan Poe stories, among them *The Fall of the House of Usher* (1960) and *The Pit and the Pendulum* (1961).

The question of the influence of film horror on literary horror during the twentieth century is enormously complex and certainly beyond the scope of this brief introduction. Still, it is interesting to note that in the mid-1960s, after three-plus decades of being saturated by the images of celluloid horror, the reading public suddenly rediscovered the pleasures of horror literature. During this decade a new phenomenon (some might say a new monster) appeared: the mass-market horror best-seller. Beginning with *Rosemary's Baby* in 1967, a string of hugely popular horror novels appeared, each going quickly from hardcover to paperback and selling millions of copies in the process. The high points in this phenomenon include Fred Mustard Stewart's *The Mephisto Waltz* (1969), Thomas Tryon's *The Other* (1971), William Peter Blatty's *The Exorcist* (1971), Ira Levin's *The Stepford Wives* (1972), Stephen King's *Carrie* (1973) and *Salem's Lot* (1975), and Anne Rice's *Interview with the Vampire* (1976). Significantly, each novel—with the exception of Rice's *Interview*—was made into a popular film within three years. (Rice's novel, with its obvious homoeroticism, had to wait nearly twenty years to be filmed.) What exactly this frantic intermingling of genres—film and literature—produced remains problematic, but certainly among its effects was a rapid increase in the proliferation—and evolution—of the mass-market horror novel. The immediate and enormous popularity of *The Exorcist*—with its shockingly transgressive suggestions of rape, incest, and pedophilia—was probably the watershed event in this regard. At any rate, by the late 1970s hundreds of horror novels were being published each year, and a greatly increased emphasis on graphic sex and violence had become the norm rather the exception. With the arrival on the horror scene of Clive Barker in the early 1980s—both in film and fiction—the transgressive limits of horror were explored as never before, in the *Hellraiser* films, for example, and especially in the *Books of Blood* series. Here, in stories featuring acts of rape, torture, dismemberment, cannibalism, and necrophilia, Barker created a chaotic world in which identity is terrifyingly fluid and uncertain and the time-honored oppositions of good and evil, pleasure and pain, and life and death are juggled with a certain undeniable glee.

It might be tempting to see in the late twentieth century's suddenly increased fascination with sex, gore, and violence a moment of disjuncture, a break with the past—the advent, perhaps, of postmodern horror. But when viewed within the context of historical development and evolution, it is clear that the change signaled here is merely one of degree. Horror literature has always been a literature of extremes—has always located itself just on the edge of things, ready at any moment to cross over—and whenever one human boundary is crossed, another tends to appear just beyond it.

THE ATTRACTION OF HORROR

Because horror literature involves crossing boundaries into fearful domains, an obvious question arises: Why do people enjoy works that are intended to evoke painful, negative emotions? To attempt an answer to this question, it might be helpful to consider briefly two celebrated, highly influential theories that contend with the human desire to experience the horrifying.

ARISTOTLE AND THE THEORY OF CATHARSIS

The first theory was provided by the Greek philosopher Aristotle in a fourth-century B.C. treatise known as *The Poetics*. Aristotle wondered why his fellow Greeks so obviously enjoyed the spectacle of dramatic tragedy, a genre that typically depicts human anguish and suffering and that so often ends in the deaths of its main characters. Aristotle's solution to the "problem" (or paradox) of tragedy remains a cornerstone of classical literary theory. He concluded that tragedy, through the representation on stage of painful events, first arouses in its audience the negative emotions of fear and pity and then allows for the expulsion or purgation of those emotions. This purgation of fear and pity, tragedy's ultimate purpose, Aristotle called catharsis, and for Aristotle, catharsis was pleasurable largely because it was therapeutic, resulting in a kind of emotional cleansing. (The term *catharsis* appears far more often in Greek medical writings than anywhere else.)

Essential to an application of Aristotle's catharsis theory to horror art is the concept of aesthetic distance. This concept suggests that an audience is able to "enjoy" the painful experiences of tragedy because it can recognize that those experiences are aesthetic—the product of art—and not "real." The degree to which an audience's negative emotions can be manipulated is largely a function of distance, a metaphor meant to explain how aesthetic experiences can be made to appear more or less real. An audience greatly "distanced" from an aesthetic experience—the events depicted in a poorly made horror film, for example—is too aware that the experience is artificial and is thus too emotionally detached from the experience to be moved by it. (As Stephen King delightfully puts it, when the audience can spot the zipper on the monster suit, the question of genuine horror is pretty much out the window.) As a general rule, horror art seeks to shrink aesthetic distance, bringing its audience imaginatively closer to the experience and thus facilitating the production of negative emotions.

FREUD AND PSYCHOANALYTIC THEORY

In the modern era, Sigmund Freud, the principal founder of psychoanalysis, has been by far the most important influence in horror art theory and criticism. Central to Freud's psychoanalytic theory—and to its use in the analysis of art and literature of all kinds—are two related concepts: the unconscious and repression. In Freudian theory, the term *unconscious* identifies a realm of human thought maintained as separate from consciousness or awareness. *Repression,* simply put, is the dynamic mental process whereby certain forbidden desires (in the form of ideas) are kept confined to the unconscious.

Working according to a kind of pneumatic model, Freud held that the more psychic "pressure" required to keep an idea successfully repressed, the more likely the idea is to escape into the conscious mind. Thus, because repressed ideas *will* escape (the repressed will "return"), the mind employs several defense mechanisms that allow these ideas to enter consciousness, primarily through dreams, fantasies, and symptoms, in disguised forms that mask the true content of the repressed ideas.

For students of art and literature, the most interesting of these defense mechanisms are condensation and displacement. *Condensation* refers to a process by which one repressed idea comes to stand for several others, and *displacement* to a process by which seemingly dissimilar ideas become linked together. In art and literature as well as myth, condensation can produce ambiguity and can often be seen expressing itself through metaphor, but "all symbolism [a key element in art and literature] is a kind of displacement."[4]

From a Freudian perspective, the unconscious becomes a

storehouse for ideas that cannot safely be allowed free and undisguised entry into the conscious mind. Most of these ideas originate in childhood and concern desires that are judged to be taboo or are otherwise prohibited. (Cultural prohibitions play the largest role in determining which ideas must be repressed, but Freud also believed that some repression is primal, a process built into the human mind as a result of long centuries of evolution.) Because all human cultures have a vital interest in regulating human reproduction, many of these ideas are inevitably sexual in nature and involve such complicated and potentially contentious issues as sexual desire and sexual identity.

HORROR ART AND THE REPRESSION MODEL

For anyone interested in the analysis of horror art, the implications of the Freudian repression model are extremely compelling. Horror art is strongly marked by its transgressive tendencies, its tendencies to challenge the sociocultural status quo. Working within this model, the sociocultural status quo emerges quite clearly as a set of normative boundaries determined by the agency of repression (what one should do and what one shouldn't do, ironically enough, determine one another), and horror art becomes a means by which repressed ideas—suitably disguised, of course—can be brought out into the open. Horror art's attraction, then, may very well lie in its capacity to create a space within which its audience can enjoy a certain degree of "safe play" with forbidden, fearful ideas, thereby allowing for the maintenance of a healthy psychic equilibrium.

The vampire, modern horror art's single-most popular monster, provides an instructive example of this principle. For the vampire, traditional cultural prohibitions have no meaning. The vampire kills to survive, and kills more or less indiscriminately, with impunity, and the vampire's "kiss," involving the penetration of both male and female bodies, along with the exchange of bodily fluids, is both literally and figuratively sexual. The vampire defies the most basic physical laws, shifting shape at will, becoming a bat, a wolf, even mist. Not even death limits the vampire. In fact, except for sunlight and certain religious symbols, nothing whatsoever limits or prohibits the immediate and direct enactment of the vampire's desire. In short, the vampire *is* desire, desire incarnate and unbridled, and is thus the natural enemy of repression.

The vampire may be a monster, but one reason it remains so very attractive a monster may be that it makes possible the "projection" (a type of displacement) of so many dark, repellent desires that must normally be kept hidden under the blanket of repression. The end result—as perhaps with horror art in general—may be a form of pleasure that is analogous to catharsis: The vicarious enjoyment of the vampire's transgressive behavior allows for the safe, socially sanctioned release of potentially dangerous, disruptive emotions.

EXPLAINING THE UNEXPLAINABLE

Although theoretical discussions of the attraction of horror art are thought-provoking and therefore intellectually beneficial, nothing suggests that horror art will ever be fully explained—much less explained away—regardless of the critical energies focused on that task. Nor does anything suggest that, even if some final explanation were forthcoming, that the popular fascination with horror art would in any way abate. The roots of horror extend too deeply into the collective human psyche for that to happen at any time in the foreseeable future.

NOTES

1. David Punter, *The Literature of Terror.* New York: Longman, 1996, p. 1
2. James B. Twitchell, *The Living Dead.* Durham, NC: Duke University Press, 1981, p. 81.
3. Leslie Fiedler, *Love and Death in the American Novel.* New York: Stein and Day, 1966, p 29.
4. Richard Caldwell, *The Origin of the Gods: A Psychoanalytic Study of Greek Theogonic Myth.* New York: Oxford University Press, 1989, p. 59.

CHAPTER 1

Understanding Horror and Its Attractions

 Horror

The Appeal of the Unknown

H.P. Lovecraft

Called by horror novelist Stephen King "the twentieth century horror story's dark and baroque prince,"
H(oward) P(hillips) Lovecraft (1890–1937) is a figure
of major importance in modern horror literature.
Although virtually unknown during his lifetime,
after his death Lovecraft became an important influence on the next two generations of horror writers.
The following selection is taken from the first chapter of *Supernatural Horror in Literature*, his study of
American and English horror fiction from the eighteenth until the early twentieth centuries. Here,
Lovecraft formulates an aesthetic of the supernatural
horror story (which he calls the "weird tale"). For
anyone interested in Lovecraft's own work, especially those stories based on what came to be known
as the "Cthulhu Mythos," his conclusions regarding
"cosmic fear" are particularly germane.

The oldest and strongest emotion of mankind is fear, and
the oldest and strongest kind of fear is fear of the unknown.
These facts few psychologists will dispute, and their admitted truth must establish for all time the genuineness and
dignity of the weirdly horrible tales as a literary form.
Against it are discharged all the shafts of a materialistic sophistication which clings to frequently felt emotions and external events, and of a naively inspired idealism which dep-
recates the aesthetic motive and calls for a didactic
literature to "uplift" the reader toward a suitable degree of
smirking optimism. But in spite of all this opposition the
weird tale has survived, developed, and attained remarkable heights of perfection; founded as it is on a profound
and elementary principle whose appeal, if not always uni-

Excerpted from *Supernatural Horror in Literature*, by H.P. Lovecraft (New York: B.
Abramson, 1945).

versal, must necessarily be poignant and permanent to minds of the requisite sensitiveness.

The appeal of the spectrally macabre is generally narrow because it demands from the reader a certain degree of imagination and a capacity for detachment from everyday life. Relatively few are free enough from the spell of the daily routine to respond to rappings from outside, and tales of ordinary feelings and events, or of common sentimental distortions of such feelings and events, will always take first place in the taste of the majority; rightly, perhaps, since of course these ordinary matters make up the greater part of human experience. But the sensitive are always with us, and sometimes a curious streak of fancy invades an obscure corner of the very hardest head; so that no amount of rationalisation, reform, or Freudian analysis can quite annul the thrill of the chimney-corner whisper or the lonely wood. There is here involved psychological pattern or tradition as real and as deeply grounded in mental experience as any other pattern or tradition of mankind; coeval with the religious feeling and closely related to many aspects of it, and too much a part of our innermost biological heritage to lose keen potency over a very important, though not numerically great, minority of our species.

THE FEAR OF THE UNKNOWN

Man's first instincts and emotions formed his response to the environment in which he found himself. Definite feelings based on pleasure and pain grew up around the phenomena whose causes and effects he understood, whilst around those which he did not understand—and the universe teemed with them in the early days—were naturally woven such personifications, marvelous interpretations, and sensations of awe and fear as would be hit upon by a race having few and simple ideas and limited experience. The unknown, being likewise the unpredictable, became for our primitive forefathers a terrible and omnipotent source of boons and calamities visited upon mankind for cryptic and wholly extraterrestrial reasons, and thus clearly belonging to spheres of existence whereof we know nothing and wherein we have no part. The phenomenon of dreaming likewise helped to build up the notion of an unreal or spiritual world; and in general, all the conditions of savage dawn-life so strongly conducted toward a feeling of the supernatural, that we need not wonder at the thoroughness with which man's very hereditary essence has become saturated with religion and superstition. That saturation must, as a matter of plain scientific fact, be regarded as virtually permanent so far as the subconscious mind and inner instincts are concerned; for though the area of the unknown has been steadily contracting for thousands of years, an infinite reservoir of mystery still engulfs most of the outer cosmos, whilst a vast residuum of powerful inherited associations clings round all the objects and processes that were once mysterious, however well they may now be explained. And more than this, there is an actual physiological fixation of the old instincts in our nervous tissue, which would make them obscurely operative even were the conscious mind to be purged of all sources of wonder.

Cosmic Fear

Because we remember pain and the menace of death more vividly than pleasure, and because our feelings toward the beneficent aspects of the unknown have from the first been captured and formalised by conventional religious rituals, it has fallen to the lot of the darker and more maleficent side of cosmic mystery to figure chiefly in our popular supernatural folklore. This tendency, too, is naturally enhanced by the fact that uncertainty and danger are always closely allied; thus making any kind of an unknown world a world of peril and evil possibilities. When to this sense of fear and evil the inevitable fascination of wonder and curiosity is superadded, there is born a composite body of keen emotion and imaginative provocation whose vitality must of necessity endure as long as the human race itself. Children will always be afraid of the dark, and men with minds sensitive to hereditary impulse will always tremble at the thought of the hidden and fathomless worlds of strange life which may pulsate in the gulfs beyond the stars, or press hideously upon our own globe in unholy dimensions which only the dead and the moonstruck can glimpse.

With this foundation, no one need wonder at the existence of a literature of cosmic fear. It has always existed, and always will exist; and no better evidence of its tenacious vigour can be cited than the impulse which now and then drives writers of totally opposite leanings to try their hands at it in isolated tales, as if to discharge from their minds cer-

> **FEAR IS THE PRIME MOVER**
> *Harlan Ellison, prolific author, essayist, and sometime
> television commentator, is the premier modern master of
> "dark fantasy"—a genre perfectly suited to his iconoclastic bril-
> liance and grim view of human society. In the following quote,
> taken from an essay entitled "3 Faces of Fear," Ellison sounds
> very much like a contemporary Lovecraft.*
>
> Since the first night of Man, hunkered down hairy and hungry
> by the primeval lightning-borne food fire, fear has been the
> prime mover. Forget momma love and posterity and man's un-
> quenchable curiosity. Fear is the primary mode of locomotion
> of *homo sapiens,* as [comic/director] Mel Brooks suggests.
> Show hairy Man a pair of yellow eyes just outside the ring of
> light thrown by that first fire, and within twenty minutes he'll
> have invented the crossbow, the arbalest, the mace, Thompson
> submachine guns and klieg lights to chase that mother away.
>   We walk through all the days and nights of our lives terri-
> fied. Of the world that surrounds us, of one another, of the un-
> known, of ourselves. Fear is the hammer that leaves us
> stunned and speechless. Fear is the goad that sends us to
> places we fear to be in, to find out things we're scared witless
> to know. Fear.
>
> Harlan Ellison, *Edgeworks: Volume 1.* Clarkston, GA: White Wolf Publishing,
> 1999, p. 23.

tain phantasmal shapes which would otherwise haunt them.
Thus [Charles] Dickens wrote several eerie narratives;
[Robert] Browning, the hideous poem *Childe Roland;* Henry
James, *The Turn of the Screw;* Dr. Holmes, the subtle novel
Elsie Venner; F. Marion Crawford, *The Upper Berth* and a
number of other examples; Mrs. Charlotte Perkins Gilman,
social worker, *The Yellow Wall Paper;* whilst the humorist,
W.W. Jacobs, produced that able melodramatic bit called *The
Monkey's Paw.*

ASPECTS OF THE WEIRD TALE

This type of fear-literature must not be confounded with a
type externally similar but psychologically widely different:
the literature of mere physical fear and the mundanely
gruesome. Such writing, to be sure, has its place, as has the
conventional or even whimsical or humorous ghost story
where formalism or the author's knowing wink removes
the true sense of the morbidly unnatural; but these things

are not the literature of cosmic fear in its purest sense. The true weird tale has something more than secret murder, bloody bones, or a sheeted form clanking chains according to rule. A certain atmosphere of breathless and unexplainable dread of outer, unknown forces must be present; and there must be a hint, expressed with a seriousness and portentousness becoming its subject, of that most terrible conception of the human brain—a malign and particular suspension or defeat of those fixed laws of Nature which are our only safeguard against the assaults of chaos and the daemons of unplumbed space.

Naturally we cannot expect all weird tales to conform absolutely to any theoretical model. Creative minds are uneven, and the best of fabrics have their dull spots. Moreover, much of the choicest weird work is unconscious; appearing in memorable fragments scattered through material whose massed effect may be of a very different cast. Atmosphere is the all-important thing, for the final criterion of authenticity is not the dovetailing of a plot but the creation of a given sensation. We may say, as a general thing, that a weird story whose intent is to teach or produce a social effect, or one in which the horrors are finally explained away by natural means, is not a genuine tale of cosmic fear; but it remains a fact that such narratives often possess, in isolated sections, atmospheric touches which fulfill every condition of true supernatural horror-literature. Therefore we must judge a weird tale not by the author's intent, or by the mere mechanics of the plot; but by the emotional level which it attains at its least mundane point. If the proper sensations are excited, such a "high spot" must be admitted on its own merits as weird literature, no matter how prosaically it is later dragged down. The one test of the really weird is simply this— whether or not there be excited in the reader a profound sense of dread, and of contact with unknown spheres and powers; a subtle attitude of awed listening, as if for the beating of black wings or the scratching of outside shapes and entities on the known universe's utmost rim. And of course, the more completely and unifiedly a story conveys this atmosphere, the better it is as a work of art in the given medium.

Some Defining Elements of Horror

Stephen King

Stephen King is the best-selling author of a staggering number of novels and short stories, many of
which have been made into films. He has probably
sold more books than any author in history and is
without doubt the single most important figure in
twentieth-century horror. Among his best-known
horror novels are *Carrie, Salem's Lot, The Shining,
The Stand,* and *Misery.* Here, in a selection from
Danse Macabre, a series of chatty, funny, and often
irreverent reflections on horror fiction and horror
films, King discusses a number of important issues
regarding horror art from a craftsman's perspective.
King asserts that horror and monstrosity are difficult
to critically define, but he suggests that the key to
understanding these terms lies in how far they stray
from commonly held notions of what is normal.

The first issue of Forrest Ackerman's gruesomely jovial
magazine *Famous Monsters of Filmland* that I ever bought
contained a long, almost scholarly article by Robert Bloch
on the difference between science fiction films and horror
films. It was an interesting piece of work, and while I do not
recall all of it after eighteen years, I do remember Bloch saying that the Howard Hawks/Christian Nyby collaboration on
The Thing (based on John W. Campbell's classic science fiction novella "Who Goes There?") was science fiction to the
core in spite of its scary elements, and that the later film
Them!, about giant ants spawned in the New Mexico desert
(as the result of A-bomb tests, naturally), was a pure horror
film in spite of its science fiction trappings.

This dividing line between fantasy and science fiction (for
properly speaking, fantasy is what it is; the horror genre is

only a subset of the larger genre) is a subject that comes up at some point at almost every fantasy or science fiction convention held (and for those of you unaware of the subculture, there are literally hundreds each year). If I had a nickel for every letter printed on the fantasy/sf dichotomy in the columns of the amateur magazines and the prozines of both fields, I could buy the island of Bermuda.

PROBLEMS OF DEFINITION

It's a trap, this matter of definition, and I can't think of a more boring academic subject. Like endless discussions of breath units in modern poetry or the possible intrusiveness of some punctuation in the short story, it is really a discussion of how many angels can dance on the head of a pin, and not really interesting unless those involved in the discussion are drunk or graduate students—two states of roughly similar incompetence. I'll content myself with stating the obvious inarguables: both are works of the imagination, and both try to create worlds which do not exist, cannot exist, or do not exist yet. There is a difference, of course, but you can draw your own borderline, if you want—and if you try, you may find that it's a very squiggly border indeed. *Alien,* for instance, is a horror movie even though it is more firmly grounded in scientific projection than *Star Wars. Star Wars* is a science fiction film, although we must recognize the fact that it's sf of the E.E. "Doc" Smith/Murray Leinster whack-and-slash school: an outer space western just overflowing with PIONEER SPIRIT.

Somewhere in between these two, in a buffer zone that has been little used by the movies, are works that seem to combine science fiction and fantasy in a nonthreatening way—*Close Encounters of the Third Kind,* for instance.

With such a number of divisions (and any dedicated science fiction or fantasy fan could offer a dozen more, ranging from Utopian Fiction, Negative Utopian Fiction, Sword and Sorcery, Heroic Fantasy, Future History, and on into the sunset), you can see why I don't want to open this particular door any wider than I have to.

Let me, instead of defining, offer a couple of examples, and then we'll move along—and what better example than *Donovan's Brain?*

Horror fiction doesn't necessarily have to be nonscientific. Curt Siodmak's novel *Donovan's Brain* moves from a scientific basis to outright horror (as did *Alien*). It was adapted twice for the screen, and both versions enjoyed fair popular success. Both the novel and the films focus on a scientist who, if not quite mad, is certainly operating at the far borders of rationality. Thus we can place him in a direct line of descent from the original Mad Labs proprietor, Victor Frankenstein. This scientist has been experimenting with a technique designed to keep the brain alive after the body has died—specifically, in a tank filled with an electrically charged saline solution.

In the course of the novel, the private plane of W.D. Donovan, a rich and domineering millionaire, crashes near the scientist's desert lab. Recognizing the knock of opportunity, the scientist removes the dying millionaire's skull and pops Donovan's brain into his tank.

So far, so good. This story has elements of both horror and science fiction; at this point it could go either way, depending on Siodmak's handling of the subject. The earlier version of the film tips its hand almost at once: the removal operation takes place in a howling thunderstorm and the scientist's Arizona laboratory looks more like Baskerville Hall. And neither film version is up to the tale of mounting terror Siodmak tells in his careful, rational prose. The operation is a success. The brain is alive and possibly even thinking in its tank of cloudy liquid. The problem now becomes one of communication. The scientist begins trying to contact the brain by means of telepathy . . . and finally succeeds. In a half-trance, he writes the name *W.D. Donovan* three or four times on a scrap of paper, and comparison shows that his signature is interchangeable with that of the millionaire.

In its tank, Donovan's brain begins to change and mutate. It grows stronger, more able to dominate our young hero. He begins to do Donovan's bidding, said bidding all revolving around Donovan's psychopathic determination to make sure the right person inherits his fortune. The scientist begins to experience the frailties of Donovan's physical body (now moldering in an unmarked grave): low back pain, a decided limp. As the story builds to its climax, Donovan tries to use the scientist to run down a little girl who stands in the way of his implacable, monstrous will. . . .

The final tip-off comes at the very end of the book, when Donovan's nephew (or perhaps it was his bastard son, I'll be damned if I can remember which) is hanged for murder.

Three times the scaffold's trapdoor refuses to open when the switch is thrown, and the narrator speculates that Donovan's spirit still remains, indomitable, implacable . . . and hungry.

For all its scientific trappings, *Donovan's Brain* is as much a horror story as M.R. James's "Casting the Runes" or H.P. Lovecraft's nominal science fiction tale, "The Colour Out of Space."

Now let's take another story, this one an oral tale of the sort that never has to be written down. It is simply passed mouth to mouth, usually around Boy Scout or Girl Scout campfires after the sun has gone down and marshmallows have been poked onto green sticks to roast above the coals. You've heard it, I guess, but instead of summarizing it, I'd like to tell it as I originally heard it, gape-mouthed with terror, as the sun went down behind the vacant lot in Stratford where we used to play scratch baseball when there were enough guys around to make up two teams. Here is the most basic horror story I know:

"This guy and his girl go out on a date, you know? And they go parking up on Lover's Lane. So anyway, while they're driving up there, the radio breaks in with this bulletin. The guy says this dangerous homicidal maniac named The Hook has just escaped from the Sunnydale Asylum for the Criminally Insane. They call him The Hook because that's what he's got instead of a right hand, this razor-sharp hook, and he used to hang around these lover's lanes, you know, and he'd catch these people making out and cut their heads off with the hook. He could do that 'cause it was so sharp, you know, and when they caught him they found like about fifteen or twenty heads in his refrigerator. So the news guy says to be on the lookout for any guy with a hook instead of a hand, and to stay away from any dark, lonely spots where people go to, you know, get it on.

"So the girl says, Let's go home, okay? And the guy—he's this real big guy, you know, with muscles on his muscles—he says, I'm not scared of that guy, and he's probably miles from here anyway. So she goes, Come on, Louie, I'm scared, Sunnydale Asylum isn't that far from here. Let's go back to my house. I'll make popcorn and we can watch TV.

"But the guy won't listen to her and pretty soon they're up on The Outlook, parked at the end of the road, makin' out like bandidos. But she keeps sayin' she wants to go home because they're the only car there, you know. That stuff about

The Hook scared away everybody else. But he keeps sayin', Come on, don't be such a chicken, there's nothin' to be afraid of, and if there was I'd protectcha, stuff like that.

"So they keep makin' out for awhile and then she hears a noise—like a breakin' branch or something. Like someone is out there in the woods, creepin' up on them. So then she gets real upset, hysterical, crine and everything, like girls do. She's beggin' the guy to take her home. The guy keeps sayin' he doesn't hear anything at all, but she looks up in the rear-view mirror and thinks she sees someone all hunkered down at the back of the car, just peekin' in at them, and grinnin'. She says if he doesn't take her home she's never gonna go out parkin' with him again and all that happy crappy. So finally he starts up the car and really peels out cause he's so jacked-off at her. In fact, he just about cracks them up.*

"So anyway, they get home, you know, and the guy goes around to open her door for her, and when he gets there he just stands there, turnin' as white as a sheet, and his eyes are gettin' so big you'd think they was gonna fall out on his shoes. She says Louie, what's wrong? And he just faints dead away, right there on the sidewalk.*

"She gets out to see what's wrong, and when she slams the car door she hears this funny clinking sound and turns around to see what it is. And there, hanging from the doorhandle, is this razor-sharp hook."*

The story of The Hook is a simple, brutal classic of horror. It offers no characterization, no theme, no particular artifice; it does not aspire to symbolic beauty or try to summarize the times, the mind, or the human spirit. To find these things we must go to "literature"—perhaps to Flannery O'Connor's story "A Good Man Is Hard to Find," which is very much like the story of The Hook in its plot and construction. No, the story of The Hook exists for one reason and one reason alone: to scare the shit out of little kids after the sun goes down.

One could jigger the story of The Hook to make him—it— a creature from outer space, and you could attribute this creature's ability to travel across the parsecs to a photon drive or a warp drive; you could make it a creature from an alternate earth à la Clifford D. Simak. But none of these sf conventions would turn the story of The Hook into science fiction. It's a flesh-crawler pure and simple, and in its direct point-to-point progress, its brevity, and its use of story only as a means to get to the effect in the last sentence, it is remarkably similar to John Carpenter's *Halloween* ("It *was* the boogeyman," Jamie Lee Curtis says at the end of that film. "Yes," Donald Pleasance agrees softly. "As a matter of fact, it was.") or *The Fog*. Both of these movies are extremely frightening, but the story of The Hook was there first.

The point seems to be that horror simply *is*, exclusive of definition or rationalization. . . .

LEVELS OF HORROR

The closest I want to come to definition or rationalization is to suggest that the genre exists on three more or less separate levels, each one a little less fine than the one before it. The finest emotion is terror, that emotion which is called up in the tale of The Hook and also in that hoary old classic, "The Monkey's Paw." We actually *see* nothing outright nasty in either story; in one we have the hook and in the other there is the paw, which, dried and mummified, can surely be no worse than those plastic dogturds on sale at any novelty shop. It's what the mind sees that makes these stories such quintessential tales of terror. It is the unpleasant speculation called to mind when the knocking on the door begins in the latter story and the grief-stricken old woman rushes to answer it. Nothing is there but the wind when she finally throws the door open . . . but what, the mind wonders, *might* have been there if her husband had been a little slower on the draw with that third wish?

As a kid, I cut my teeth on William B. Gaines's horror comics—*Weird Science, Tales from the Crypt, Tales from the Vault*—plus all the Gaines imitators (but like a good Elvis record, the Gaines magazines were often imitated, never duplicated). These horror comics of the fifties still sum up for me the epitome of horror, that emotion of fear that underlies terror, an emotion which is slightly less fine, because it is not entirely of the mind. Horror also invites a physical reaction by showing us something which is physically wrong.

One typical E.C. screamer goes like this: The hero's wife and her boyfriend determine to do away with the hero so they can run away together and get married. In almost all the weird comics of the '50s, the women are seen as slightly overripe, enticingly fleshy and sexual, but ultimately evil: castrating, murdering bitches who, like the trapdoor spider, feel an almost instinctual need to follow intercourse with cannibalism. These two heels, who might have stepped whole and breathing from a James M. Cain novel, take the poor slob of a husband for a ride and the boyfriend puts a bullet between his eyes. They wire a cement block to the corpse's leg and toss him over a bridge into the river. Two or three weeks later, our hero, a living corpse, emerges from the river, rotted and eaten by the fish. He shambles after wifey and her friend . . . and not to invite them back to his place for a few drinks, either, one feels. One piece of dialogue from this story which I've never forgotten is, "I am coming, Marie, but I have to come slowly . . . because little pieces of me keep falling off . . ."

In "The Monkey's Paw," the imagination alone is stimulated. The reader does the job on himself. In the horror comics (as well as the horror pulps of the years 1930–1955), the viscera are also engaged. As we have already pointed out, the old man in "The Monkey's Paw" is able to wish the dreadful apparition away before his frenzied wife can get the door open. In *Tales from the Crypt*, the Thing from Beyond the Grave is still there when the door is thrown wide, big as life and twice as ugly.

Terror is the sound of the old man's continuing pulsebeat in "The Tell-Tale Heart"—a quick sound, "like a watch wrapped in cotton." Horror is the amorphous but very physical "thing" in Joseph Payne Brennan's wonderful novella "Slime" as it enfolds itself over the body of a screaming dog.

But there is a third level—that of revulsion. This seems to be where the "chest-burster" from *Alien* fits. Better, let's take another example from the E.C. file as an example of the Revolting Story—Jack Davis's "Foul Play" from *The Crypt of Terror* will serve nicely, I think. And if you're sitting in your living room right now, putting away some chips and dip or maybe some sliced pepperoni on crackers as you read this, maybe you'd just better put the munchies away for awhile, because this one makes the chest-burster from *Alien* look like a scene from *The Sound of Music*. You'll note that the story lacks any real logic, motivation, or character development, but, as in the tale of The Hook, the story itself is little more than the means to an end, a way of getting to those last three panels.

"Foul Play" is the story of Herbie Satten, pitcher for Bayville's minor league baseball team. Herbie is the apotheosis of the E.C. villain. He's a totally black character, with absolutely no redeeming qualities, the Compleat Monster.

He's murderous, conceited, egocentric, willing to go to any lengths to win. He brings out the Mob Man or Mob Woman in each of us; we would gladly see Herbie lynched from the nearest apple tree, and never mind the Civil Liberties Union.

With his team leading by a single run in the top of the ninth, Herbie gets first base by deliberately allowing himself to be hit by an inside pitch. Although he is big and lumbering, he takes off for second on the very next pitch. Covering second is Central City's saintly slugger, Jerry Deegan. Deegan, we are told, is "sure to win the game for the home team in the bottom of the ninth." The evil Herbie Satten slides into second with his spikes up, but saintly Jerry hangs in there and tags Satten out.

Jerry is spiked, but his wounds are minor . . . or so they appear. In fact, Herbie has painted his spikes with a deadly, fast-acting poison. In Central City's half of the ninth, Jerry comes to the plate with two out and a man in scoring position. It looks pretty good for the home team guys; unfortunately, Jerry drops dead at home plate even as the umpire calls strike three. Exit the malefic Herbie Satten, smirking.

The Central City team doctor discovers that Jerry has been poisoned. One of the Central City players says grimly: "This is a job for the police!" Another responds ominously, "No! Wait! Let's take care of him ourselves . . . our way."

The team sends Herbie a letter, inviting him to the ballpark one night to be presented with a plaque honoring his achievements in baseball. Herbie, apparently as stupid as he is evil, falls for it, and in the next scene we see the Central City nine on the field. The team doctor is tricked out in umpire's regalia. He is whisking off home plate . . . which happens to be a human heart. The base paths are intestines. The bases are chunks of the unfortunate Herbie Satten's body. In the penultimate panel we see that the batter is standing in the box and that instead of a Louisville Slugger he is swinging one of Herbie's severed legs. The pitcher is holding a grotesquely mangled human head and preparing to throw it. The head, from which one eyeball dangles on its stalk, looks as though it's already been hit over the fence for a couple of home runs, although as Davis has drawn it . . . one would not expect it to carry so far. It is, in the parlance of baseball players, "a dead ball."

The Old Witch followed this helping of mayhem with her own conclusions, beginning with the immortal E.C. Chuckle:

"Heh, heh! So that's my yelp-yarn for this issue, kiddies. Herbie, the pitcher, went to pieces that night and was taken out ... of existence, that is ..."

As you can see, both "The Monkey's Paw" and "Foul Play" are horror stories, but their mode of attack and their ultimate effect are light-years apart. ...

So: terror on top, horror below it, and lowest of all, the gag reflex of revulsion. My own philosophy as a sometime writer of horror fiction is to recognize these distinctions because they are sometimes useful, but to avoid any preference for one over the other on the grounds that one effect is somehow better than another. The problem with definitions is that they have a way of turning into critical tools—and this sort of criticism, which I would call criticism-by-rote, seems to me needlessly restricting and even dangerous. I recognize terror as the finest emotion (used to almost quintessential effect in Robert Wise's film *The Haunting*, where, as in "The Monkey's Paw," we are never allowed to see what is behind the door), and so I will try to terrorize the reader. But if I find I cannot terrify him/her, I will try to horrify; and if I find I cannot horrify, I'll go for the gross-out. I'm not proud. ...

Well, let all that go for the moment. Let's talk monsters.

Exactly what is a monster?

Begin by assuming that the tale of horror, no matter how primitive, is allegorical by its very nature; that it is symbolic. Assume that it is talking to us, like a patient on a psychoanalyst's couch, about one thing while it means another. I am not saying that horror is *consciously* allegorical or symbolic; that is to suggest an artfulness that few writers of horror fiction or directors of horror films aspire to. ...

The element of allegory is there only because it is built-in, a given, impossible to escape. Horror appeals to us because it says, in a symbolic way, things we would be afraid to say right out straight, with the bark still on; it offers us a chance to exercise (that's right; not *exorcise* but *exercise)* emotions which society demands we keep closely in hand. The horror film is an invitation to indulge in deviant, antisocial behavior by proxy—to commit gratuitous acts of violence, indulge our puerile dreams of power, to give in to our most craven fears. Perhaps more than anything else, the horror story or horror movie says it's okay to join the mob, to become the total tribal being, to destroy the outsider. It has never been done better or more literally than in Shirley Jackson's short story "The

Lottery," where the entire concept of the outsider is symbolic, created by nothing more than a black circle colored on a slip of paper. But there is no symbolism in the rain of stones which ends the story; the victim's own child pitches in as the mother dies, screaming "It's not fair! It's not fair!"

Nor is it an accident that the horror story ends so often with an O. Henry twist that leads straight down a mine shaft. When we turn to the creepy movie or the crawly book, we are not wearing our "Everything works out for the best" hats. We're waiting to be told what we so often suspect—that everything is turning to shit. In most cases the horror story provides ample proof that such is indeed the case, and I don't believe, when Katharine Ross falls prey to the Stepford Men's Association at the conclusion of *The Stepford Wives* or when the heroic black man is shot dead by the numbnuts sheriff's posse at the end of *Night of the Living Dead,* that anyone is really surprised. It is, as they say, a part of the game.

And monstrosity? What about that part of the game? What sort of handle can we get on that? If we don't define, can we at least exemplify? Here is a fairly explosive package, my friends.

What about the freaks in the circus? The carny aberrations observed by the light of naked hundred-watt bulbs? What about Cheng and Eng, the famous Siamese twins? A majority of people considered them monstrous in their day, and an even greater number no doubt considered the fact that each had his own married life even more monstrous. America's most mordant—and sometimes funniest—cartoonist, a fellow named Rodrigues, has rung the changes on the Siamese-twin theme in his Aesop Brothers strip in the *National Lampoon,* where we have our noses rubbed in almost every possible bizarre exingency of life among the mortally attached: the sex lives of, the bathroom functions of, the love lives, the sicknesses. Rodrigues provides everything you ever wondered about in regard to Siamese twins . . . and fulfills your darkest surmises. To say that all of this is in poor taste may be true, but it's still a futile and impotent criticism—the old *National Enquirer* used to run pictures of car-wreck victims in pieces and dogs munching happily away at severed human heads, but it did a land-office business in grue before lapsing back into a quieter current of the American mainstream.

What about the other carny freaks? Are they classifiable as monstrosities? Dwarves? Midgets? The bearded lady? The fat lady? The human skeleton? At one time or another most of us have been there, standing on the beaten, sawdust-strewn dirt with a chili-dog or a paper of sweet cotton candy in one hand while the barker hucksters us, usually with one sample of these human offshoots standing nearby as a specimen—the fat lady in her pink little girl's tutu, the tattooed man with the tail of a dragon curled around his burly neck like a fabulous hangman's noose, or the man who eats nails and scrap metal and light bulbs. Perhaps not so many of us have surrendered to the urge to cough up the two bits or four bits or six bits to go inside and see them, plus such all-time favorites as The Two-Headed Cow or The Baby in a Bottle (I have been writing horror stories since I was eight, but have never yet attended a freak show), but most of us have surely felt the impulse. And at some carnivals, the most terrible freak of all is kept out back, kept in darkness like some damned thing from Dante's Ninth Circle of Hell, kept there because his performance was forbidden by law as long ago as 1910, kept in a pit and dressed in a rag. This is the geek, and for an extra buck or two you could stand at the edge of his pit and watch him bite off the head of a live chicken and then swallow it even as the decapitated bird fluttered in his hands. . . .

THE ABNORMAL REAFFIRMS THE NORMAL

Perhaps I've not touched your idea of monstrosity in real life even yet, and perhaps I won't, but for just a moment consider such an ordinary thing as left-handedness. Of course, the discrimination against left-handed people is obvious from the start. If you've attended a college or high school with the more modern desks, you know that most of them are built for inhabitants of an exclusively right-handed world. Most educational facilities will order a few left-hand desks as a token gesture, but that's all. And during testing or composition situations, lefties are usually segregated on one side of the lecture hall so they will not jog the elbows of their more normal counterparts.

But it goes deeper than discrimination. The roots of discrimination spread wide, but the roots of monstrosity spread both wide and deep. Left-handed baseball players are all considered screwballs, whether they are or not. The French for left, bastardized from the Latin, is *la sinistre*, from which comes our word *sinister*. According to the old superstition, your right side belongs to God, your left side to that other fellow. Southpaws have always been suspect. My mother was a leftie, and as a schoolgirl, so she told my brother and me, the teacher would rap her left hand smartly with a ruler to make her change her pen to her right hand. When the teacher left she would switch the pen back again, of course, because with her right hand she could make only large, childish scrawls—the fate of most of us when we try to write with what New Englanders call "the dumb hand." A few of us, such as Branwell Brontë (the gifted brother of Charlotte and Emily), can write clearly and well with either hand. Branwell Brontë was in fact so ambidextrous that he could write two different letters to two different people *at the same time*. We might reasonably wonder if such an ability qualifies as monstrosity . . . or genius.

In fact, almost every physical and mental human aberration has been at some point in history, or is now, considered monstrous—a complete list would include widows' peaks (once considered a reliable sign that a man was a sorcerer), moles on the female body (supposed to be witches' teats), and extreme schizophrenia, which on occasion has caused the afflicted to be canonized by one church or another.

Monstrosity fascinates us because it appeals to the conservative Republican in a three-piece suit who resides within all of us. We love and need the concept of monstrosity because it is a reaffirmation of the order we all crave as human beings . . . and let me further suggest that it is not the physical or mental aberration in itself which horrifies us, but rather the lack of order which these aberrations seem to imply.

The late John Wyndham, perhaps the best writer of science fiction that England has ever produced, summarized the idea in his novel *The Chrysalids* (published as *Rebirth* in America). It is a story that considers the ideas of mutation and deviation more brilliantly than any other novel written in English since World War II, I think. A series of plaques in the home of the novel's young protagonist offer stern counsel: ONLY THE IMAGE OF GOD IS MAN; KEEP PURE THE STOCK OF THE LORD; IN PURITY OUR SALVATION; BLESSED IS THE NORM; and most telling of all: WATCH THOU FOR THE MUTANT! After all, when we discuss monstrosity, we are expressing our faith and belief in the norm and watching for the mutant. The writer of horror fiction is neither more nor less than an agent of the status quo.

The Paradox of Horror

Noël Carroll

Noël Carroll is the Monroe C. Beardsley Professor of Art at the University of Wisconsin–Madison. In addition to the celebrated but controversial *The Philosophy of Horror*, from which the following selection has been excerpted, he has written *A Philosophy of Mass Art* and *The Philosophy of Art: A Contemporary Introduction*. Here Carroll confronts horror art's central question: Why is horror interesting and compelling? Carroll's response is "cognitive" in nature, involving what he sees as the innate human fascination with monsters. To Carroll, horror narratives pique a reader's curiosity, and the reader is willing to confront the disturbing or disgusting aspects of the genre in order to reach the pleasure of a satisfying narrative conclusion.

WHY HORROR?

There is a theoretical question about horror which, although not unique to horror, nevertheless is not one that readily arises with respect to other popular genres, such as mystery, romance, comedy, the thriller, adventure stories, and the western. The question is: why would anyone be interested in the genre to begin with? Why does the genre persist? I have written a lot about the internal elements of the genre; but many readers may feel that in doing that their attention has been deflected away from the central issue concerning horror—viz., how can we explain its very existence, for why would anyone *want* to be horrified, or even art-horrified?

This question, moreover, becomes especially pressing if my analysis of the nature of horror is accepted. For we have seen that a key element in the emotion of art-horror is repulsion or disgust. But—and this is the question of "Why horror?" in its primary form—if horror necessarily has something repulsive about it, how can audiences be attracted to it? Indeed, even if horror only caused fear, we might feel justified in demanding an explanation of what could motivate people to seek out the genre. But where fear is compounded with repulsion, the ante is, in a manner of speaking, raised. . . .

THE PARADOX OF HORROR

[Previously] I explored, with relation to horror, what might be called the paradox of fiction—the question of how people can be moved (e.g., be horrified) by that which they know does not exist. [Now] I shall take a look at another apparent paradox that pertains to the genre: what might be called the paradox of horror. This paradox amounts to the question of how people can be attracted by what is repulsive. That is, the imagery of horror fiction seems to be necessarily repulsive and, yet, the genre has no lack of consumers. Moreover, it does not seem plausible to regard these consumers—given the vast number of them—as abnormal or perverse in any way that does not beg the question. Nevertheless, they appear to seek that which, under certain descriptions, it would seem natural for them to avoid. How is this ostensible conundrum to be resolved?

That the works of horror are in some sense both attractive and repulsive is essential to an understanding of the genre. Too often, writing about horror only emphasizes one side of this opposition. Many journalists, reviewing a horror novel or movie, will underscore only the repellent aspects of the work—rejecting it as disgusting, indecent, and foul. Yet this tack fails to offer any account of why people are interested in partaking of such exercises. Indeed, it renders the popularity of the genre inexplicable.

On the other hand, defenders of the horror genre or of a specific example of it will often indulge in allegorical readings that make their subjects appear wholly appealing and that do not acknowledge their repellent aspects. Thus, we are told that the Frankenstein myth is really an existential parable about man thrown-into-the-world, an "isolated sufferer." But where in this allegorical formulation can we find an explanation for the purpose of the unsettling effect of the charnel house imagery? That is, if *Frankenstein* is part *Nausea*, it is also part nauseating. . . .

The need to account for the peculiar nature of horror had

already begun to strike writers in the eighteenth century. John and Anna Laetitia Aikin, in their essay "On the Pleasure Derived From Objects of Terror," write that " . . . the apparent delight with which we dwell upon objects of pure terror, where our moral feelings are not in the least concerned and no passion seems to be excited but the depressing one of fear, is a paradox of the heart . . . difficult of solution." This question, of course, was not unique to tales of terror and horror. At roughly the same time, [critic David] Hume published his "Of Tragedy," wherein he seeks to explain how the audiences of such dramas are "pleased in proportion as they are afflicted." Hume, in turn, cites Jean-Baptiste Dubos and Bernard Le Bovier Fontenelle as earlier theoreticians concerned with the problem of how pleasure is to be derived from that which is distressful, while the Aikins themselves tackle this general problem in their "An Enquiry into those Kinds of Distress which excite agreeable Sensations.". . . Thus, the paradox of horror is an instance of a larger problem, viz., that of explaining the way in which the artistic presentation of normally aversive events and objects can give rise to pleasure or can compel our interests. . . .

LOOKING AT THE LARGER NARRATIVE

In order to appreciate the way Hume's observations on tragedy can contribute to answering the paradox of horror, it is important to keep in mind that the horror genre, like that of tragedy, most generally takes a narrative form. . . . That horror is often narrative suggests that with much horror, the interest we have and the pleasure we take may not primarily be in the object of art-horror as such—i.e., in the monster for its own sake. Rather, the narrative may be the crucial locus of our interest and pleasure. For what is attractive—what holds our interest and yields pleasure—in the horror genre need not be, first and foremost, the simple manifestation of the object of art-horror, but the way that manifestation or disclosure is situated as a functional element in an overall narrative structure.

That is, in order to give an account of what is compelling about the horror genre, it may be wrong to ask only what it is about the monster that gives us pleasure; for the interest and pleasure we take in the monster and its disclosure may rather be a function of the way it figures in a larger narrative structure.

Speaking of the presentation of melancholy events by orators, Hume notes that the pleasure derived is not a response to the event as such, but to its rhetorical framing. When we turn to tragedy, plotting performs this function. The interest that we take in the deaths of Hamlet, Gertrude, Claudius, et al. is not sadistic, but is an interest that the plot has engendered in how certain forces, once put in motion, will work themselves out. Pleasure derives from having our interest in the outcome of such questions satisfied. . . .

Similarly, the Aikins look to the plot, in large measure, to account for the interest and pleasure taken in the objects of terror. They think the question may be stated badly if we attempt to account for the pleasure derived from terror fictions solely in terms of saying how the objects—monsters, for our purposes—are attractive or pleasurable for their own sake. . . .

One need not buy everything that Hume and the Aikins assert wholesale. . . . However, their shared notion, that the aesthetic contrivance of normally upsetting events depends upon their contextualization in structures like narrative, is particularly suggestive with respect to the paradox of horror.

For, as noted, a great deal of the horror genre is narrative. Indeed, I think it is fair to say that in our culture, horror thrives above all as a narrative form. Thus, in order to account for the interest we take in and the pleasure we take from horror, we may hypothesize that, in the main, the locus of our gratification is not the monster as such but the whole narrative structure in which the presentation of the monster is staged. This, of course, is not to say that the monster is in any way irrelevant to the genre, nor that the interest and pleasure in the genre could be satisfied through and/or substituted by any old narrative. For, as I have argued earlier, the monster is a functional ingredient in the type of narratives found in horror stories, and not all narratives function exactly like horror narratives. . . .

Disclosing the Monster

These stories, with great frequency, revolve around proving, disclosing, discovering, and confirming the existence of something that is impossible, something that defies standing conceptual schemes. It is part of such stories—contrary to our everyday beliefs about the nature of things—that such monsters exist. And as a result, audiences' expectations revolve around whether this existence will be confirmed in the story.

Often this is achieved, as Hume says of narrative "secrets" in general, by putting off the conclusive information that the monster exists for quite a while. Sometimes this information may be deferred till the very end of the fiction. And even where this information is given to the audience right off the bat, it is still generally the case that the human characters in the tale must undergo a process of discovering that the monster exists, which, in turn, may lead to a further process of confirming that discovery in an ensuing scene or series of scenes. That is, the question of whether or not the monster exists may be transformed into the question of whether and when the human characters in the tale will establish the existence of the monster. Horror stories are often protracted series of discoveries: first the reader learns of the monster's existence, then some characters do, then some more characters do, and so on; the drama of iterated disclosure—albeit to different parties—underwrites much horror fiction.

Even in overreacher plots, there is a question of whether the monsters exist—i.e., of whether they can be summoned, in the case of demons, or of whether they can be created by mad scientists and necromancers. Furthermore, even after the existence of the monster is disclosed, the audience continues to crave further information about its nature, its identity, its origin, its purposes, and its astounding powers and properties, including, ultimately, those of its weaknesses that *may* enable humanity to do it in.

Thus, to a large extent, the horror story is driven explicitly by curiosity. It engages its audience by being involved in processes of disclosure, discovery, proof, explanation, hypothesis, and confirmation. Doubt, skepticism, and the fear that belief in the existence of the monster is a form of insanity are predictable foils to the revelation (to the audience or to the characters or both) of the existence of the monster.

Horror stories, in a significant number of cases, are dramas of proving the existence of the monster and disclosing (most often gradually) the origin, identity, purposes and powers of the monster. Monsters, as well, are obviously a perfect vehicle for engendering this kind of curiosity and for supporting the drama of proof, because monsters are (physically, though generally not logically) impossible beings. They arouse interest and attention through being putatively inexplicable or highly unusual vis-à-vis our standing cultural categories, thereby instilling a desire to learn and to know about them. And since they are also outside of (justifiably) prevailing definitions of what is, they understandably prompt a need for proof (or the fiction of a proof) in the face of skepticism. Monsters are, then, natural subjects for curiosity, and they straightforwardly warrant the ratiocinative energies the plot lavishes upon them.

All narratives might be thought to involve the desire to know—the desire to know at least the outcome of the interaction of the forces made salient in the plot. However, the horror fiction is a special variation on this general narrative motivation, because it has at the center of it something which is given as in principle *unknowable*—something which, *ex hypothesi*, cannot, given the structure of our conceptual scheme, exist and that cannot have the properties it has. This is why, so often, the real drama in a horror story resides in establishing the existence of the monster and in disclosing its horrific properties. Once this is established, the monster, generally, has to be confronted, and the narrative is driven by the question of whether the creature can be destroyed. However, even at this point, the drama of ratiocination can continue as further discoveries—accompanied by arguments, explanations, and hypotheses—reveal features of the monster that will facilitate or impede the destruction of the creature. . . .

HORROR LOGICALLY FULFILLS READERS' EXPECTATIONS

Applied to the paradox of horror, these observations suggest that the pleasure derived from the horror fiction and the source of our interest in it resides, first and foremost, in the processes of discovery, proof, and confirmation that horror fictions often employ. The disclosure of the existence of the horrific being and of its properties is the central source of pleasure in the genre; once that process of revelation is consummated, we remain inquisitive about whether such a creature can be successfully confronted, and that narrative question sees us through to the end of the story. Here, the pleasure involved is, broadly speaking, cognitive. . . .

Moreover, it should be clear that these particular cognitive pleasures, insofar as they are set in motion by the relevant kind of unknowable beings, are especially well served by horrific monsters. Thus, there is a special functional relationship between the beings that mark off the horror genre and the pleasure and interest that many horror fictions sustain. That interest and that pleasure derive from the disclosure of unknown and impossible beings, just the sorts of things that seem to call for proof, discovery, and confirmation. Therefore, the disgust that such beings evince might be seen as part of the price to be paid for the pleasure of their disclosure. That is, the narrative expectations that the horror genre puts in place is that the being whose existence is in question be something that defies standing cultural categories; thus, disgust, so to say, is itself more or less mandated by the kind of curiosity that the horror narrative puts in place. The horror narrative could not deliver a successful, affirmative answer to its presiding question unless the disclosure of the monster indeed elicited disgust, or was of the sort that was a highly probable object of disgust.

That is, there is a strong relation of consilience between the objects of art-horror, on the one hand, and the revelatory plotting on the other. The kind of plots and the subjects of horrific revelation are not merely compatible, but fit together or agree in a way that is highly appropriate. That the audience is naturally inquisitive about that which is unknown meshes with plotting that is concerned to render the unknown known by processes of discovery, explanation, proof, hypothesis, confirmation, and so on.

Of course, what it means to say that the horrific being is "unknown" here is that it is not accommodated by standing conceptual schemes. Moreover, . . . things that violate our conceptual scheme, by (for example) being interstitial, are things that we are prone to find disturbing. Thus, that horrific beings are predictably objects of loathing and revulsion is a function of the ways they violate our classificatory scheme.

If what is of primary importance about horrific creatures is that their very impossibility vis à vis our conceptual categories is what makes them function so compellingly in dramas of discovery and confirmation, then their disclosure, insofar as they are categorical violations, will be attached to some sense of disturbance, distress, and disgust. Consequently, the role of the horrific creature in such narratives—where their disclosure captures our interest and delivers pleasure—will simultaneously mandate some probable revulsion. That is, in order to reward our interest by the disclosure of the putatively impossible beings of the plot, said beings ought to be disturbing, distressing, and repulsive in the way that theorists . . . predict phenomena that ill fit cultural classifications will be.

So, as a first approximation of resolving the paradox of horror, we may conjecture that we are attracted to the majority of horror fictions because of the way that the plots of discovery and the dramas of proof pique our curiosity, and abet our interest, ideally satisfying them in a way that is pleasurable. But if narrative curiosity about impossible beings is to be satisfied through disclosure, that process must require some element of probable disgust since such impossible beings are, *ex hypothesi,* disturbing, distressful, and repulsive.

One way of making the point is to say that the monsters in such tales of disclosure have to be disturbing, distressful, and repulsive, if the process of their discovery is to be rewarding in a pleasurable way. Another way to get at this is to say that the primary pleasure that narratives of disclosure afford—i.e., the interest we take in them, and the source of their attraction— resides in the processes of discovery, the play of proof, and the dramas of ratiocination that comprise them. It is not that we crave disgust, but that disgust is a predictable concomitant of disclosing the unknown, whose disclosure is a desire the narrative instills in the audience and then goes on to gladden. Nor will that desire be satisfied unless the monster defies our conception of nature which demands that it probably engender some measure of repulsion.

In this interpretation of horror narratives, the majority of which would appear to exploit the cognitive attractions of the drama of disclosure, experiencing the emotion of art-horror is not our absolutely primary aim in consuming horror fictions, even though it is a determining feature for identifying membership in the genre. Rather, art-horror is the price we are willing to pay for the revelation of that which is impossible and unknown, of that which violates our conceptual schema. The impossible being does disgust; but that disgust is part of an overall narrative address which is not only pleasurable, but whose potential pleasure depends on the confirmation of the existence of the monster as a being that violates, defies, or problematizes standing cultural classifications. Thus, we are attracted to, and many of us seek out, horror fictions of this sort despite the fact that they provoke disgust, because that disgust is required for the pleasure involved in engaging our curiosity in the unknown and drawing it into the processes of revelation, ratiocination, etc.

Five Characteristics of Postmodern Horror

Isabel Cristina Pinedo

Isabel Cristina Pinedo is a professor of Media and Cultural Studies in the Department of Communications at Hunter College of the City University of New York. In the following selection, taken from the first chapter of *Recreational Terror: Women and the Pleasures of Horror Film Viewing,* Pinedo identifies and discusses "five characteristics that operate together to constitute the postmodern horror film." While Pinedo concerns herself exclusively with horror films, it is important to note that, like most contemporary film theorists, she tends to treat films both as narratives and as *texts,* making her insights directly applicable to literary horror—and not just to recent or "postmodern" literary horror.

In *Monsters and Mad Scientists: A Cultural History of the Horror Movie,* Andrew Tudor (1989) charts the development of the Anglo-American horror genre. The primary distinction he draws is between the pre-sixties (1931–1960) and the post-sixties (1960–1984) genre, terms that roughly correspond to my use of "classical" and "postmodern." Tudor parenthetically aligns the post-1960s genre with postmodernism and the "legitimation crisis" of postindustrial society by which he means the failure of traditional structures of authority. Although Tudor does not involve himself in discussions of postmodernism per se, he does point out that the legitimation crisis of late capitalism may be the salient social context in which to ground the contradictions of the post-sixties horror genre. . . .

The classical horror film is exemplified in films such as *Dracula* (1931), *Frankenstein* (1931), and *Dr. Jekyll and Mr. Hyde* (1931). The creature feature films of the post-war period—including *The Thing* (1951), *Invasion of the Body Snatchers* (1956), and *The Blob* (1958)—share a similar narrative structure, which Tudor lays out. The film opens with the violent disruption of the normative order by a monster, which can take the form of a supernatural or alien invader, a mad scientist, or a deviant transformation from within. The narrative revolves around the monster's rampage and people's ineffectual attempts to resist it. In the end, male military or scientific experts successfully employ violence and/or knowledge to defeat the monster and restore the normative order. The boundary between good and evil, normal and abnormal, human and alien is as firmly drawn as the imperative that good must conquer evil, thus producing a secure Manichean worldview in which the threats to the social order are largely external and (hu)man agency prevails, largely in the figure of the masterful male subject. . . .

In the fifties, the gothic monsters largely receded into the background, and what emerged was an amalgam of science-fiction and horror elements known as the creature feature. This hybrid combines science fiction's focus on the logically plausible (especially through technology) with horror's emphasis on fear, loathing, and violence. The fifties films generally locate the monster in a contemporary American city, sometimes a small town, thus drawing the danger closer to home, but they retain the exotic in the monster's prehistoric or outer space origins.

The postmodern horror film is exemplified by films such as *Night of the Living Dead* (1968), *The Texas Chain Saw Massacre* (1974), *Halloween* (1978), *The Thing* (1982), *A Nightmare on Elm Street* (1984), and *Henry: Portrait of a Serial Killer* (1990). Again, drawing on Tudor's analysis we can summarize the narrative structure as follows. Such films usually open with the violent disruption of the normative order by a monster, which can take the form of a supernatural or alien invader, a deviant transformation from within, a psychotic, or a combination of these forms. Like its classical predecessors, the postmodern horror film revolves around the monster's graphically violent rampage and ordinary people's ineffectual attempts to resist it with violence. In the end, the inefficacy of human action and the repudiation of narrative closure combine to produce various forms of the open ending: the monster triumphs (*Henry*); the monster is defeated but only temporarily (*Hal-*

loween), or the outcome is uncertain (*Night of the Living Dead, Texas Chain Saw Massacre, The Thing, Nightmare on Elm Street*). The boundary between living and dead, normal and abnormal, human and alien, good and evil, is blurred, sometimes indistinguishable. In contrast to the classical horror film, the postmodern film locates horror in the contemporary everyday world, where the efficacious male expert is supplanted by the ordinary victim who is subjected to high levels of explicit, sexualized violence, especially if female. Women play a more prominent role as both victims and heroes. The postmodern genre promotes a paranoid worldview in which inexplicable and increasingly internal threats to the social order prevail. . . .

CHARACTERISTICS OF THE HORROR GENRE

Despite the enormous breadth of films falling under the rubric of horror, there are identifiable elements that define horror in general, classical horror, and postmodern horror. I locate five characteristics that *operate together* to constitute the postmodern horror film:

1. Horror constitutes a violent disruption of the everyday world.
2. Horror transgresses and violates boundaries.
3. Horror throws into question the validity of rationality.
4. Postmodern horror repudiates narrative closure.
5. Horror produces a bounded experience of fear. . . .

Each characteristic operates in the *context* of the others; none is constitutive of the genre in and of itself. But together they form an interlocking web that constitutes the genre. This is a working definition, not an exhaustive list of qualifying criteria, and as such, this provisional definition is subject to the ongoing historical changes of the genre. The postmodern genre operates on the principles of disruption, transgression, undecidability and uncertainty.

HORROR CONSTITUTES A VIOLENT DISRUPTION OF THE EVERYDAY WORLD

Contrary to popular criticism, violence in the horror film is not gratuitous but is rather a constituent element of the genre. The horror narrative is propelled by violence, manifested in both the monster's violence and the attempts to destroy the monster. Horror is produced by the violation of what are tellingly called natural laws—by the disruption of our presuppositions about the integrity and predictable character of objects, places, animals, and people. Violence disrupts the world of everyday life; it explodes our assumptions about normality. The impermeability of death is violated when corpses come back to life (*Dracula* [1931], *Night of the Living Dead* [1968]). The integrity of self is breached when the body undergoes a radical transformation (*Dr. Jekyll and Mr. Hyde* [1931], *The Fly* [1986]).

The horror film throws into question our assumptions about reality and unreality. . . . It disorients the viewer's taken-for-granted reality. Horror violates our assumption that we live in a predictable, routinized world by demonstrating that we live in a minefield, by demanding a reason to trust in the taken-for-granted realm of "ordered normality."

In the classical paradigm, the violent disruption is often located in or originates from a remote, exotic location. In contrast, the postmodern paradigm treats violence as a constituent element of everyday life. . . . The disruption takes the form of physical violence against the body: (typically nonsexual) invasion of body cavities or of body surfaces to create cavities, the release of body fluids through stabbing and slashing, the tearing of body parts from each other, the wrenching transformation of bodies. Gore—the explicit depiction of dismemberment, evisceration, putrefaction, and myriad other forms of boundary violations with copious amounts of blood—takes center stage.

The postmodern paradigm is characterized by the forceful importance of what Philip Brophy calls the act of *showing* the spectacle of the ruined body. In contrast, the classical paradigm focuses on the more circumspect act of *telling*. This difference in the approach to violence is one of the primary distinctions between the classical and postmodern paradigms. The latter's fascination with the spectacle of the mutilated body, the creative death, necessitates its high level of explicit violence and privileging of the act of showing. The dismembered body, the body in bits and pieces, occupies center stage in the postmodern paradigm. Pete Boss, following Brophy, claims that the primacy of *body horror* is central to the contemporary horror genre, which he too characterizes as postmodern. Characteristically, everything else, including narrative and character development, is subordinated to "the demands of presenting the viewer with the uncompromised or privileged detail of human carnage" presented in an emotionally detached manner so that what fascinates is not primarily the suffering of the victim but her or his bodily ruination. . . .

HORROR TRANSGRESSES AND VIOLATES BOUNDARIES

Although violence is a salient feature of the genre, it must be situated in the context of monstrosity, culturally defined as an unnatural force. As [critic] Stephen Neale remarks,

> what defines the specificity of [the horror] genre is not the violence as such, but its conjunction with images and definitions of the monstrous. What defines its specificity with respect to the instances of order and disorder is their articulation across terms provided by categories and definitions of "the human" and "the natural."

Horror violates the taken-for-granted "natural" order. It blurs boundaries and mixes categories that are usually regarded as discrete to create what [critic] Mary Douglas calls "[im]purity and danger." The anomaly manifests itself as the monster: a force that is unnatural, deviant, and possibly malformed. The monster violates the boundaries of the body in a two-fold manner: through the use of violence against other bodies as discussed above and through the disruptive qualities of its own body. The monster's body is marked by the disruption of categories; it embodies contradiction. The pallor of the vampire, the weirdly oxymoronic "living dead," signifies death, yet the sated vampire's veins surge with the blood of its victim. The monster disrupts the social order by dissolving the basis of its signifying system, its network of differences: me/not me, animate/inanimate, human/nonhuman, life/death. The monster's body dissolves binary differences. . . .

HORROR QUESTIONS THE VALIDITY OF RATIONALITY

Horror exposes the limits of rationality and compels us to confront the irrational. The realm of rationality represents the ordered, intelligible universe that can be controlled and predicted. In contrast, the irrational represents the disordered, ineffable, chaotic, and unpredictable universe which constitutes the underside of life. In horror, irrational forces disrupt the social order. The trajectory of the classical narrative is to deploy science and force (often together as when science is put into the service of the military) to restore the rational, normative order, whereas the postmodern narrative is generally unable to overcome the irrational, chaotic forces of disruption. Because of this narrative structure, the classical paradigm's critique of science is necessarily limited. It takes the form, as in *Frankenstein,* of the hubris-inspired overreacher who aspires to be like God. Or the form of military science gone awry as in *Them!* (1954) in which exposure to radiation causes ants to mutate into giants. . . .

Horror films assert that not everything can or should be dealt with in rational terms. As the parapsychologist warns the rational skeptic in *The Haunting* (1963), "the supernatural is something that isn't supposed to happen, but it does happen . . . if it happens to you, you're liable to have that shut door in your mind ripped right off its hinges.". . .

POSTMODERN HORROR REPUDIATES NARRATIVE CLOSURE

The classical horror film constructs a secure universe characterized by narrative closure, one in which (hu)man agency (human agency understood as male agency) prevails and the normative order is restored by film's end. In contrast, violating narrative closure has become de rigueur for the postmodern genre. The film may come to an end, but it is an open ending. . . .

In the classical horror film, the monster is an irrational Other who precipitates violence and transgresses the law. It is evil because it threatens the social order; the suppression of the unleashed menace is a priority for the agents of order. The violence of the law restores repression, and the social order is reestablished. . . .

In the postmodern horror film either the monster triumphs or the outcome is uncertain. . . .

HORROR PRODUCES A BOUNDED EXPERIENCE OF FEAR

Horror is an exercise in recreational terror, a simulation of danger not unlike a roller coaster ride. Like the latter, people in a confined space are kept off-balance through the use of suspense and precipitous surprises achieved by alternating between seeing what lies ahead and being in the dark (for instance, tunnels and other shadowy regions, closed or shielded eyes). Throughout, the element of control, the conviction that there is nothing to be afraid of turns stress/arousal (beating heart, dry mouth, panic grip) into a pleasurable sensation. Fear and pleasure commingle. Indeed, the physical and emotional thrills experienced by a horror audience may be akin to the biochemical reactions stimulated by the intense physical excitement of a rollercoaster ride. . . .

The horror film is an exquisite exercise in coping with the terrors of everyday life. Earlier I argued that the horror film violates everyday life. This is true on the narrative level, but on the level of unconscious operations, it is more accurate to say that horror exposes the terror *implicit* in everyday life: the pain of loss, the enigma of death, the unpredictability of events, the inadequacy of intentions. It seems odd to talk about everyday life in terms of terror precisely because terror is a routinely repressed aspect of everyday life. According to Henri Lefebvre in *Everyday Life in the Modern World,* the repression of terror is incessant and ubiquitous; repression operates "at all levels, at all times and in every sphere of experience." Ironically, repression is effective precisely because everyday life seems spontaneous and "natural" and, therefore, exempt from repression.

Horror denaturalizes the repressed by transmuting the "natural" elements of everyday life into the unnatural form of the monster. In *Night of the Living Dead,* the mindless malevolence of a racist society (here and in Southeast Asia) is transmuted into the rampage of a group of zombies. This transmutation renders the terrors of everyday life at least emotionally accessible. By monstrifying quotidian terrors, horror unearths the repressed. This process is similar to the dream work described by Freud (1966). Much as dreams displace and condense repressed thoughts and feelings, so horror films introduce monstrous elements to disguise the quotidian terrors of everyday life. Much as dreams are unconscious attempts to express conflicts and resolve tensions, so horror films allow the audience to express and thus, to some extent, master feelings too threatening to articulate consciously. The horror film is the equivalent of the cultural nightmare, processing material that is simultaneously attractive and repellent, displayed and obfuscated, desired and repressed. Just as Freud regards dreams, even distressing ones, as wish fulfillments of repressed desires, so I regard the horror film as an amalgam of desire and inhibition, fascination and fear.

CHAPTER 2

The Gothic
and the
Grotesque

 Horror

The Gothic Novel, 1764–Present

Anne Williams

A scholar specializing in eighteenth-century British literature, Anne Williams is professor of English at the University of Georgia. She is the author of numerous articles and of two booklength studies: *Prophetic Strain: The Greater Lyric in the Eighteenth Century* and *Art of Darkness: A Poetics of Gothic*. The following article traces the development of the Gothic novel in British and American literature from its beginnings in eighteenth-century England through the end of the twentieth century. Here Williams discusses Horace Walpole's *The Castle of Otranto*—generally considered the first Gothic novel in English—as well as two early, and highly influential, Gothic novels: Ann Radcliffe's *The Mysteries of Udolpho* and M.G. Lewis's *The Monk*. Within this context, she considers eighteenth-century theories of terror and horror, and briefly touches upon the conventions common to the genre. Her conclusion—that today "the Gothic tradition may at last be drawing to a close"—is both challenging and provocative.

In 1764 a book called *The Castle of Otranto: A Gothic Story* was published anonymously in London. In the first chapter, a giant helmet comes crashing down into the courtyard of the Castle, killing Conrad, only son of Prince Manfred. With suspicious alacrity, Manfred responds to the loss of his heir by proposing to divorce his aging wife Hippolyta and to marry Isabella, his son's betrothed. He conducts his implicitly incestuous but quite literal pursuit of this princess through the dark vaults and dim corridors of the Castle, spaces uncannily furnished with weeping statues and sighing ancestral portraits.

Excerpted from "Edifying Narratives: The Gothic Novel, 1764–1997," by Anne Williams in *Gothic: Transmutations of Horror in Late 20th Century Art*, edited by Christoph Grunenberg. Reprinted with permission from the MIT Press.

But Manfred is doomed to failure at every turn. He accidentally kills his other child, Matilda, and he learns that his own claim to the throne he inherited is illegitimate. A young "peasant," Theodore, effects the fall of the House of Manfred, both literally and figuratively: "The walls of the castle behind Manfred were thrown down with a mighty force, and the form of Alphonso [patriarch of the family line and owner of the giant helmet] appeared in the centre of the ruins: 'Behold in Theodore the true heir of Alphonso!' said the vision." Manfred and Hippolyta retire to separate convents; Theodore (who had been in love with Matilda) marries Isabella, intending to pass the remainder of his life "in the society of one, with whom he could forever indulge the melancholy that had taken possession of his soul."

A MYTH OF ORIGINS

This slender volume was an immediate best-seller. With the second edition, the author disclosed his identity; he was Horace Walpole, son of the great Prime Minister, and a noted antiquarian, raconteur, collector, and dilettante, who had spent the previous decade in remodeling his country house, Strawberry Hill, in "Gothick" style. Walpole declared that his story had its origins in his dream of an enormous gauntlet resting on the balustrade of the staircase, a vision so compelling that he sat down and began to write, completing his narrative in a mere six weeks.

No historian of the Gothic novel fails to repeat this story of Walpole's dream house and house dream. It is, however, somewhat misleading as a myth of origins. There was very little novel (in the sense of "new") in either the plot or decor of *The Castle of Otranto*. The word "Gothic" in the subtitle signified in Walpole's time "medieval" as well as "rude and barbarous." A taste for all these qualities had been developing throughout the eighteenth century. Antiquarianism—interest in the past both for its own sake and as a source of national identity—was flourishing. . . . The "graveyard school" of the 1740s had taught readers of poetry to appreciate "the gloomy horrors of the tomb.". . . And Edmund Burke's *Philosophical Enquiry into the Origins of the Sublime and the Beautiful* (1759), had claimed aesthetic respectability for the grand, the indeterminate, the boundless, the infinite, the dark.

Furthermore, *The Castle of Otranto* was not, technically speaking, a "novel" at all. Literary scholars generally reserve that term for designating prose fiction in a realistic mode, narratives that accurately mirror social and historical conditions. *Otranto* (and all so-called Gothic novels) are more properly called "romances," lurid fictions driven by the wish-fulfillment dreams, or the nightmares, of author and audience. To give Walpole his due, however, one must acknowledge that his "Gothic Story" hit upon a set of images and conventions that was to preoccupy the literary imagination of Great Britain quite obsessively until around 1820, and then to disappear, reemerging periodically in a series of "Gothic Revivals." Walpole placed a dynastic family plot within a Gothic ("rude," "barbarous," "medieval") setting. This combination seemed particularly effective in evoking those emotions, terror and melancholy, that the reading public by 1764 found pleasurable. And he published it in the newly popular medium of the novel, cheaply marketed and widely distributed.

THE GOTHIC TRADITION IN LITERATURE

The Gothic tradition has not been highly regarded by literary scholars, despite the fact that it has attracted many canonical writers, such as Coleridge, Keats, the Brontës, Melville, and Faulkner. . . . Reasons for their low opinion no doubt include the Gothic tradition's intermittent but often extreme popularity, the sensational and subversive nature of its materials, and its long and close association with women writers as well as readers. Jane Austen's affectionate satire of the Gothic in *Northanger Abbey* (1818) acknowledges the dangers of such company; Isabella Thorpe, who initiates the heroine Catherine Morland into the delights of the Gothic with her list of "truly horrid" books, is an exceptionally silly and superficial girl. In addition, "the novel" itself had to struggle for respectability during the nineteenth century; it did so by growing increasingly preoccupied with the social and ethical issues best dealt with in a more realistic narrative mode. In their themes and topics, novelists seemed to express a growing conviction that if "the novel" was to be taken seriously, it had better claim the high seriousness that only realism affords. . . .

And yet Walpole appears to have assumed that his "Gothic Story" might instruct as well as delight. He agreed with the old idea that the author bears a responsibility to edify the audience. Walpole's tone in both his prefaces is ironic; but

when he (posing as translator) piously suggests "the author"
of *Otranto* might have hit upon a "more useful moral" than
that "the sins of the fathers are visited on their children to
the third and fourth generations," he both articulates his
book's theme and accepts the premise that stories should be
instructive. . . . A generation later, Ann Radcliffe's *The Mysteries of Udolpho* (1794), the most popular and influential of
all early Gothics, still conforms to this didactic convention. It
concludes with this rousing peroration: "O! useful may it be
to have shewn, that, though the vicious can sometimes pour
affliction upon the good, their power is transient and their
punishment certain; and that innocence, though oppressed
by injustice, shall, supported by patience, finally triumph
over misfortune!"

While these claims may sound a bit disingenuous to our
ears, they should not be entirely dismissed, even though the
explicit morals the authors intended to convey are not the
most interesting lessons the Gothic teaches. Certainly
Gothic conventions have had remarkable staying power,
which implies that their reappearances, their continual rebirth in various guises, reveals something constant—and
anxiety-provoking—in Anglo-American culture of the past
two centuries. By 1820 the public taste for Gothic fiction had
sharply declined, assuming a less prominent place in Victorian literary subculture.

The Gothic reemerged spectacularly, however, with *Dracula* (1897). In contrast to the "historical" settings of the earlier Gothic novels, Bram Stoker makes his contemporary:
London of the 1890s, populated by Darwinian-minded scientists and the "new woman," that alarming creature who
has learned to type and presumes to expect equality and
partnership in marriage. Thus, not only does Stoker's vampire imply the fearful, ancient, foreign "other," he also en-
codes late-Victorian anxieties about "nature red in tooth and
claw" and a resurgent female principle in the culture.

Since *Dracula* was contemporary with the invention of cin-
ema, and this new medium (like the appearance of "the
novel" in the eighteenth century) proved effective in the dif-
fusion of Gothic imagery, Stoker's blood-sucking aristocrat, as
well as the monster in Mary Shelley's earlier *Frankenstein*
(1819) were quickly exploited as material for the Grade B horror flick. And in the 1960s Gothic reappeared as best-selling
mass-market paperback fiction. Hundreds of novels emulat-

ing Victoria Holt's *Mistress of Mellyn* (1960) were sold with an iconic cover illustration: a woman wearing a look of terror and a diaphanous gown flees from a darkened mansion with one lighted window. A complementary strain of supernatural Gothic also reemerged at about the same time, with Ira Levin's *Rosemary's Baby* (1965) and Stephen King's first novel, *Carrie* (1974). This latest Gothic revival subsided in the early 1970s, when the mode of historical romance known as the "bodice-ripper" inundated the paperback market.

GOTHIC CONVENTIONS

It is easy to enumerate Gothic narrative formulas; it is more difficult to determine, however, the roots of their appeal. I would suggest that those elements that continually reappear may be read as complex cultural metaphors. The haunted castle, for instance: as Walpole's title, *The Castle of Otranto* declares, this genre was at first identified with a particular kind of edifice. In later variations any kind of enclosed space, so long as it is associated with mysteries or secrets, may serve. Gothics usually feature several other elements: characters who are types rather than realistic and sharply individualized people; complex plots full of exciting and violent action; situations derived from the conflict between individual desire and social constraints, such as the necessity of marrying "appropriately;" supernatural or seemingly supernatural events; suspense motivated by family secrets, such as inheritance or kinship. . . .

A haunted castle, so crucial to early Gothic, connotes many inherited traditions, such as the structures of political power and families, which are not only inherited but potentially imprisoning: in short, the Gothic novel evokes the weight of the past. . . .

It is perfectly logical . . . that the castle should be, or seems to be, haunted. Not only is the patriarchal "family romance" an inherently Gothic tale; we can also see that the early Gothic novelists' insistence on the "historicity" of their stories allows them to deploy their culture's fantasies of a past imagined as dark indeed: violent, cruel, despotic, superstitious. The broad structures and themes of the Gothic novel, therefore, demonstrate the effects of the Enlightenment on the popular imagination: Gothic fictions are the fantasies, quasi-memories, of a culture newly conscious of itself as different from its past: not rude, not barbarous, not despotic, not superstitious. It is equally logical that the fascination with Gothic darkness that had grown for at least a century prior to Walpole's book finally exploded in the Gothic novel of the 1790s, the decade immediately following the French Revolution. This event marked the final collapse of several ancient hierarchies: the monarchy, an inflexible class system, and the hegemony of the Roman Catholic Church. . . .

One might speculate, therefore, that the Gothic simply offers a nostalgic fantasy of a more orderly past. But this hypothesis, while partially true, is inadequate to explain the genre's recurrent popularity. Why it should be so becomes clearer if we turn to the most important of Gothic conventions: these tales aim to please readers by scaring them.

GOTHIC TERROR, GOTHIC HORROR: *UDOLPHO* AND *THE MONK*

According to eighteenth-century aesthetic theory, there are two kinds of fear: horror and terror. They are, though complementary, very different responses. Horror is physical revulsion at some gruesome object; terror is imaginative, aroused by contemplation of the dark, the dangerous, the unknown. To come across a worm-eaten corpse (a common early Gothic experience) arouses horror; to awaken in a crypt and fear that it might contain a worm-eaten corpse (another common experience) creates terror. By the 1790s, readers began to notice that Gothic novelists tended to specialize in one or the other of these effects. Ann Radcliffe consciously sought to create terror, which she justified on the grounds established by Burke. In his scandalous novel *The Monk* (1796), however, which was not published in an unexpurgated edition between 1797 and 1950, M.G. Lewis exemplifies the techniques of "horror." The differences between "horror" and "terror" reveal an unexpected theme at the core of the Gothic tradition.

Radcliffe's terror plot is a familiar story, at least to women readers, the Ur-plot of Charlotte Brontë's *Jane Eyre* (1847), of Daphne du Maurier's *Rebecca* (1938), and of the countless variations that appeared in the mass-market Gothic revival of the 1960s. In *The Mysteries of Udolpho,* the orphaned Emily St. Aubert is sent to live with her vulgar, social-climbing aunt who decries her niece's proposed engagement to Valencourt, a most charming young man, but a younger son. This aunt marries a mysterious Italian, Count Montoni, who carries her and

Emily off to Udolpho, his brooding, half-ruined castle in the Apennines. There Emily experiences all kinds of terrors, and suffers, too, at the hands of Montoni, who intends to trick her out of her inheritance and to marry her to his friend, the lecherous Count Murano. Eventually, she and her maid Annette escape Udolpho and make their way back toward France, where they happen to be shipwrecked on a beach owned by Emily's long-lost cousin, the Vicomte de Villeroi. It turns out that Emily's aunt was the Vicomtesse, murdered by Laurentini di Udolpho. She is cousin of Montoni and avatar of Charlotte Brontë's Bertha Mason, the madwoman in the attic: a wild, bad girl who poisons her lover's wife and goes mad upon immuring herself in a convent. At last Valencourt and Emily are reunited, reconciled, and married. They return to Emily's childhood home, presumably to live happily ever after.

In contrast, the horrors of *The Monk*, precociously published by the nineteen-year-old M.G. Lewis portray a world far less benign. The main plot concerns Ambrosio, an infant abandoned on the steps of a monastery and reared by the monks to be perfectly virtuous. Famous throughout Seville for his sermons on chastity, he secretly yields to the wiles of Matilda, a beautiful young woman who resembles the Monk's painting of the Madonna, and who has disguised herself as a novice in order to seduce him. She succeeds without much difficulty. Once fallen, Ambrosio becomes ever more lustful, appropriating Matilda's now revealed magical powers in order to abduct and rape a fair maiden, Antonia, killing her mother Elvira in the process. Having satisfied his desires, the Monk kills Antonia as well.

Meanwhile, we also read of Agnes, who is forced to take the veil against her will. She attempts to elope with her beloved Lorenzo, disguising herself as "The Bleeding Nun," a specter that appears in her aunt's German castle every five years at midnight on May 5. Lorenzo mistakes the ghost for Agnes, and finds himself inadvertently wed to the Nun, who turns out to be his ancestress (another mad, bad girl) who had broken her holy vows and then murdered her lover. Meanwhile, Agnes is incarcerated in the Convent of St. Clare. When the cruel Abbess discovers that the young woman is pregnant, she imprisons her in the vaults, where she gives birth to a son who dies because she didn't know how to nurse an infant. She goes mad. Rescuing Agnes, Lorenzo discovers Antonia's body. Ambrosio, imprisoned for murder, strikes a desperate bargain with Lucifer, who gleefully discloses that Matilda was a demon disguised as a woman, sent to effect the proud Monk's fall from virtue. And more: Antonia was his sister, Elvira his mother. He has committed not only fornication but incest, not only murder but matricide. The demon carries him away from prison and drops him in a desert gorge where he dies an excruciating death.

Although these two novels have exotic settings and complex plots hinging on the discovery of family secrets, their differences are equally significant. Radcliffe's novel is broadly comic in its narrative structure: hero and heroine survive their terrors and learn from them. (Emily's experiences illustrate the connection between "apprehension" as "fear" and "apprehension" as "understanding"). The heroine is finally united with her beloved and married; the ghosts are all explained. Radcliffe thus creates a world that is ultimately explicable, in which an orphaned, isolated young woman may not only survive, but triumph. *The Monk*, however, is, like *Otranto*, tragic; it traces a hero's fall from greatness to destruction or death. The ghosts are real, and nothing is to be trusted. . . .

Terror expresses the power of mind; horror demonstrates the power of nature. "Horror" and "terror" imply contrasting cultural attitudes about the nature of "the female" in the literal and symbolic sense, including the "feminine" nature and materiality. (It is not a coincidence that our words "matter" and "mother" both come from the Latin *mater*.) Since ancient Greece, (male) philosophers and theologians have conceived of "the female" as "otherness"—dark and disorderly and dangerous. In this view even woman's quasi-miraculous powers of maternity align her with irrational power and loathsome materiality, since birth is always followed by death. The plot, the decor, and the structure of *The Monk* enact such assumptions about women and maternity. As the fate of its female characters implies, *The Monk* is profoundly misogynistic. The seductive demon Matilda, who presents herself in the guise of the Holy Mother, awakens Ambrosio's carnality and so destroys him. Another woman he kills in pursuit of that lust turns out to be his mother. A frenzied crowd literally beats the cruel Mother Abbess of St. Clare to a bloody pulp; Agnes the mad mother refuses to part with the worm-eaten corpse of her infant, which the narrator describes as a sight disgusting to any eye "but a mother's." The Bleeding Nun, most potent of Lewis' horrific fantasies, uncannily violates almost all patriarchal taboos about female sexuality. . . .

"Horror," therefore, springs out of a fundamentally conservative world view that adheres to the ancient Western model of reality, though to foreground the horrible in fiction or any art, paradoxically brings it to consciousness. "Terror," on the other hand, is thoroughly revolutionary in its implications. Since terror is an experience of the individual imagination, Radcliffe narrates her stories so that we share the perspective of the heroine. Later Gothics in the terror mode almost always use a first-person narrator. But this technique has important ramifications: it replaces the "I" tacitly assumed to be male, the "I" of centuries of philosophers, theologians, and poets, with a female subject. The literary artist is no longer necessarily "a man speaking to men" (in Wordsworth's phrase); she may well be "a woman speaking to women."

THE GOTHIC AND FEMINIST CRITICISM

The recognition that such a shift is not only possible but important has recently been facilitated by the most important change to affect our reading of the Gothic since it became an object of academic interest in the 1890s: the development of feminist criticism. . . .

The emerging feminist critics' initial take on the Gothic was fairly predictable: they tended to regard it with some suspicion, since in these novels women inevitably seem to experience a fate worse than death. They are either pursued, stabbed, or raped, the helpless victims of horror Gothic, or pursued and threatened with stabbing and rape, and then married off at the end of the story in terror Gothic. This latter fate is almost as bad, since these narratives seem to imply that marriage to a wealthy man is a worthy aim—indeed the only proper aim—for a young woman. Numerous feminist critics, therefore, argued that the Gothic inculcated patriarchal standards in its readers while at the same time offering a kind of vicarious contemplation of patriarchal horrors. One may argue that in exploring the mysterious house and learning its secrets, the heroine is initiated into the implications of a male-dominated system and how to succeed in it: protect your virtue and marry as well as possible. The Walpole or Lewis kind of plot "horror" (reemerging in such bestsellers as *Rosemary's Baby* and *Carrie*) had an even more distressing subtext: the uncontrollable dangers associated with the female, dangers that must be resisted whenever possible, but that can never be conquered. And yet a feminist critic might also wish to inquire why women's writing seemed to be so preoccupied with dangers to women and bizarre distortions of reality. Furthermore, the Radcliffe formula seemed to have some kind of therapeutic or empowering effect, and it can be no coincidence that two most dramatic eruptions of Gothic in the popular press (the 1790s and the 1960s) coincided with two important outbreaks of political feminism. In *Literary Women* (1976), a pioneering work of feminist criticism, Ellen Moers coined the term "Female Gothic." In her examination of Mary Shelley, Emily Brontë, and Christina Rossetti she proposed that these writers used Gothic conventions to express their sense of women's experience in their culture. Two years later, Sandra Gilbert and Susan Gubar's magisterial book *The Madwoman in the Attic*, adopted Charlotte Brontë's imprisoned madwoman as a figure for woman writers in nineteenth-century British and American culture. . . .

The Gothic Legacy

Literature creates a virtual space that escapes the "real world," where limits are imposed by culture, consciousness, and the laws of physics; and yet imagination, invited into this place to play, may, paradoxically, return to the world with the power to revise at least two of these three limits. Following a particular character through a set of circumstances that arouse particular responses, Gothic fiction offers its readers an imaginative space that both insists on "reality," on historicity, on materiality, and at the same time liberates the reader from the constrictions of that history. Similarly paradoxical are the effects of pleasurable fear, which we find in the vicarious experience of horror and terror. The reader, particularly the female reader, may contemplate both the horrors of the ways in which the culture at large regards the female, but also some alternate possibilities in imagining the world as it appears to a female I/eye. By expressing a fascinated ambivalence toward the past, the Gothic novel both condemns that time of darkness and superstition, and revels in it. Clearly, the experience of fear in art may exorcise fear, since artistic fear is chosen, sought, and controllable.

Aside from the empowering possibilities inherent in a newly developing female literary tradition, the Gothic may have one other important legacy: the conception of the self that is most familiar nowadays in psychoanalysis. Here is another paradox. The Gothic has proved extraordinarily amenable to psychoanalytic interpretation, but perhaps this is true not because Freud had discerned a dynamics of selfhood as simply true and universal, one which the Gothic was somehow intuiting. Instead, it may be that by means of the images and affects aroused by Gothic conventions, our culture was imagining, one century prior to Freud, some of the concepts that he would articulate: that the self is a structure, like a house; that it is haunted by history—both one's own and that of one's family; that this psychic "house" has secret chambers that need to be opened if the house is to be livable. For what is the process of psychoanalysis but the construction of a story—long, complicated, rambling, digressive— about the past which concludes when the story has been told, when all the doors of all the secret rooms have been opened?

At the end of the twentieth century, Gothic novels continue to be written and read. Anne Rice, Stephen King, Barbara Michaels, and a host of others supply the shelves with endless paperbacks. Gothic horror films continue to thrill: consider, for instance, the long series of *Halloween* movies, or the *Nightmare on Elm Street* sequence. And yet, I would speculate that the Gothic tradition may at last be drawing to a close. In the beginning its conventions seemed compelling to the greatest, as well as to quite ordinary literary minds. All the high Romantic poets exploited the possibilities of Gothic at some point in their careers; Faulkner may have been the most important writer to do so. Nowadays it seems that the popular vocabulary most likely to appeal to the serious literary artist is that of science fiction: not Montoni, one's wicked uncle by marriage, but an alien from another galaxy is more likely to be the abductor. And while the *Alien* films and many episodes of *The X-Files* use Gothic conventions (and certainly each has a heroine who is easily beleaguered), it seems that we are in the process of reimagining our place in the universe: the most frightful others reside in the vast deserts of strange planets, not in the dark vaults of our history on earth.

Elements of the Gothic

Linda Bayer-Berenbaum

The following selection is excerpted from the first
chapter of Linda Bayer-Berenbaum's *The Gothic
Imagination,* a wide-ranging study of the Gothic tradition in literature and art. Here Bayer-Berenbaum
locates the origins of the term *Gothic* in Renaissance
discussions of medieval architecture and considers
how it came to be applied to a certain body of literature produced in eighteenth-century England. In addition to considering the relationship between the
Gothic and the grotesque, she also discusses themes
and conventions common to most forms of Gothic
literature—such as death and decay, the presence of
the supernatural, the typical Gothic villain, and the
trademark Gothic castle. But for Bayer-Berenbaum,
the presence or absence of such "standard Gothic
paraphernalia" is essentially arbitrary and thus of
secondary interest. Much more important to her is
Gothic's psychological and spiritual effect: an "expansion of consciousness and reality."

The word *Gothic* originally referred to the Northern tribes
that invaded Europe during the fourth, fifth, and sixth centuries. The term was later applied by Renaissance critics to
the style of architecture that flourished in the thirteenth century, because these critics thought that the style had originated with the Goths. This architecture was held in low esteem during the Renaissance, and the word *Gothic* therefore
developed pejorative connotations suggesting the uncouth,
ugly, barbaric, or archaic. It implied the vast and the gloomy,
and subsequently denoted anything medieval. Later the word
indicated any period in history before the middle or even the
end of the seventeenth century. *Gothic* loosely referred to
anything old-fashioned or out of date. The ruins of Gothic
cathedrals and castles were naturally termed *Gothic,* and

Excerpted from *The Gothic Imagination: Expansion in Gothic Literature and Art,* by
Linda Bayer-Berenbaum. Reprinted with permission from Associated University
Presses.

soon any ruins—the process of decay itself—became associated with the Gothic as did wild landscapes and other mix-
tures of sublimity and terror.

ORIGINS OF GOTHIC LITERATURE

The Gothic movement in literature began in England during
the second quarter of the eighteenth century, and because it
encompassed a general interest in the past, in archaeology,
antiques, and ruins, particularly those of the Middle Ages,
the label *Gothic* seemed appropriate. This Gothic revival
was a reaction against earlier eighteenth-century order and
formality, and it gleaned its inspiration from medieval Romantic literature. A changing attitude toward nature and
feeling evolved; wildness and boldness came into vogue.
The Romantic qualities of yearning, aspiration, mystery, and
wonder nourished the roots of the Gothic movement. Sensu-
alism, sensationalism, and then sadism and satanism were
nurtured in an orgy of emotion. The child of Romanticism,
the Gothic movement in literature exaggerated and intensified its parent's nature.

Horace Walpole, Ann Radcliffe, Matthew Lewis, and
Charles Robert Maturin, as well as hundreds of less capable
Gothic writers, established the conventions for the Gothic
novel, which were later drawn upon by Mary Shelley, Jane
Austen, Emily Brontë, Edgar Allan Poe, Bram Stoker,
Charles Brockden Brown, William Godwin, Thomas Love
Peacock, William Beckford, Edward Bulwer-Lytton, and
Robert Louis Stevenson, to name only a few. The works of
these authors differ significantly; critics have even identified
different schools of Gothic literature—a Gothic historical
school, a school of terror, and a school of horror, for example. Nonetheless, a basic orientation to reality is apparent in
all Gothic works. The standard Gothic paraphernalia
(haunted castles, creaking staircases, vampire bats, and secret passageways) are only the trappings that may or may
not be present. More substantial characteristics reappear
from work to work, such as recurrent character types, plot
patterns, and themes, as well as common psychological and
sexual attitudes, similar treatments of fear, pain, compulsion, and disgust, and comparable views of religion and politics. Although the standard conventions for the Gothic novel
were developed during the eighteenth and nineteenth centuries, Gothicism itself is not restricted to a single time and

culture or even to a single style of writing. The origins of the Gothic sensibility predate the eighteenth century, and works that are essentially Gothic are being produced today.

IMMANENCE AND CONTRAST IN GOTHIC LITERATURE

The traditional Gothic paraphernalia, now familiar to any school child, was established in Walpole's *The Castle of Otranto* and Radcliffe's *The Mysteries of Udolpho*, the proto-types of the early Gothic novel. The graveyard and the con-vent, the moats and drawbridges, dungeons, towers, myste-rious trap doors and corridors, rusty hinges, flickering candles, burial vaults, birthmarks, tolling bells, hidden man-uscripts, twilight, ancestral curses—these became the trade-marks of the early Gothic novel. They prepare the reader for later apparitions, reducing his incredulity and encouraging a suspension of disbelief. These trademarks are symptoms of underlying Gothic assumptions. They symbolically echo the dimensions of the Gothic reality, serving as rituals that invoke that reality. However, beneath the Gothic gimmicks, the essential tenet is an expansion of consciousness and re-ality that is basic to every aspect of the Gothic, from setting to metaphysical claims.

Gothicism insists that what is customarily hallowed as real by society and its language is but a small portion of a greater reality of monstrous proportion and immeasurable power. The peculiarly *Gothic* quality of this extended reality is its immanence, its integral, inescapable connection to the world around us. The spirit does not dwell in another world; it has invaded an ordinary chair, a mirror, or a picture. The soul has not gone to heaven; the ghost lingers among the liv-ing. Furthermore, the perception of the expanded reality in-volves an expansion of consciousness. Sometimes external occurrences precipitate this heightened concentration, as when a person is so shocked by what he sees that he enters a state of complete awareness; at other times an initial heightened consciousness makes possible the detection of an external reality—such as the hovering presence of some strange apparition. Through heightened sensitivity and re-fined perception, the Gothic mind encounters a greater in-tensity or reacts to it.

The Gothic setting first introduces the expanded domain by insinuating that reality may be higher and deeper and more tangled than we ordinarily think. Persistent contrasts illustrate this greater scope. The Gothic landscape plunges from extreme to extreme; from the height of an airy bell tower to the depth of a dungeon vault; from the mass of heavy stone walls to the delicate, illusive spiderweb; from utter darkness to a candle's flicker; or from hollow silence to a high-pitched squeak. Even modern Gothic novels that have abandoned these clichés maintain extreme contrast. The shrill scream still manages to shatter silence, lightning breaks the darkness, and a sudden chill of wind stirs a hot and heavy night. In Bram Stoker's *Dracula*, for instance, Dracula himself first appears as gleaming bright eyes and white teeth against the black of his garments and the night. Later he is described as a long, black figure leaning over Lucy's frail, white form. Dracula's dark castle cuts a jagged line against the moonlight, and in the daytime a drab haziness is pierced by brilliant green grass and glowing silver tree trunks. When the full moon appears, it is accompanied by black, driving clouds, and a black bat periodically flits across its brightness. The terrible storms recorded in Nina's newspaper clipping erupt from a calm sea without warning; Renfield is violent all day and quiet all night; the men leaving the burial chamber are particularly conscious of that moment when the pure night air replaces the pungent stuffiness of the vault—such examples are virtually endless. These contrasts are included in Gothic literature because they magnify reality; between the greatest extremes lies the greatest breadth. The constant presence of polar opposites prevents us from mistaking any single dimension for the whole, and with respect to density, as opposed to scope, the mind is unable to tolerate extremes for very long. We either avoid, or forget, the unbearable or become accustomed to it, yet persistent contrast discourages adjustment, because in the clash between two states we can adjust to neither, and thus any dulling of the senses is averted. Whether by superficial color contrasts or more basic emotional and thematic juxtapositions, the Gothic novel sustains unmitigated sensitivity.

The castle (or the convent) in Gothic literature is a good study in contrast. Usually situated in a wild forest or uninhabited mountain range where the sky is unsettled and the wind howling, the calm and the stable are set amid the wild and dynamic. God's creation is pitted against man's in the clash between nature and architecture. Internally, the castle accentuates a contrast in power for its inhabitants by fortifying the power of its owner and diminishing that of his victim. By preventing the prisoner from escaping or receiving aid, the castle renders the victim more passive in comparison to the villain as does the storm that often rages outside, discouraging flight or rescue.

Contrast in Gothic literature is not limited to setting but is echoed in characterization and theme. . . . There are the villains—the interfering, brutal fathers, the officials of the Inquisition, the sadistic monks and abbots, or the ugly, monstrous foreigners; there are the victims—the helpless, innocent virgins or the naive and sensitive youths; and there are the heroes—the dauntless, gallant, handsome knights, the courageous, insistent saviors. If the victim is of noble birth, the hero is frequently a peasant. The scatterbrained, chattering domestic servant provides comic relief, but she is also important as a counter-image for the deep, intelligent, serious heroine or for any of the supermen who inhabit the Gothic world. The stereotyping of these characters is the price that must be paid for the desired contrast, yet the Gothic sensibility judges the accompanying gain in intensity well worth the loss of realistic portraiture. Many of these characters' virtues and vices, as well as many general themes in the Gothic novel, are not important in their own right but only as antithetical tendencies. Idealized femininity, for example, is extremely common in the Gothic novel and is usually more functional as a backdrop for cruelty than as a convincing description of behavior. Gushing sentimentality is set beside brutality, each to highlight the other. The restoration of nobility and hereditary rights is likewise more striking when the restored noble was initially a pauper, and savagery and revenge, violence and hate are constantly set in the context of chivalry and honor, suffering and courage, love and loyalty. The principle of contrast that dilates the mind is here, as elsewhere, more important than content.

Besides contrasting extremes, twisted convolutions in Gothic settings also extend the conception of reality. The devious and elusive nature of life is reflected in the winding staircases and underground tunnels that challenge the restrictions of three-dimensional space. In their tortuous windings, they baffle our sense of direction and threaten to lead us out of the known and into the depths of another dimension. The lack of simple forms and clear direction can also be detected in plot progression. A long, complicated story line can more easily sustain a constant level of anticipation than can a direct exposition and resolution, and therefore the Gothic novel tends to replace the climax of the novel with the constant presence of the supernatural or with ever-developing contingencies. The Gothic writer is reluctant to sacrifice any intensity to rising or falling action before or after a climax, so that when the climax is not eliminated altogether, it is often postponed until the very end of the novel. The absence of clear boundaries and distinctions in setting is compounded by haze and darkness, permitting infinite possibilities that would be dispelled by clear perception.

In time some of the contrasts became overused and, like many of the ritual Gothic trademarks, such as the castle, they lost their power through familiarity. The medieval tone began to fade in Matthew Lewis's *The Monk* and William Godwin's *Caleb Williams,* and finally vanished altogether in such works as Mary Shelley's *Frankenstein* and Oscar Wilde's *The Picture of Dorian Grey.* Although the traditional hallmarks of the Gothic had withered, the fear and thrill of a greater reality remained.

SLEEP, DEATH, AND DECAY

Gothic literature continued to portray all states of mind that intensify normal thought or perception. Dream states, drug states, and states of intoxication have always been prevalent in the Gothic novel because repressed thoughts can surface in them; under their influence inhibitions are minimized, and thus the scope of consciousness is widened. Gothic novelists are particularly fond of hypnotic trances, telepathic communications, visionary experiences, and extrasensory perceptions, for these reveal the secret recesses of the mind or powers of increased mental transmission and reception. Hallucinations augment mental images to the point of visual perception, and visions involving future occurrences challenge the confines of space and time.

Sleep, the most readily available alternative to ordinary, waking thought processes, receives considerable attention in Gothic novels, both within the stories themselves and as sources for the authors' inspiration. Horace Walpole wrote of *The Castle of Otranto:*

> Shall I even confess to you what was the origin of this romance? I waked one morning in the beginning of last June from a dream, of which all I could recover was, that I had thought my-

self in an ancient castle (a very natural dream for a head filled like mine with Gothic story) and that on the uppermost bannister of a great staircase I saw a gigantic hand in armour.

Mary Shelley similarly writes that her book *Frankenstein* was based on a dream. Within the Gothic novel, characters frequently question whether or not they are awake or merely dreaming, often describing strange states of awareness between sleep and wakefulness where neither the reality of the dream nor that of wakefulness can dispel the other so that both persist in an expanded, double encounter. Deprivation of sleep is also investigated by Gothic writers; for example, Count Dracula meets with Jonathan Harker only at night, and Harker's lack of sleep and changed sleeping patterns alter his perceptions. Gothic writers exploit night-consciousness in general, highlighting changes in temperament from morning to evening related to drowsiness and fatigue or even to the gravity of the moon and other variables. In the state of night-consciousness, as portrayed in Gothicism, a person is more susceptible to the power of suggestion, less analytical or rational, less strictly controlled; the defense mechanisms of the psyche become weary and less effective.

Gothic scenes never seem complete without their share of crumbling architectural remains, rotting old houses, ancient relics, and even decrepit, senile people. This attraction to ruins might initially appear to oppose the notion of an expanded reality by emphasizing a temporal, physical world in decay, yet considered from another angle, ruins indicate the limitless power of nature over human creation. Death and sickness lead us to acknowledge the extent of the forces that control us, and in the face of death we recognize the omnipotence of time and try to confront our own annihilation. The concept of self-extinction stretches consciousness; we probe the limits of our minds with fear, with caution, and yet with a certain thrill. We are attracted to that great beyond. . . .

The Gothic fascination with death and decay involves an admiration for power at the expense of beauty. . . . Those factors which conquer life and disintegrate matter become the object of great admiration. . . .

THE GOTHIC AND THE GROTESQUE

The grotesque aspects of Gothicism are evident in the caricatures that evolved from fifteenth-century ornamentation and in the repulsive characters and gruesome scenes from

Gothic literature. A predilection for deformity is unmistakable. Often Gothic villains have huge noses or eyes, elongated foreheads, growths or moles, enormous hands or teeth, scars, cleft palates, or hunched backs. Both caricatures and grotesques are created through exaggeration rather than by a complete departure from normality. The exaggeration of just one aspect of the beautiful can produce the hideous, and thus the Gothic intensification without regard for beauty and proportion is also operative here.

When distortion is not involved, the grotesque can be simply achieved through unusual combinations of the normal or even the beautiful, through an unexpected fusion of different realms. This aspect of the grotesque, like other aspects of the Gothic, can be described as particularly nontranscendent, for the strange creatures that appear are not totally other—they are not complete departures from the known but unusual amalgamations of the ordinary. When we dissect the purely ugly, we find that its parts are ugly, but when we dissect the grotesque, we may find that its parts are pleasing. We are left to wonder what strange power has caused the familiar to become so unfamiliar, so terrible.

The grotesque can be further understood as a demonstration of underlying chaos. . . . The grotesque insults our need for order, for classification, matching, and grouping; it violates a sense of appropriate categories. The resulting disorientation reinforces an ultimate vision of disorder at the root of the Gothic endeavor, for the rejection of all restrictions must necessarily produce chaos, a chaos similarly implied in the celebration of ruins. A certain revolt against materialism and the tyranny of the physical world is involved here, as it is whenever spirits defy matter. In its most basic implication, the Gothic quest is for the random, the wild, and the unbounded. . . .

GOTHIC TERROR

Terror is a primary Gothic ingredient not only because it is a reaction to threat but also because of its own physiological quality. The terrified person, and the reader by identification, becomes suddenly alert. He notices how chilly the room has become or how dark the night has grown. He may sense the pulsation of blood through the tips of his fingers or notice a piercing smell of sulphur in the air. In terror a person feels powerfully present, starkly alive. The words *terror* and *horror* are often used erroneously as interchangeable reactions to frightening experiences. Both involve fear and repulsion, but terror is more immediate, more emotional, and less intellectual. You may be horrified by what your friend tells you but terrified by what you yourself see. Ann Radcliffe felt that terror and horror were "so far opposite, that the first expands the soul, and awakens the faculties to a higher degree of life," while "the other contracts, freezes, and nearly annihilates." Terror is more potent and stimulating and thus the more Gothic emotion.

Terror in Gothic literature is sometimes caused by human or natural actions, but more often the formidable agent is in some sense supernatural. . . .

GOTHIC AND THE SUPERNATURAL

The Gothic supernatural appears particularly real, disturbing, and uncanny, because it is so close; it permeates the world around us, looming fantastic and immediate. By comparison the religious type of transcendent supernatural is somewhat remote, projecting a numinous realm that is more otherworldly—heavenly rather than earthly, spiritual rather than physical, sacred rather than profane. The Gothic mentality seeks to obliterate all such distinctions to render the supernatural greater and nearer, and thus it avoids the make-believe aura of the fairy tale. . . .

The supernatural in Gothicism involves the materialization of the spiritual, such as when a ghost takes form and moves a chair or when a spoken formula makes a dog turn into a fly, but also the spiritualization of the material. Magic mirrors, enchanted wands, and mysterious potions are all material objects that have taken on spiritual powers. The rejection of physical restrictions can also be interpreted as a spiritualization of the material. Ghosts and vampires are rejections of time in that they live on indefinitely, and wraiths (apparitions of living people) are in the same sense rejections of temporal and spatial limitation. A number of Gothic creatures, such as the ghoul, are neither male nor female yet somehow both, defying sexual definition. The ghoul feeds on corpses, bringing death into life, as the vampire (which is dead) feeds on life blood. The recurrent Gothic theme of the living dead or the dead alive strains the distinction between (and thus the limitations of) life and death in a manner parallel to the way the physical and spiritual realms overlap. In both cases a greater inclusion is circumscribed by the fusion of opposite categories. . . .

PERVERSE SEXUALITY IN GOTHIC

Gothicism is no more inclined to accept sexual restriction than psychological or aesthetic confinement. Sexual excess functions physically as madness does psychologically; one drive, one intention, becomes overpowering, all-consuming. Sexual perversions are important in Gothic literature for their intensity born of repression and for the expansion they provide in the range of sexual practice. Homosexuality, sodomy, incest, rape, or group copulations are inserted into ordinary experience in order to destroy the boundary line between the normal and the perverse, infecting the normal with the germ of the perverse so that all behavior becomes susceptible to possible perversion. . . .

Aberrant sexuality is frequently associated in Gothic literature with those who possess supernatural powers, such as witches and vampires. The witches' coven is held in the nude, and strange copulations with animals and sexual orgies may be involved. Such perversities contribute an additional dimension of shock to the initial, supernatural expansion.

GOTHIC AND THE POLITICS OF REVOLUTION

In terms of politics, the Gothic novel has been continually associated with revolution and anarchy. . . .

Gothicism allies itself with revolutionary movements because it cannot tolerate any restriction of the individual, and thus Gothicism is not merely revolutionary but anarchistic in its sympathies. As all forms of order disintegrate, the Gothic mind is free to invade the realms of the socially forbidden. The danger to civilization that is likely to result does not deter the Gothic spirit, which is of course drawn to ruins and destruction anyway.

The antiestablishment tenor in Gothic literature, whether directed against the church, the Inquisition, or the government, champions individuals rather than institutions, and, furthermore, the restraints on the individual necessary to insure freedom are inconsistent with the Gothic bent toward license. . . . In the Gothic conflict between the tyrant and victim, the tyrant becomes the more important figure, his magnitude rather than the depreciation of the victim being emphasized. Fear rather than pity is the essential Gothic emotion, and the victim in the story, as well as the reader, is overawed by the conqueror. Society, culture, or government is not allowed to hamper unbridled individualism, as we see in the triumph of love over social convention lauded in Gothic novels. Clearly, the revolutionary sympathies in Gothicism do not really spring from any concern for the masses or for societal injustice, but from the expansion of personal experience. . . .

In analyzing the characteristics of Gothic literature, its images, preoccupations, alignments, sources, and influences, we see that we do not have here a random collection of propensities and tidbits. A single desire motivates the Gothic spirit and can be found at the root of all its peculiarities. The integrated assault of all these factors on the reader's soul accounts for the grip of the Gothic.

The Grotesque in Literature

Bernard McElroy

In *Fiction of the Modern Grotesque,* Bernard McElroy approaches the grotesque as a primarily visual phenomenon based on various forms of distortion and deformity which—like all kinds of horror art—are both repulsive and fascinating. In this excerpt from the first chapter of his study of the grotesque, McElroy surveys grotesque art from the earliest times to the twentieth century and, using the views of the nineteenth-century British art critic John Ruskin and the famous psychoanalyst Sigmund Freud, develops a theory to help explain the attraction of the grotesque. McElroy, formerly professor of English at Chicago's Loyola University, is also the author of *Shakespeare's Mature Tragedies.*

The source of the grotesque in art and literature is man's capacity for finding a unique and powerful fascination in the monstrous. The psychic reasons for this proclivity are far from clear, but the proclivity itself has left its mark on a wide variety of cultures, from prehistory to the present, from the most primitive societies to the most sophisticated. From ice-age cave paintings to modern films, from shaman costumes and devil masks to the paintings of Dali and Picasso, from folk stories and fairy tales to the writings of Kafka, the transmutations of men, beasts, devils, and chimeras have made their bizarre progress, constantly changing with the world views of the cultures which produced them, yet still retaining the essential qualities by which we may attempt to designate them as grotesques. In few ages has this proclivity been more pronounced than in our own.

Excerpted from *Fiction of the Modern Grotesque,* by Bernard McElroy. Copyright © 1989 by Bernard McElroy. Reprinted with permission from St. Martin's Press, LLC.

THE ROOTS OF THE GROTESQUE

Though the phenomenon it designates is older than history, the word itself is of fairly recent origin, having been coined in Renaissance Italy to describe certain droll decorations unearthed in the *grotte* of Nero's House of Gold. In its comparatively short history, the term has meant very different things to different eras, and even in our own day it has a subtly graded series of connotations. In its most limited sense, it refers to a type of decorative art combining human features with lithe beasts and fantastic birds in a filigree of vines and curlicues—the style developed in ancient Rome and imitated by such Renaissance artists as Raphael and Pinturicchio. . . . On the other hand, in colloquial usage, it can mean almost anything unseemly, disproportionate, or in bad taste, and the term is routinely applied to everything from a necktie to a relationship. The first problem to face, then, is that, historically and semantically, the word has variable meanings, and the problem is further complicated by a whole skein of more or less related words whose meanings are similar to but, presumably, not synonymous with grotesque: bizarre, macabre, fantastic, weird, Gothic, arabesque—these are but a few, and much effort by previous critics has gone into trying to undo the tangle and delineate where the province of one ends and that of another begins.

I hope to avoid such hair-splitting by recognising from the outset that the limits of definition of the word must be fairly flexible. There can be no precise point at which one says, 'the grotesque stops here; commence using some other term', because the grotesque is not a genre to which a work either does or does not belong. It does not originate in a particular school or artistic theory, but antedates all schools and theories. Nor is it an absolute which is either fully present or not at all. Rather, it is a continuum which may be present in varying degrees in otherwise disparate works. . . .

SOURCES OF TERROR IN THE GROTESQUE

The most enduring and valuable discussion of the subject remains John Ruskin's *The Stones of Venice*. Its strength is in the simplicity and rightness of its central assertion: 'that the mind, under certain phases of excitement, *plays* with *terror*'. . . .

For Ruskin, the source of the terror of the grotesque is not a specific situation but the human condition itself, ' . . . not the sudden, selfish, and contemptible fear of immediate danger, but the fear which arises out of the contemplation of great powers in destructive operation, and generally from the perception of the presence of death'. This account is all right as far as it goes, but it leaves a number of important questions unanswered. All people fear cataclysm and death, but is there a special kind of fear that manifests itself in images of the grotesque? In the time since Ruskin, such special fear—the eerie, unsettled feeling, the combination of fascination and revulsion so difficult to define but so unmistakable in our felt response to certain situations and certain kinds of art—has been most effectively dealt with by Freud under the heading of the *'Unheimlich'*, literally the 'unhomely', but more usually in translation, the 'uncanny'.

In exploring this feeling (to which he claimed to be only very slightly susceptible himself), Freud used as a point of departure E.T.A. Hoffman's story, 'The Sandman'. It narrates the tale of a young man driven to insanity and suicide by a sinister and possibly supernatural figure who appears in various guises, all of them avatars of the Sandman, a childhood bogy that throws sand in the eyes, causing them to pop out. Freud interprets the story as an expression of infantile castration anxiety, and attributes its uncanny effect to the recurrence of repressed emotion.

However, as he surveys other examples of the uncanny in life and literature, he finds that a second psychological stimulus which can induce the strange sensation is a partial reversion to 'the old animistic conception of the universe'. In the world views of many primitive peoples, the external environment is endowed with anthropomorphic consciousness, with intentions, benign or malevolent, toward the individual, and with powers to influence the course of events. [In the "Uncanny", Freud writes] 'It seems as if each one of us has been through a phase of individual development corresponding to this animistic stage in primitive men, that none of us has passed through it without preserving certain residues and traces of it which are still capable of manifesting themselves, and that everything which now strikes us as "uncanny" fulfils the condition of touching those residues of animistic mental activity within us and bringing them to expression'.

Thus, there are two kinds of psychological material that, separately or in combination, can produce a sense of the un-

canny: repressed infantile anxieties, and surmounted modes
of primitive thought. . . .

I suggest that our response to the grotesque, whether in
life or in art, has as a fundamental component that sense of
the uncanny which arises from the reassertion of the primitive, magical view of the world. It seems to me inescapable
that the grotesque is linked definitively to aggression in human nature, both the impulse to commit aggression and
even more, the fear of being the victim of aggression: and I
do not mean merely natural aggression, but aggression by
impossible, all-powerful means—which is to say aggression
by magic. . . .

This, then, is the first quality of the special kind of terror
that discharges itself in images of the grotesque: it is primitive, magical, uncanny. The grotesque transforms the
world from what we 'know' it to be to what we fear it might
be. It distorts or exaggerates the surface of reality in order
to tell a qualitative truth about it. The grotesque does not address the rationalist in us or the scientist in us, but the vestigial primitive in us, the child in us, the potential psychotic
in us. This magical, animistic quality prevails in the
grotesque art of the most disparate periods and cultures. In
primitive art, images that appear to the modern eye
grotesque are conjured up by an animistic view of the world
and the spirits that control it—fertility figures and gods who
are both anthropomorphic and theriomorphic. In the Middle
Ages, the demonic provided the material for one of the rich-
est strains in the history of grotesque art, culminating in the
fantastic hellscapes of Hieronymus Bosch. The same concern with magic, especially aggression by magic, dominates
the work of modern writers of the grotesque. Once the world
of familiar surfaces has been transformed into the world of
grotesque possibilities, events abound that can only be
called magical, and almost invariably they centre around
victimisation and efficacy.

It is no accident, I think, that the word 'grotesque' came
into currency at exactly the time when rationalism and em-
piricism were assuming an increasingly important role in
Western man's address to the world. A primitive in a demon
mask strikes *us* as a grotesque, but he scarcely could seem
so to himself or to those who believe what he represents actually exists. The very concept of the grotesque in the modern sense would be impossible, for it implies a differentia-

tion from the norm. For the modern, the grotesque is by nature something exceptional, something set apart or aberrant, and in its most extreme forms, situated in the realm of fantasy, dream, or hallucination—in the realm, that is, of unreality. The primitive makes no such distinction, nor does a very young child, and it is upon the vestige of precisely that mentality in us that the grotesque exerts its power. The word 'grotesque' differentiates that which we want to have separate from our sense of reality, but still powerfully experience as real. . . .

PERCEIVING THE GROTESQUE

As an aesthetic category, the grotesque is physical, predominantly visual. Its true habitat is pictorial and plastic art; in literature it is created by narration and description which evoke scenes and characters that can be visualised as grotesque. There is no such thing as an abstract grotesque. . . .

The perception of the grotesque in the world need not even involve the mediation of art. A wide variety of perfectly natural creatures induce in most people that combination of aversion and fascination that characterises our response to the grotesque. Spiders, bats, and virtually the whole kingdom of reptiles usually make perfectly calm, self-controlled people get quickly out of the way, and the depiction of such beasts is a notable feature of much grotesque art. The reason for this strange reaction to certain perfectly natural and often quite harmless creatures is a mystery. Freud discussed animal phobias among children in terms of sexual symbols and father fears. More recently, physiological psychologists, working mostly with lower animals, have postulated innate releasing mechanisms imprinted in the nervous system and transmitted genetically. A newly hatched chick, for instance, which has never seen a hawk, will react defensively when it does see one or even a properly painted effigy of one; the response cannot have been learned, but is innate. It is conceivable (though just barely) that some defense mechanism, developed who knows where on the evolutionary chain and passed on for who knows how long, remains vestigial in modern man and prompts an instinctive aversion to certain kinds of insects and animals. Whatever the case, an effect of that aversion is that the imagination is readily stimulated to endow such creatures with enormous size and magical powers and then to imagine what it might be like to be at their mercy. Among the more puzzling coincidences of cultural history is that man created in his imaginative dragon lore reptilian monsters strikingly similar to animals that actually lived, completely unknown to man, millions of years before him. On a more mundane level, the common housefly is a pest but not a grotesque—until we see one through a microscope.

In a similar vein, severe deformity in human beings unsettles us in ways that go beyond rational explanation and evoke Freud's sense of the uncanny. 'Monstrous' births have been universally attributed to magic or divine intervention, and such explanations are still evident in the attitudes of many moderns. Such events are more than misfortunes; they seem to resurrect primitive fears about human identity, inexplicable influence, and the possibility of some malign principle at work in the very processes of nature. . . .

IMAGINING THE GROTESQUE

Once again, grotesque art presents us not with the world as we know it to be, but with the world as we fear it might be. The artist of the grotesque does not merely combine surfaces; he creates a context in which such distortion is possible. To imagine a monstrosity is to imagine a world capable of producing that monstrosity. . . .

The most pervasive effect of such animalism and corporeal degradation in grotesque art is to direct our attention to the undignified, perilous, even gross physicality of existence, and to emphasise it by exaggeration, distortion, or unexpected combination. The result may be thought of as an arc ranging from the entirely animal, through the human-animal, to the entirely human. A gradation of the continuum might go as follows:

A. The depiction of real or imaginary animals which combine aversive appearance with real or imaginable dangers (dinosaurs, other reptiles, large insects);

B. The combination of disparate animal parts to produce chimeras and mythical beasts, sometimes jovial, but more often ominous (griffins, gargoyles, dragons);

C. The combination of human and animal features and traits to produce a hybrid man-beast (totem masks and figures, anthrotheriomorphic gods, the kinds of demons most often depicted by Bosch);

D. The depiction of humans so deformed as to be astonishingly ugly and suggest an aberration of nature (gnomes, extreme hydrocephalics, persons with very distorted faces or bodies; in a light vein, some clowns);

E. The depiction of humans is some state so bizarre, macabre, or gross that human dignity is obliterated and even identity is threatened (decomposed corpses, skeletons; cannibalism, some behavior of the insane).

To these examples we may add others less typical but still encountered in the art of the grotesque: animalistic or humanoid plants; the combination of mechanical devices with animal forms (the flying stork-boat and wheeled spire-fish of Bosch's *The Temptation of Saint Anthony*); combinations of machines and humans (some robots, the title character of Pynchon's *V.*); or gruesome machines that take on life of their own (the execution contraption in Kafka's 'In the Penal Colony'). No doubt, many other isolated examples could be cited, but we are here in the area of borderline instances.

A primitive, magical reading of experience, corporeal degradation, and animalism—these are common properties of the kind of terror embodied in the grotesque. . . .

THE GROTESQUE IN MODERN LITERATURE

It is not surprising that grotesque fiction of the twentieth century is concerned mostly with the same issues as non-grotesque modern literature. Man is usually presented as living in a vast, indifferent, meaningless universe in which his actions are without significance beyond his own, limited, personal sphere. The physical world of his immediate surroundings is alien and hostile, directing its energies to overwhelming the individual, denying him a place and identity even remotely commensurate with his needs and aspirations, surrounding him on every side with violence and brutalisation, offering him values that have lost their credibility, manipulating and dehumanising him through vast, faceless institutions, the most ominous of which are science, technology, and the socio-economic organisation. . . .

Literature of the modern grotesque usually focuses on the unequal struggle between the self and such a hostile environment, and the most common theme linking the novels discussed here is dominance and submission. In one frequently encountered format, the individual is persecuted by a patently insane world which is capable of overwhelming him by means that go beyond the limits of physical possibility. Kafka's fiction provides example after example. Or, in another format, the individual, aware of what he is up against, endows himself with magical powers by which he is suddenly able to deal brilliantly with his surroundings, though he usually loses in the end. Oskar Matzerath in *The Tin Drum* is a prime example of such a character.

In depicting a vindictive, persecuting world, the grotesque can be put to several uses, separately or in combination. The simplest is radical satire, in which the grotesque world is a caricature of the real world accessible to the senses. More effectively, the grotesque can be used as a heightening device by which the conflict between self and other is intensified by expanding it to magical proportions. The attack on the individual, being magical, is irresistible, and it is also physical. A person is not merely cowed psychologically; his body is attacked, transformed, rendered grotesque—and not by the physically possible means of mutilation or torture, but in uncanny, bizarre, and often magical ways. For example, on the literal level of Ken Kesey's *One Flew Over the Cuckoo's Nest*, an oppressive and bigoted society has reduced Chief Bromden to a state of catatonic withdrawal. But in his own deranged view, which is the viewpoint of the novel, he believes that the Combine has planted machines in his body and has wired up the world with gadgets to control it completely, even to the passage of time. The limits of the actual and the possible have been abolished in order to heighten the conflict between self and other and clarify its nature. Such transformations are frequent in the literature of the modern grotesque. . . .

At its most effective, as in, say, the best stories of Kafka, the modern grotesque serves not only to satirise and to heighten, but to expose. The rationalisations and compensations of everyday life are stripped away to bare the substratum of terror which underlies the seemingly mundane. A widely used phrase coined by Hannah Arendt posits 'the banality of evil' in the modern world. Huge atrocities are perpetrated not by monsters but by mediocrities. The evils of the world arise not from satanic grandeur but from the millionfold repetition of shabby vices, most of which boil down to greed and stupidity. The modern grotesque reverses that banality and portrays modern evil in trappings more dramatically compelling, more commensurate with the terrible outcome. . . .

Though some modern writers have used great ingenuity

to create grotesque renditions of the external world, even more attention has been lavished in the grotesque inner life of twentieth-century man. In earlier art, the source of the grotesque was usually the external realm, natural or supernatural. In societies where men felt themselves to be at the day to day mercy of potent, malevolent spiritual powers, the grotesque often embodied that which, though invisible, was presumed to exist. But in the modern Western world, deeply aware of the rift between the external, objective world and the internal, subjective interpretation of it, the source of the grotesque has moved inward and is found in the fears, guilts, fantasies, and aberrations of individual psychic life. The modern grotesque is internal, not infernal, and its originator is recognised as neither god nor devil but man himself.

Even in those novels which depict the external world as being grotesque itself, the emphasis is usually not so much upon man's predicament before a powerful and dehumanising world as upon the protagonist's inner reaction to that predicament. Irrational fears and primitive dreads are made actual; fantasies, delusions, and hallucinations often mingle freely with physical existence in the external world. Not supernatural demons or devouring chimeras, but external powerlessness and psychic dissolution are the fears with which the modern grotesque plays, and that is the most modern thing about it. Awareness of the gulf between self and other has become total and obsessive, but if the other is sterile and dehumanising, the self is abject and contemptible; and yet contemptible as it may be, the self is the only thing man has left to fight for if he wishes to retain some semblance of control over his actions and identity. . . .

Finally, the modern grotesque is not merely an assault upon the idea of a rational world; it is an assault upon the reader himself, upon his sensibilities, upon his ideals, upon his feeling of living in a friendly, familiar world or his desire to live in one.

The Gothic Tradition in American Literature

Joyce Carol Oates

A professor in the Creative Writing Program at Princeton University, Joyce Carol Oates is the highly acclaimed author of several dozen novels and short story collections, including *Gothic* and *Zombie*. Among her many literary awards are the PEN/Faulkner Bernard Malamud Lifetime Achievement Award for the short story and the Bram Stoker Award for Lifetime Achievement presented by the Horror Writers of America. Here, in the Introduction to her anthology entitled *American Gothic Tales*, Oates examines the importance of the Gothic tradition in American literature by discussing its connection to Puritanism and by pointing to Gothic elements and influences in the works of several great American authors, including Edgar Allan Poe, Nathaniel Hawthorne, and Herman Melville.

"Though in many of its aspects this visible world seems formed in love, the invisible spheres were formed in fright."
—Herman Melville, *MOBY DICK*

How uncanny, how mysterious, how unknowable and infinitely beyond their control must have seemed the vast wilderness of the New World, to the seventeenth-century Puritan settlers! The inscrutable silence of Nature—the muteness that, not heralding God, must be a dominion of Satan's; the tragic ambiguity of human nature with its predilection for what Christians call "original sin," inherited from our first parents, Adam and Eve. When Nature is so vast, man's need for control—for "settling" the wilderness—becomes obsessive. And how powerful the temptation to project mankind's divided self onto the very silence of Nature.

THE AMERICAN GOTHIC AND ITS PURITAN BACKGROUND

It was the intention of those English Protestants known as Puritans to "purify" the Church of England by eradicating everything in the Church that seemed to have no biblical justification. The most radical Puritans, "Separatists" and eventually "Pilgrims," settled Plymouth, Massachusetts, in the 1620s; others who followed, in subsequent years, were less zealous about defining themselves as "Separatists" (from the mother country England). Yet all were characterized by the intransigence of their faith; their fierce sense of moral rectitude and self-righteousness. The New England Puritans were an intolerant people whose theology could not have failed to breed paranoia, if not madness, in the sensitive among them. Consider, for instance, the curious Covenant of Grace, which taught that only those men and women upon whom God sheds His grace are saved, because this allows them to believe in Christ; those excluded from God's grace lack the power to believe in a Savior, thus are not only not saved, but damned. *We never had a chance!* those so excluded might cry out of the bowels of Hell. *We were doomed from the start.* The extreme gothic sensibility springs from such paradoxes: that the loving, paternal God and His son Jesus are nonetheless willful tyrants; "good" is inextricably bound up with the capacity to punish; one may wish to believe oneself free but in fact all human activities are determined, from the perspective of the deity, long before one's birth.

It comes as no surprise, then, that the very titles of celebrated Puritan works of the seventeenth and early eighteenth centuries strike a chord of anxiety. *The Spiritual Conflict, The Holy War, Day of Doom, Thirsty Sinner, Groans of the Damned, The Wonders of the Invisible World, Man Knows Not His Time, Repentant Sinners and Their Ministers, Memorable Providences Relating to Witchcraft and Possessions*— these might be the titles of lurid works of gothic fiction, not didactic sermons, prose pieces and poetry. The great Puritan poet Edward Taylor was also a minister; Taylor's subtle, intricately wrought metaphysical verse dwells upon God's love and terror almost exclusively, and man's insignificance in the face of God's omnipotence: "my Will is your Design." Taylor's poetry suggests a man of uncommon gifts, intelligence and sensitivity trapped in a fanatic religion as in a straitjacket; here is the gothic predilection for investing all things, even the most seemingly innocuous (weather, insects) with cosmological meaning. Is there nothing in the gothic imagination that can mean simply—"nothing"?

EARLY NIGHTMARISH TALES

Our first American novelist of substance, Charles Brockden Brown, was born of a Philadelphia Quaker family; but his major novel *Wieland, or The Transformation* (1798) is suffused with the spirit of Puritan paranoia—"God is the object of my supreme passion," Wieland declares. Indeed, the very concept of rational self-determinism is challenged by this dark fantasy of domestic violence. Though Charles Brockden Brown provides a naturalistic explanation for Wieland's maniacal behavior, it is clearly not plausible; the novel is a nightmare expression of the fulfillment of repressed desire, anticipating Edgar Allan Poe's similarly claustrophobic tales of the grotesque. Wieland's deceased father was a Protestant religious fanatic who seems to have been literally immolated by guilt; Wieland Jr. is a disciple of the Enlightenment who is nonetheless driven mad by "voices" urging him to destruction.

> I was dazzled. My organs were bereaved of their activity. My eyelids were half-closed. . . . A nameless fear chilled my veins, and I stood motionless. This irradiation did not retire or lessen. It seemed as if some powerful effulgence covered me like a mantle. . . . It was the element of heaven that flowed around.

But the "element of heaven" demands that Wieland sacrifice those he loves best—his wife and children.

Such assaults upon individual autonomy and identity characterize the majority of the tales . . . by Washington Irving, Nathaniel Hawthorne, Edgar Allan Poe, Charlotte Perkins Gilman, H.P. Lovecraft and more recent twentieth-century writers for whom the "supernatural" and the malevolent "unconscious" have fused. Even in the more benign "enchanted region" of Washington Irving's Sleepy Hollow (of *The Sketch Book*, 1820), an ordinary, decent man like Ichabod Crane is subjected to an ordeal of psychic breakdown; Irving's imagination is essentially comic, but of that cruel, mordant comedy tinctured by sadism.

Descendant of one of the judges of the notorious Salem witch trials of 1692–93, Nathaniel Hawthorne became a historian-fantasist of his own Puritan forbears in such sym-

bolist romances as *The Scarlet Letter* and *The House of the
Seven Gables* and in the parable-like stories gathered in
Mosses from an Old Manse (1846), of which "Young Good-
man Brown" is the most frequently reprinted and "The Man
of Adamant". . . is exemplary, though relatively little-known.
Here is a chilling tale of a developing psychosis in the guise
of religious piety: a radical Puritan preacher adopts "a plan of
salvation . . . so narrow, that, like a plank in a tempestuous
sea, it could avail no sinner but himself." In true gothic fashion, the man of adamant suffers a physical transformation
commensurate with his spiritual condition: he becomes a
calcified, embalmed corpse. (The gothic-grotesque sensibility, graphically expressed by such artists as Hieronymus
Bosch, Goya, Francis Bacon, insists upon the *physicality* of
such spiritual transformations.) Unusual for any gothic tale,
Herman Melville's surreal, dream-like allegory "The Tartarus of Maids" is informed by a political vision, the writer's
appalled sympathy with the fates of girls and women condemned to factory work in New England mills—and condemned to being female in a wholly patriarchal society. Usually paired with the cheery, jocose "The Paradise of
Bachelors," which is set in an affluent gentlemen-lawyers'
club in London, "The Tartarus of Maids" is a remarkable
work for its time (the 1850s) in its equation of sexual/bio-
logical and social determinism: "At rows of blank-looking
counters sat rows of blank-looking girls, with blank, white
folders in their blank hands, all blankly folding blank paper." Yet somehow the paper-mill to which the girls are condemned to work like slaves is also the female body. The narrator is led through it by an affable guide named Cupid and
learns that to be female, to be male chattel, to be condemned
by impregnation by male seed, is for the virginal females
their Tartarus, that region of Hades reserved for punishment
of the wicked. Of what are these girls and women guilty except having been born of a debased female sex?—into a body
"that is a mere machine, the essence of which is unvarying
punctuality and precision."

EDGAR ALLAN POE: THE MADMAN'S VOICE

"The Tartarus of Maids" is notable for exhibiting a rare feat
of sexual identification, for virtually no male writers of Melville's era, or any other, have made the imaginative effort of
trying to see from the perspective of the "other sex," let alone

trying to see in a way highly critical of the advantages of masculinity. A more psychologically realistic portrayal of the trapped female, in this case a wife and mother of an economically comfortable class (her husband is a physician), is Charlotte Perkins Gilman's classic "The Yellow Wallpaper" whose inspired manic voice derives from Poe but whose vision of raging female despair is the author's own. In the work of our premier American gothicist, Edgar Allan Poe, from whose *Tales of the Grotesque and Arabesque* (1840), so much of twentieth-century horror and detective fiction springs, there are no fully realized female characters, indeed no fully realized characters at all; but the female is likely to be the obsessive object of desire, and her premature death, as in "The Fall of the House of Usher," "Ligeia," and . . . "The Black Cat," is likely to be the precipitating factor.

"The Black Cat" demonstrates Poe at his most brilliant, presenting a madman's voice with such mounting plausibility that the reader almost—*almost*—identifies with his unmotivated and seemingly unresisted acts of insane violence against the affectionate black cat Pluto, and eventually his own wife. Like "The Tell-Tale Heart," with which it bears an obvious kinship, "The Black Cat" explores from within a burgeoning, blossoming evil; an evil exacerbated by alcohol, yet clearly a congenital evil unprovoked by the behav-. ior of others. Ironically, the nameless narrator is one who has enjoyed since childhood the company of animals, and he and his wife live amid a Peaceable Kingdom of pets— "birds, a gold-fish, a dog, rabbits, a small monkey, and *a cat.*" The narrator, drawn by degrees to escalating acts of cruelty, gouges out Pluto's eye with a pen-knife, and later hangs the mutilated creature: "And then came, as if to my final and irrevocable overthrow, the spirit of PERVERSE-NESS." In Poe's gothic cosmology, not the "I" but the "imp of the perverse" rules. With the logic of dream retribution, the murdered Pluto reappears in the guise of another one-eyed black cat who haunts the narrator in his own household and, after the narrator's murder of his wife, and his walling-up of her corpse in his cellar, brings about the murderer's arrest by police. The black cat trapped in the wall (or tomb) recalls not only the tell-tale heart of another brutally murdered victim but the prematurely entombed Madeline Usher of "The Fall of the House of Usher." Like Wieland, whose grotesque "confession" would have been known to

Poe, this husband kills his wife for no apparent, or conscious, reason.

HENRY JAMES AND EDITH WHARTON

Perhaps the most artistically realized gothic tale in American literature is Henry James's enigmatic *The Turn of the Screw*. (It has certainly been the most analyzed.) James's ghost stories are masterpieces of style, irony, ambiguity; though distinguished by James's characteristic subtlety, in which "gothic" effects are subordinate to psychological drama, each of the tales—"The Romance of Certain Old Clothes," "The Friends of the Friends," "Maud-Evelyn," "Sir Edmund Orme" and "The Jolly Corner"—differs surprisingly from the others. ("Maud-Evelyn" is perhaps the most ingenious in conception; the very early, "The Romance of Certain Old Clothes," written when James was in his twenties, is the most conventional in gothic terms, presenting covert female sexual rivalry as the dynamic of the story and ending with an eruption of "real" ghostly revenge.) Like her one-time mentor James, Edith Wharton wrote a number of exquisitely crafted psychological ghost stories: "Pomegranate Seed," "The Eyes," "All Souls," and "Afterward.". . . Wharton's tales of the supernatural, genteel by gothic standards, ponder questions of individual conscience and destiny in a social context very different from that of the more sensational gothic writers, like Poe and Ambrose Bierce; often, they dramatize a distinctly female, perhaps feminist angle of vision, as in the not-quite-gothic story "A Journey," in which a young wife endures a nightmare train journey accompanied by the corpse of her husband. Edith Wharton and Henry James are virtually alone in their experimentation with gothic forms of fiction even as they forged distinguished literary careers as "realists" of the social and domestic American scene.

These canonical writers of the gothic-grotesque were all born, fittingly, in the nineteenth century. With the rise of realism in prose fiction in the late nineteenth century, and the more radical, more grindingly materialist school of naturalism derived from [Gustav] Flaubert and [Emile] Zola, educated readers turned to the work of such writers as Stephen Crane, Frank Norris, Hamlin Garland and Theodore Dreiser. In the toughly Darwinian masculine-urban worlds of such writers, with their exposure of social and political corruption and their frank depiction of adult sexual relations, a subject largely taboo in gothic fiction, there would seem to have been no place, still less sympathy, for the idiosyncrasies of the gothic imagination.

H.P. LOVECRAFT: POE'S HEIR

If there is a single gothic-grotesque writer of the American twentieth century to be compared with Poe, it is H.P. Lovecraft, born in 1890. The child of psychotic parents (his father died of tertiary syphilis when Lovecraft was three, his mother, a schizophrenic, died institutionalized), Lovecraft was a precocious, prolific talent who chose to live a reclusive life, producing a unique body of horror stories and novellas before his premature death, of cancer, at the age of forty-seven, in 1937. Long a revered cult figure to admirers of "weird fiction" (Lovecraft's own, somewhat deprecatory term for his art), Lovecraft is associated with crude, obsessive, rawly sensationalist and overwrought prose in the service of naming the unnameable. Like Poe, he may have been creating counter-worlds in which to speak his heart in frank, if codified terms: "Unhappy is he to whom the memories of childhood bring only fear and sadness. Wretched is he who looks back upon lone hours in vast and dismal chambers with . . . maddening rows of antique books," begins "The Outsider," an atypically compressed story. Lovecraft's compulsion is again and again to approach the horror that is a lurid twin of one's self, or that very self seen in an unsuspected mirror:

> I beheld in full, frightful vividness the inconceivable, indescribable, and unmentionable monstrosity . . . I cannot even hint what it was like, for it was a compound of all that is unclean, uncanny, unwelcome, abnormal, and detestable. It was the ghoulish shade of decay, antiquity, and dissolution; the putrid, dripping eidolon of unwelcome revelation, the awful baring of that which the merciful earth should always hide.

In short, the unloved monster-child sired by unknown parents, abandoned to a universe of infinite mystery in which he will always be an "outsider."

The accumulating horrors of "The Rats in the Walls," the lurid final epiphany of "The Dunwich Horror," the terrifying bizarrerie of "The Shadow Out of Time," the prophetic reasonableness of "The Colour Out of Space"—Lovecraft's influence upon twentieth-century horror writers has been incalculable, and in certain quarters he is prized for the very traits (lurid excess, overstatement, fantastical and repetitive contrivance) for which, in more "literary" quarters, he is despised. The gothic imagination melds the sacred and the profane in startling and original ways, suggesting its close kinship with the religious imagination; Lovecraft's cosmology of demonic extraterrestrial beings (The Great Old Ones) whose intrusion into the human world brings disaster to human beings is readily recognizable as a mystic's vision in which God has become numerous Cronus-gods bent upon devouring their unacknowledged offspring. There is a melancholy, operatic grandeur in Lovecraft's most passionate work; a curious elegiac poetry of loss, of adolescent despair and yearning; an existential loneliness so pervasive, so profound and convincing that it lingers in the reader's memory long after the rudiments of Lovecraftian plot have faded. Lovecraft is a hybrid of the traditional gothic and "science fiction" but his temperament is clearly gothic. His "science" is never future-oriented but a mystic's minute, compulsive scrutinizing of the inner self or soul. Some tragic, prehistoric conjunction of the "human" and the "inhuman" has blighted what should have been a natural life; and nature itself is consequently contaminated. ("The Colour Out of Space" with its meticulous, poetic descriptions of a once-fertile and now blighted New England landscape seems uncannily to be prophesizing ecological devastation.) Here is the wholly obverse vision of American destiny; the repudiation of American-Transcendentalist optimism, in which the individual is somehow divine, or shares in nature's divinity. In the gothic imagination, there has been a profound and irrevocable split between mankind and nature in the romantic sense, and a tragic division between what we wish to know and what may be staring us in the face. So "The Colour Out of Space" concludes elegiacally: "It was just a colour out of space—a frightful messenger from unformed realms of infinity beyond all Nature as we know it . . ."

Poe and the Gothic

Clark Griffith

Edgar Allan Poe did not invent the tale of terror, but he certainly worked diligently to perfect the form in such famous stories as "The Tell-Tale Heart," "The Black Cat" and "The Fall of the House of Usher." In the following article Clark Griffith, author of *The Long Shadow: Emily Dickinson's Tragic Poetry* and formerly professor of English at the University of Oregon, examines Poe's connection to the Gothic tradition and argues that, while Poe may have "borrowed" from that tradition, he ultimately developed a new, internalized and "psychologized" Gothic in which terror derives from the mind of the first-person narrator.

Despite the emphasis in his criticism upon a need for novelty, Poe's tales of terror are clearly indebted to some literary forebears. From Gothic fiction of the English eighteenth century, Poe took the *imagery* of terror: the blighted, oppressive countryside: the machinery of the Inquisition; in particular, the haunted castle, swaddled in its own atmosphere of morbidity and decay. From the nineteenth-century Gothicized tales in *Blackwood's Magazine,* which he both ridiculed and admired, he took the *form* of terror: a first-person narrator, lingering typically over a single, frightening episode, and bringing matters to a climax in which he has grown deaf to every sound except the noise of his unique sensations. So close are the resemblances that one passes from [Gothic novelist] Anne Radcliffe's architecture to the effusions of a *Blackwood's* speaker, convinced that Poe's effects often result from his combining the murky details of the one with the inveterate, uninterrupted talkativeness of the other. Yet I wish to argue that even as Poe borrowed, he also made a significant contribution. Imperfectly at first, but then with greater assurance, he was concerned with shifting what I shall call the locus of the terrifying. This change in stance is one measure of his originality as a practicioner in the Gothic mode. And to watch him make it is to find special meaning in his famous declaration that the terror of which he wrote came not from Germany but from the soul.

As the basis for contrast, let us glance briefly at [Anne Radcliffe's character] Emily St. Aubert, before the Castle of Udolpho [from the novel of the same name]. Confronting it for the first time, she can only see the castle as a real and utterly objective fact. For Emily is a true child of the *Essay Concerning the Human Understanding*. It would please her to suppose that she has somehow been transported into "one of those frightful fictions in which the wild genius of the poet delights." But aware that there is nothing in the mind not first in the senses, she recognizes that she has no grounds for distrusting her perceptions; hence she must scorn as "delusion" and "superstition" the notion that the source of her agitation is anywhere except in the world around her. In Emily's case, therefore (as throughout Mrs. Radcliffe and the eighteenth-century Gothic generally), the direction of the horrifying is from without to within: from setting to self. . . .

"PSYCHOLOGIZING" THE GOTHIC

The situation seems identical in the early portions of [Poe's] "MS. Found in a Bottle" (1833). The storm at sea, which overtakes Poe's narrator, or the engulfing waves that "surpass . . . anything [he] had imagined possible": both appear to be examples of the received, physical ordeal, such as . . . Mrs. Radcliffe had devised. Halfway through "MS.," however, a change in emphasis occurs. Now, for the first time, the narrator speaks of strange "conceptions" which are arising from inside his mind. They consist of "feelings" and "sensations" to which no name can be given; nevertheless, they cause him to spell out the word "Discovery" as he beholds—in any case, apparently beholds—an entire new order of experience. At this point, I suggest, Poe has commenced to modify the traditional Gothic relationship. If terror is to be the effect of inner conceptions, it is no longer necessary to regard his narrator as a "mere man," beset and beleaguered by appalling circumstances. Instead, one can as readily think of him as Creative Man, and of the circumstances themselves as the products of his terrible creativity. At least potentially, the locus of the terrifying has passed from the spectacle into the spectator.

Admittedly, though, the change remains no more than implied and potential in "MS. Found in a Bottle." It breaks down ultimately, because the scenery in the tale still seems too much founded upon the eighteenth-century convention of the "outer wonder." What Poe needed, if he intended to psychologize the Gothic, was nothing so spacious or openly exotic as the South Indian Ocean. He required the smaller, less public *mise-en-scène*, one which could more plausibly be transfigured by his narrators, and, above all, one which would dramatize the processes of transfiguration in action. He is best off, in short, when he returns to the dark, secluded interiors of eighteenth-century fiction, but portrays them in such a way that the interiors are made suggestive of the human mind itself. And this of course is the technique he has perfected two years later, with the publication in 1835 of "Berenice," his first example of a genuinely new Gothic.

Sitting within his ancestral mansion, Poe's Egaeus turns out to be both projector and voice, the source of a strange predicament as well as its spokesman. He has spent a lifetime gazing for "long unwearied hours" at objects which he half-suspects are trivial and without purpose—and watching while, gradually and inexplicably, they acquire some momentous significance. The story makes it clear, however, that the details present this heightened aspect only to Egaeus's "mind's eye"; whatever the meaning they come to possess, it is due solely to his fierce concentration upon them. Obviously, then, there has ceased to be any distance, or difference, between the terror and the terrified. Egaeus's realities are the realities of his own making; his world resembles a mirror in a madhouse, wherein distortions and phantasms appear, but only as the reflections of a particular sort of observer. And nowhere is this fact more evident than in his obsession with the teeth of Berenice:

> The teeth!—the teeth! they were here, and there, and everywhere, and visibly and palpably before me; long, narrow, and excessively white, with the pale lips writhing about them. . . .

At first glance, we are likely to be struck by the sheer, intense *physicalness* of these dreadful molars. Superficially, in fact, they may well seem of a kind with the highly tangible horrors which [Matthew Lewis's] *The Monk* presents. Yet they function in quite another way. M.G. Lewis's ghoulish occurrences were rooted in a thoroughly Lockean landscape. The putrefying head, in the convent vaults at St. Clare, had to exist independently of Agnes de Medina, first to accost Agnes's senses and then to register on her appalled sensibility. By contrast, the teeth in Poe have no meaningful existence outside a sensibility; as Egaeus acknowledges, *"tous ses dents étaient des idées."* ["all her teeth were ideas"]. What the teeth might be like apart from Egaeus, or whether, for that matter, they even have an identity except in his vision of them: these are issues of no real moment. So successfully has Poe internalized the Gothic that the old "outer wonders" of the eighteenth century now disappear into the stream of consciousness. They have become the conditions and consequences (if one likes, the "objective correlatives") of a psychic state.

THE INTERNALIZED NARRATOR IN "USHER"

The strategy of "Berenice" is one that with the slightest variations Poe would continue to utilize for the rest of his life. Barring the allegorical "Masque of the Red Death" and the fact-bound *Pym* (with its return to a glamorous out-of-doors),

---

THE FALL OF THE HOUSE OF USHER

As Clark Griffith points out in "Poe and the Gothic," Poe's use of first-person narrators allowed him a degree of insight into human psychological processes that no earlier writer in the Gothic tradition had ever attained. In fact, as the long, eerie, and unsettling opening paragraph of "The Fall of the House of Usher" suggests, Poe's mastery of first-person narration has probably never been surpassed.

During the whole of a dull, dark, and soundless day in the autumn of the year, when the clouds hung oppressively low in the heavens, I had been passing alone, on horseback, through a singularly dreary tract of country; and at length found myself, as the shades of the evening drew on, within view of the melancholy House of Usher. I know not how it was—but, with the first glimpse of the building, a sense of insufferable gloom pervaded my spirit. I say insufferable; for the feeling was unrelieved by any of that half-pleasurable, because poetic, sentiment, with which the mind usually receives even the sternest natural images of the desolate or terrible. I looked upon the scene before me—upon the mere house, and the simple landscape features of the domain—upon the bleak walls—upon the vacant eye-like windows—upon a few rank sedges—and upon a few white trunks of decayed trees—with an utter depression of soul which I can compare to no earthly sensation more

I know of none of the horror tales in which the perceiving mind does not seem much more nearly the originator of the terrifying than it is a mere passive witness. Moreover, I am convinced that to read them as though they were notes composed from within is often to clarify and enrich the stories. For example, the real key to the somewhat baffling "Fall of the House of Usher" (1839) appears to me to lie in the way it opens by re-enacting an episode out of Mrs. Radcliffe, but repeats the event for a totally different purpose.

Like Emily St. Aubert, Poe's speaker also rides up, at the end of a long day's journey, before an apparently haunted castle. He too feels it to be a massive and brooding presence in the foreground. And then, in an effort to dispel the alarm with which it quickly envelopes him, he decides to examine the place from a different perspective. But when he reins in his horse and proceeds to the new location, nothing happens. Where Emily could always look forward to being physically delivered from peril, the physical change in Poe only

properly than to the after-dream of the reveller upon opium—the bitter lapse into everyday life—the hideous dropping off of the veil. There was an iciness, a sinking, a sickening of the heart—an unredeemed dreariness of thought which no goading of the imagination could torture into aught of the sublime. What was it—I paused to think—what was it that so unnerved me in the contemplation of the House of Usher? It was a mystery all insoluble; nor could I grapple with the shadowy fancies that crowded upon me as I pondered. I was forced to fall back upon the unsatisfactory conclusion, that while, beyond doubt, there *are* combinations of very simple natural objects which have the power of thus affecting us, still the analysis of this power lies among considerations beyond our depth. It was possible, I reflected, that a mere different arrangement of the particulars of the scene, of the details of the picture, would be sufficient to modify, or perhaps to annihilate its capacity for sorrowful impression; and, acting upon this idea, I reined my horse to the precipitous brink of a black and lurid tarn that lay in unruffled lustre by the dwelling, and gazed down—but with a shudder even more thrilling than before—upon the remodelled and inverted images of the gray sedge, and the ghastly tree-stems, and the vacant and eye-like windows.

Edgar Allan Poe, *Complete Stories and Poems.* Garden City, NY: Doubleday and Company, Inc., 1966, pp. 177–78.

means that his narrator seems menaced anew. The "ghastly tree stems" and "vacant eyelike windows" continue to glare back at him with the same old ominousness.

Of course nothing happens. The truth about the speaker in "Usher" is that he has all along been engaged in a kind of symbolic homecoming. When at length he crosses the causeway and goes indoors, he finds himself among rooms and furnishings that are oddly familiar, because he has arrived at nothing less than the depths of his own being. Thereafter, it is not his talkativeness—his descriptive abilities, in the usual sense—that summon up Roderick and Madeline. The Ushers are products of the narrator's psyche; for they and their behavior become the embodiments of his trance, or they appear as the *personae* in his dream vision, or perhaps their incestuous relationship is a working out of his own, dark, tabooed, and otherwise inexpressible desires. Thus every subsequent event in "Usher" is prepared for by an opening tableau in which the power to terrorize could not be blotted from the landscape, because it had actually been brought into the landscape by the mind of the narrator. The organic unity, of which Poe makes so much, is a unity between the single creating self at the center of the story, and those shapes and forms which radiate outward as the marks of his continuous creative act. To me at least, no other interpretation of the tale can justify the amount of attention paid its narrator, or is so true to the form and manner of his narration.

POE AND THE ROMANTIC MOVEMENT

Poe's tinkerings with tradition are probably less eccentric and ultra-personal than, at first look, they appear to be. Behind them, after all, one discerns nothing more remarkable than a particular manifestation of the Romantic Movement. If the terrors of the eighteenth century were accountable in terms of [Thomas] Locke's *Essay*, then what is terror for Poe except an adjunct to the thirteenth chapter of the *Biographia Literaria*? That is, the horrifying now looms up out of a world in which the imagination "dissolves, diffuses, dissipates, in order to recreate" and wherein imaginative tendencies are "essentially *vital*, even as all objects *(as* objects) are essentially fixed and dead."

Granted that they represent extreme cases, Poe's narrators have to be understood as figures who are deeply involved in just the activity that [Samuel Taylor] Coleridge describes.

Poe received wide acclaim for his macabre poem "The Raven."

Until their inner lives impinge upon the outer, the outer, if it is consequential at all, remains a dull and prosaic affair. It gains its extraordinary qualities, as we have seen, through the transforming and the transfiguring capacities of an imaginative self. To cite a last example, we are told by the speaker in "Ligeia" (1838) of how the *décor* in Lady Rowena's bedchamber "partook of the true character of the Arabesque only when regarded from a single point of view." As we read, however, it is to find that the single point of view has nothing to do with physical positioning. Rather, it seems expressive of the narrator's personality, an extension of his inward state. One concludes therefore that it is akin to Coleridge's "secondary imagination." In Poe's hands this faculty has become more nearly an instrument of the appalling than it is a strictly aesthetic principle. Nevertheless, it still operates as the means of discovering relevance, pattern, even a certain sort of beauty and ideality in objects which, left to themselves, would be "essentially fixed and dead."

Small wonder, consequently, that Poe's fiction is better unified but, at the same time, darker and much gloomier than the eighteenth-century Gothic had been. With their stress upon horror as an objective phenomenon, the earlier Gothic writers could introduce a whole range of tones and effects. As they evoked terror from the outside, so they were likewise free to suspend and withdraw it from without. Having opened what amounted to a trapdoor into the world of menace, they found it possible to snap the door shut again, and so to conduct their characters back into a world of happy endings: of order, security and (typically) the celebration of marriage vows. The waking nightmare succeeded by the nuptials! It is the regular drift of events from [Horace Walpole's] *The Castle of Otranto* to *The Monk* and on into *Blackwood's*.

THE DOWNWARD JOURNEYS OF POE'S NARRATORS

But Poe possessed no such latitude. Since the stimulus for terror comes from within, there can, in the tale he tells, be no real survivors, no remissions of the terrible, no protagonists who, by pluck or by luck, either earn or are at least vouchsafed the right to turn backward through the trapdoor. Self-afflicted and self-victimized (so to speak, their own executioners), Poe's characters must perform a persistently downward journey, sinking further and further into voluble wonderment at themselves, until they arrive at one of those shattering silences with which their narratives customarily end. And yet, even as they descend, they are granted a kind of glory which no hero of the earlier Gothic could ever have matched. We may feel that the next step for Poe's narrators will be the tomb or the lunatic asylum. During a single, transcendent moment, however, they have had the privilege of calling up out of their very beings a totally new order of reality. They are Romantic heroes without peer, for they have been the masters, because the creators, of all that they survey.

And small wonder, finally, that *their* creator was fascinated by what he called "the power of words." Once he had got hold of his true theme, it was never enough for Poe simply to set a scene, describe an action, use words to provoke a shudder or two; that was the business of those attuned to the terrors of Germany. The test of language in his work lay in its ability to delve deeply within and bring to light the most hidden crannies of a suffering, yet oddly prolific self. Thus the descriptive devices of his Gothic predecessors reemerge as Poe's metaphors of mind; their rhetorical flourishes are turned by him into a rhetoric of revelation. Out of the magic of words, Poe brings forth the symbolic countryside, self-contained and self-sustaining, utterly devoid of connections with the world as it is, yet recognizable still in the terms of its own special topography. And behind the countryside, he shows us the figure of the owner. This is the soul of man, cloaked in the works which it has made, and rendered thereby into a visible and articulate entity.

CHAPTER 3

Three Classic Horror Novels

 Horror

Biographical Contexts for *Frankenstein*

Wendy Lesser

Wendy Lesser is founding editor of *The Threepenny Review* in Berkeley, California, and the author of *The Life Below Ground: A Study of the Subterranean in Literature and History* and *His Other Half: Men Looking at Women Through Art.* The following article is taken from her introduction to the 1992 Everyman edition of *Frankenstein, or The Modern Prometheus.* Here Lesser develops a series of biographical contexts which help the reader understand the complicated origins of *Frankenstein.* In particular, Lesser focuses on Mary Shelley's somewhat problematic relationship with her father, the English radical philosopher William Godwin, and on her own painful experiences with motherhood. Lesser concludes that one of *Frankenstein*'s major thematic concerns involves a "steely examination of parenthood."

One's first response to *Frankenstein* is amazement that a girl just turning nineteen could have composed such a work. Then one pauses to rethink. Would it be any less amazing if an Oxford don of forty-five had written *Frankenstein*? Such arguments are reminiscent of those which attempt to prove that Shakespeare's plays were really written by this or that duke or earl—the presumption being that noble birth or classical education or wealth or worldly experience could explain the existence of Shakespeare's plays, whereas *nothing* can really explain them. And this is also true of *Frankenstein.*

I do not mean to suggest that *Frankenstein* is the same kind of precisely wrought work of literature as, say, *Richard III* or *King Lear.* . . . Shakespeare's rich genius can be located in specific words and sentences; Mary Shelley's is harder to pin down. *Frankenstein* is simultaneously gripping and silly, well constructed and full of rough places, tragic but also (if we step back from it) somehow laughable. As Philip Stevick has pointed out in his essay '*Frankenstein* and Comedy', Mary Shelley's masterpiece, like those of Poe and Kafka, has the zany truth of a dream.

A BOOK FROM A DREAM

This makes sense, for the novel originated in a dream, as the author famously recounts in her 1831 preface to the book. Writing fifteen years after the work's initial composition, having just finished revising *Frankenstein* for its second edition, Mary Shelley recalled the circumstances which led to the writing of her first novel. '"We will each write a ghost story," said Lord Byron, and his proposition was acceded to. There were four of us.' They included the already renowned Byron ('the noble author', as she calls him in the 1831 preface); his friend Percy Bysshe Shelley, who at twenty-four had published *Queen Mab* and was beginning to make his reputation; a doctor friend of theirs whom Mary refers to in the preface as 'poor Polidori'; and Mary herself.

In June of 1816, when this gathering in Switzerland took place, she was not yet Mary Shelley, for she was not to marry Percy Shelley until December of that year, a few weeks after his first wife had drowned herself. In June she was still Mary Wollestonecraft Godwin, bearing her name like a badge of her illustrious parentage, a testimonial to two of the most notorious radicals in late eighteenth-century England, Mary Wollestonecraft and William Godwin. She was not yet Percy Shelley's wife, but by June of 1816, at the age of eighteen, she had already borne him two children—one a girl, dead a few weeks after birth, and the other a little boy named William. Like her mother (who had married Godwin only when she was several months into her pregnancy with Mary, having already borne one out-of-wedlock daughter as a result of a previous love affair), Mary Shelley exhibited a fine disregard for the social proprieties. She came from a circle of social radicals, and she joined a circle of social radicals. (Byron, at that point, had just fathered an illegitimate daughter borne by Mary's stepsister, with whom Percy Shelley was also, it seems likely, having an affair.) Yet there is some evidence to suggest that Mary, vigorously as she threw herself into this excessively romantic way of life, also had some reservations about its possibilities for making her happy. She was both adventurous and sceptical, willing to cross boundaries and yet well aware of the need for containment. In short, she was exactly the sort of person who could retrieve a dream like *Frankenstein* from the depths of her unconscious and deliver it to us—I was going to say 'unflinchingly', but that is not accurate, for she was intelligent and sensitive enough to flinch at all its terrors.

The dream was so frightening that even fifteen years afterward, recounting it to us in her preface, she flinches a bit in the interpretation. First she describes the scene itself: 'I saw—with shut eyes, but acute mental vision—I saw the pale student of unhallowed arts kneeling beside the thing he had put together. I saw the hideous phantasm of a man stretched out, and then, on the working of some powerful engine, show signs of life and stir with an uneasy, half-vital motion.' But instantly as we are wont to do in the telling of our dreams, Mary Shelley begins to impose connections and causalities, to shape the untamed, unwilled dream toward a moral lesson: 'Frightful must it be, for supremely frightful would be the effect of any human endeavor to mock the stupendous mechanism of the Creator of the world. His success would terrify the artist; he would rush away from his odious work, horrorstricken.' In the preface, she justifies this sudden departure on scientific grounds: 'He would hope that, left to itself, the slight spark of life which he had communicated would fade, that this thing which had received such imperfect animation would subside into dead matter, and he might sleep in the belief that the silence of the grave would quench forever the transient existence of the hideous corpse which he had looked upon as the cradle of life.' But the 'hideous phantasm', the 'hideous corpse', does not just die off politely; instead, it nastily, horridly, coldly intrudes on its maker: 'He sleeps; but he is awakened; he opens his eyes; behold, the horrid thing stands at his bedside, opening his curtains and looking on him with yellow, watery, but speculative eyes.'

'I opened mine in terror' is how Mary Shelley begins the next paragraph, forging an implicit though unacknowledged connection between herself and the monster, both of whom clearly possess 'speculative eyes'. Realizing that this horrific vision can be used to fulfill Lord Byron's challenge, she instantly writes down the dream, beginning her ghost story with the words 'It was on a dreary night in November.' Yet if

you look at the chapter which now begins with those words—
—the description of the monster's awakening, buried deep in
the book as Chapter 5—you will find that in her preface
Mary Shelley has done some violence to the dream, and to
the novel it gave rise to. For the novel is far more sympa-
thetic than the preface to the hideous creature himself, and
far less so to his vacillating creator. . . .

MONSTROUS DREAMS WITHIN DREAMS

In her prefatory description of her own dream, Mary Shelley
summarizes the bedside apparition of 'the horrid thing' in a
few distant words. But in her novel she brings us much
closer to the monster, hinting at tender feelings and im-
pulses within him through gestures that only scare away the
obtuse Frankenstein. 'He held up the curtain of the bed; and
his eyes, if eyes they may be called, were fixed on me,' says
our irretrievably dense narrator. 'His jaws opened, and he
muttered some inarticulate sounds, while a grin wrinkled his
cheeks. He might have spoken, but I did not hear; one hand
was stretched out, seemingly to detain me, but I escaped and
rushed downstairs.' Even we, who have no more acquaintance with this new species of man-made creature than
Frankenstein himself has, may suspect that the monster's
gestures signify friendliness rather than aggression; and the
creature eventually confirms these suspicions when he gets
to tell his own story in Volume Two of the three-volume
novel. But Victor Frankenstein is too frightened and too
guilt-ridden to see his child's first sounds, tentative smile
and outstretched hand as anything other than menacing.

Between Frankenstein's initial departure from the lab
and his bedside sighting of the monster comes a dream
within a dream, Victor's own nightmarish fantasy embed-
ded in Mary Shelley's. Frankenstein dreams that he sees his
beloved Elizabeth walking in the streets of his university
town. 'Delighted and surprised, I embraced her, but as I imprinted the first kiss on her lips, they became livid with the
hue of death; her features appeared to change, and I
thought that I held the corpse of my dead mother in my
arms; a shroud enveloped her form, and I saw the grave-
worms crawling in the folds of the flannel.' This foreshad-
ows much else in *Frankenstein.* . . . It is a premonition of
Elizabeth's eventual death at the hands of the monster,
which is virtually a parody of wedding-night sexual ecstasy,

complete with swoon (Victor's, again, of course). As such, the dream is evidence that Victor's protestations of ignorance and helplessness in regard to Elizabeth's death (he thought the monster was after *him*) ring a little hollow, at least in terms of his unconscious suspicions. His dream also draws the essential link between life and death that pervades the novel: the monster's life, which stems from death ('the hideous corpse'), also leads to a number of deaths—including, ultimately, his creator's and (possibly) his own. Beyond all this, the dream rises up out of its context in *Frankenstein* to break its restraining bonds—literary, social, chronological—and prefigure the relations between sons and mothers that were not to be so graphically stated again until D.H. Lawrence and Sigmund Freud. . . .

FRANKENSTEIN AND PARENTHOOD

The novel is filled with dead or absent mothers—in Victor Frankenstein's dream, in his life (his beloved mother died soon after he went off to the university), in Elizabeth's past (she was adopted by Victor's family because her mother died in childbirth), and even in the motherless DeLacey family, who make a cameo appearance in the monster's part of the narrative. Mary Shelley's own mother died of puerperal fever, a complication following childbirth, when Mary was only ten days old, and her revered memory (not to mention her prominently placed portrait) was a constant presence in the Godwin household. But it was a presence mainly noticeable as an absence. Like *King Lear, Frankenstein* is essentially a world without mothers, a world where fathers have to fulfill the range of maternal and paternal roles, from the narrow-minded harshness of Henry Clerval's businessman father to the softhearted kindness of Victor's father and the yielding, dependent tenderness of old Mr. DeLacey.

Victor Frankenstein himself has to be both father and mother (not that he is particularly good at being either) to the unfortunate monster he has created. The novel is at times explicit about the extent to which it addresses the subject of parenthood. Contemplating his creation before he finishes it, Victor blithely reflects: 'A new species would bless me as its creator and source; many happy and excellent natures would owe their being to me. No father could claim the gratitude of his child so completely as I should deserve theirs.' This boast comes back to mock him later, as the renounced, exiled monster (who has already mourned his orphan state, complaining that 'No father had watched my infant days, no mother had blessed me with smiles and caresses') confronts Frankenstein with the words: 'I learned from your papers that you were my father, my creator; and to whom could I apply with more fitness than to him who had given me my life?'

It is difficult at this distance to assess exactly what kind of father William Godwin was, particularly since his irritating characteristics (and he had many) have led generations of writers and philosophers to portray him as the most irksome of literary ancestors. In recent years this tendency has been exacerbated by feminist critics' desire to see him as the removed but repressive patriarch who ruined Mary's life. The real story, as usual, appears to be more complicated than that. At least during Mary's infancy and childhood, he involved himself personally in his precocious daughter's upbringing and education, generously treated Fanny Imlay (Mary Wollestonecraft's illegitimate daughter) as his own child, and allowed both girls to participate to the full in the intellectual life of the household—which included, at one point, listening to Coleridge read aloud the just-completed 'Rime of the Ancient Mariner'. . . .

Still, . . . William Godwin could not have been an easy father. He had a deep and unyielding belief in his own rightness, manifested in his emphatic prose as well as his personal behaviour. When people disagreed with him or, worse, disobeyed him, he simply cut them off—as he did, for instance, with Mary's beloved childhood nanny, whom she never saw again after the age of three. When Mary's half-sister Fanny committed suicide (this happened in October of 1816, during the composition of *Frankenstein),* Godwin refused to have her body brought back to the house, and insisted that this once-favoured child be buried in a pauper's grave. Godwin's reasons for this were unlikely to be religious or conventional; his primary motive appears to have been a very personal anger at being abandoned. The same seems true of his attitude toward Mary. When this rebellious sixteen-year-old ran off with the married Percy Bysshe Shelley—her father's friend, disciple and financial supporter—Godwin stopped speaking to her. During the time she was writing *Frankenstein,* he would have nothing to do with the young couple beyond a continued acceptance of

funds. Mary unabashedly complained about this treatment
in the form of her portrait of Victor Frankenstein, a man who
so self-righteously marches away from his ill-favoured progeny that he never does acknowledge the extent to which the
creature's crimes are his own fault. . . .

Mary Shelley's steely examination of parenthood goes far
beyond the working-off of her gripes against her father. If Victor Frankenstein and his monster (two halves of the same
soul, as our modern conflation of them in 'Frankenstein' suggests) can be seen as representing William Godwin, they are
no less a portrait of Mary Shelley herself. She was a mother as
well as a daughter, and in this novel she gave the first and
most pathetic victim—Victor's youngest brother, William—
the same name as her own little boy. One needs to understand
the degree of emotional risk involved here. For an author who
has children of her (or his) own, it takes a self-lacerating
courage to imagine and write about the death of *any* child. If
little William Shelley were to die (and he did die, less than
three years after Mary conceived of his fictional death), then
this emotional gamble would take on even higher stakes, and
his mother would be bound to see herself as responsible for
the terrifying fantasy that had become reality. Nor was this a
remote and inconceivable possibility in Mary's life, for all her
children but one were to die before growing up, and one infant had already died before she began to write *Frankenstein.*
A few weeks after her first child died, when Mary was only
seventeen, she wrote in her diary: 'Dream that my little baby
came to life again; that it had only been cold, and that we
rubbed it before the fire, and it lived. Awake and find no baby.
I think about the little thing all day.' *Frankenstein* is that
dream brought to life and turned to nightmare.

In this novel, parents are not just parents; they are 'creators', which can mean 'gods'. The monster explicitly compares his and Frankenstein's relation to that of Adam and
God: 'Remember that I am thy creature; I ought to be thy
Adam, but I am rather the fallen angel, whom thou drivest
from joy for no misdeed.' Later, with an eye toward asking
Frankenstein to make him a female counterpart, he mentions that 'no Eve soothed my sorrows nor shared my
thoughts; I was alone'. This is not just any Adam, but specifically Milton's, for *Paradise Lost* is one of the formative works
of the monster's education, one of the three books through
which he learns to read. (The other two are Plutarch's *Lives*

and Goethe's *Sorrows of Werther.*) Like *Paradise Lost,* *Frankenstein* asks to be admitted instantly to the realm of our mythic literature—mythic not just in its use of fantasy, but in its stature among our cultural memories and explanations.

MARY SHELLEY'S "HIDEOUS PROGENY"

Unlike Victor Frankenstein, Mary Shelley is a relatively loving parent: she feels affection not only for her novel, but for the monster who is *its* hideous progeny. She also stimulates in us, the readers, a comparable affection for him, and she makes this kind of affection, this kind of sympathy, a crucial point of the novel. How *Frankenstein* works on our readerly sympathies is not a technical adjunct of the novel's meaning; it *is* its meaning. Through the feelings created in us by the manipulation of language (the monster's language, in particular, but also other people's), we arrive at moral judgements about the reasonableness of various characters' behaviour, which we in turn generalize into moral principles. All novels work this way to some extent, but in Mary Shelley's case the enterprise is central to both the plot of *Frankenstein* and its structure.

Anticipating later writers like Emily Brontë, Wilkie Collins and Joseph Conrad, Mary Shelley elaborated a complex technique of narrative frames and multiple viewpoints. The structure of *Frankenstein* is not linear, but circular: we bore our way into the 'heart of darkness' (which is also the heart of feeling, of sympathy) and then come back out again. We begin with letters from the explorer Walton, who then gives us the narrative of Victor Frankenstein, who in turn gives way to the monster's own telling of his tale. After the monster's speech (which takes up most of Volume Two in the original three-volume edition), we then come back out to Frankenstein, and thence to Walton. In story-telling terms, this technique has wonderful advantages: it allows us to get a central character's firsthand, eyewitness account, and at the same time permits us to learn about his death (as we can't normally do in a first-person narrative, where the tale dies before the teller). In emotional terms, the method plays complicatedly with our capacities for sympathy, as each new character seems first a fearful stranger, then our closest intimate. (This is particularly true of the monster, who is utterly obscure to us in Frankenstein's account, utterly appealing in his own.) And in philosophical or moral terms, the use of multiple narratives is itself a commentary on the complex nature of truth. In *Frankenstein*, there are no given facts; everything we are told is a function of someone or other's viewpoint. This applies even to the monster's death or disappearance at the end. Walton, watching from the cabin of his ship, tells us that the creature 'was soon borne away by the waves and lost in darkness and distance'. But this doesn't literally mean he was lost at sea; it simply means that Walton lost sight of him.

The doubtfulness of all the information we receive in *Frankenstein* is set against the pressure on us to respond to the characters emotionally. This is a novel which, heightening our emotions through the portrayal of horrific or catastrophic events, asks us to feel strongly. . . . At the same time, *Frankenstein* asks us to question all the sources of those strong feelings. Sympathy and antipathy are our crucial responses in this as in every novel; yet *Frankenstein* tells us that our sympathies, our antipathies, can be wrong. This applies massively to the monster himself (who is rejected instantly, by everybody, purely because of his 'hideous' appearance), but it also applies to other characters in the novel, as if to show that not just monsters suffer from this unfair fate. Walton, for instance, describes in an early letter to his sister the extremely noble, kind, self-sacrificing Russian who serves as his ship's master, but then adds that 'he is silent as a Turk, and a kind of ignorant carelessness attends him, which, while it renders his conduct the more astonishing, detracts from the interest and sympathy which otherwise he would command'. The monster's history is only the most extreme example of the way we tend to allocate our sympathies on the basis of nice manners and superficial appearances rather than essential moral worth.

Lost to Walton's sight he may have been, but Frankenstein's creature reappears to us with frequent regularity, in numerous different forms—from the first theatrical adaptation in 1823 (which Mary Shelley attended and enjoyed) to the dozens of film and television versions, both serious and parodic, in our own century. As that century hurtles to its terrifying close—amidst toxic spills, nuclear threats, devastating climatic changes, angry homeless people, ineducable crack babies, starving war victims and all the other catastrophes we have come to take for granted—it might help us to recall, with Mary Shelley's help, that we make our own monsters.

Death and Birth in *Frankenstein*

Ellen Moers

Ellen Moers is the author of *Harriet Beecher Stowe and American Literature, The Dandy: Brummell to Beerbohm,* and *Literary Women.* In this celebrated and highly influential article, Ellen Moers first coined the term "Female Gothic" to describe the work of various early nineteenth-century women authors in England, particularly Ann Radcliffe. Moers places *Frankenstein* within that context, but she sees Shelley's novel as marking a "major turning point in the tradition." In the following excerpt Moers discusses themes of birth and death in *Frankenstein* as they emerge from Shelley's genuinely original story of a mad scientist who "works at creating human life, only to find that he has made a monster."

Ann Radcliffe's novels suggest that, for her, Gothic was a device to set maidens on distant and exciting journeys without offending the proprieties. In the power of villains, her heroines are forced to scurry up the top of pasteboard Alps and penetrate bandit-infested forests. They can scuttle miles along castle corridors, descend into dungeons, and explore secret chambers without a chaperone, because the Gothic castle, however ruined, is an indoor and therefore freely female space. In Mrs. Radcliffe's hands the Gothic novel became a feminine substitute for the picaresque, where heroines could enjoy all the adventures and alarms that masculine heroes had long experienced, far from home, in fiction.

She also made the Gothic novel into a make-believe puberty rite for young women. Her heroines are always good daughters, her villains bad, cruel, painfully attractive father figures, for which her lovers are at last accepted as palely

Excerpted from "Female Gothic: The Monster's Mother," by Ellen Moers, *New York Review of Books.* Reprinted with permission from the author's husband, Martin Mayer.

satisfactory substitutes, but only after paternal trials and tortures are visited upon the heroine. . . .

As early as the 1790s, Ann Radcliffe firmly set the Gothic in one of the ways it would go ever after: a novel in which the central figure is a young woman who is simultaneously persecuted victim and courageous heroine. But what are we to make of the next major turning of the Gothic tradition that a woman brought about a generation later? Mary Shelley's *Frankenstein,* in 1818, made over the Gothic novel into what today we call science fiction. *Frankenstein* brought a new sophistication to literary terror, and it did so without a heroine, without even an important female victim. Paradoxically, however, no other Gothic work by a woman writer, perhaps no other literary work of any kind by a woman, better repays examination in the light of the sex of its author. For *Frankenstein* is a birth myth, and one that was lodged in the novelist's imagination, I am convinced, by the fact that she was herself a mother.

GIVING BIRTH TO *FRANKENSTEIN*

Much in Mary Shelley's life was remarkable. She was the daughter of a brilliant mother (Mary Wollstonecraft) and father (William Godwin). She was the mistress and then wife of the poet Shelley. She read widely in five languages, including Latin and Greek. She had easy access to the writings and conversation of some of the most original minds of her age. But nothing so sets her apart from the generality of writers of her own time, and before, and for long afterward, than her early and chaotic experience, at the very time she became an author, with motherhood. Pregnant at sixteen, and almost constantly pregnant throughout the following five years; yet not a secure mother, for she lost most of her babies soon after they were born; and not a lawful mother, for she was not married—not at least when, at the age of eighteen, Mary Godwin began to write *Frankenstein.* So are monsters born.

What in fact has the experience of giving birth to do with women's literature? In the eighteenth and nineteenth centuries very few important women writers, except for Mary Shelley, bore children; most of them, in England and America, were spinsters and virgins. With the coming of Naturalism late in the century, and the lifting of the Victorian taboo against writing about physical sexuality (including pregnancy and labor), the subject of birth was first brought to literature in realistic form by male novelists, from Tolstoy and Zola to William Carlos Williams. . . .

Mary Shelley was a unique case, in literature as in life. She brought birth to fiction not as realism but as Gothic fantasy, and thus contributed to Romanticism a myth of genuine originality. She invented the mad scientist who locks himself in his laboratory and secretly, guiltily, works at creating human life, only to find that he has made a monster.

> It was on a dreary night of November, that I beheld the accomplishment of my toils. With an anxiety that almost amounted to agony, I collected the instruments of life around me, that I might infuse a spark of being into the lifeless thing that lay at my feet. . . . The rain pattered dismally against the panes, and my candle was nearly burnt out, when, by the glimmer of the half-extinguished light, I saw the dull yellow eye of the creature open; it breathed hard, and a convulsive motion agitated its limbs . . . . His yellow skin scarcely covered the work of muscles and arteries beneath; his hair was of a lustrous black, and flowing . . . ; but these luxuriances only formed a more horrid contrast with his watery eyes, that seemed almost of the same colour as the dun white sockets in which they were set, his shrivelled complexion and straight black lips.

That is very good horror, but what follows is more horrid still: Frankenstein, the scientist, runs away and abandons the newborn monster, who is and remains nameless. Here, I think, is where Mary Shelley's book is most interesting, most powerful, and most feminine: in the motif of revulsion against newborn life, and the drama of guilt, dread, and flight surrounding birth and its consequences. Most of the novel, roughly two of its three volumes, can be said to deal with the retribution visited upon monster and creator for deficient infant care. *Frankenstein* seems to be distinctly a woman's mythmaking on the subject of birth precisely because its emphasis is not upon what precedes birth, not upon birth itself, but upon what follows birth: the trauma of the after-birth.

Fear and guilt, depression and anxiety are commonplace reactions to the birth of a baby, and well within the normal range of experience. But more deeply rooted in our cultural mythology, and certainly in our literature, are the happy maternal reactions: ecstasy, a sense of fulfillment, and the rush of nourishing love which sweep over the new mother when she first holds her baby in her arms. . . .

INFLUENCES ON SHELLEY

From what we know about the strange young woman who wrote *Frankenstein*, Mary Shelley . . . rejoiced at becoming a mother and loved and cherished her babies as long as they lived. But her journal is a chilly and laconic document, mostly concerned with the extraordinary reading program she put herself through at Shelley's side. Her own emphasis on books in the journal has set the tone of most of the discussion of the genesis of *Frankenstein*. Mary Shelley is said—and rightly—to have based her treatment of the life of her monster on the ideas about education, society, and morality held by her father and her mother. She is shown to have been influenced directly by Shelley's genius, and by her reading of Coleridge and Wordsworth and the Gothic novelists. She learned from Sir Humphry Davy's book on chemistry and Erasmus Darwin on biology. In Switzerland, during the summer she began *Frankenstein*, she sat by while Shelley, Byron, and Polidori discussed the new sciences of mesmerism, electricity, and galvanism, which promised to unlock the riddle of life, and planned to write ghost stories.

Mary Shelley herself was the first to point to her fortuitous immersion in the romantic and scientific revolutions of her day as the source of *Frankenstein*. Her extreme youth, as well as her sex, has contributed to the generally held opinion that she was not so much an author in her own right as a transparent medium through which passed the ideas of those around her. . . .

FRANKENSTEIN AND THE OVERREACHER TRADITION

Passive reflections, however, do not produce original works of literature, and *Frankenstein*, if not a great novel, was unquestionably an original one. The major Romantic and minor Gothic tradition to which it *should* have belonged was the literature of the overreacher: the superman who breaks through normal human limitations to defy the rules of society and infringe upon the realm of God. . . .

But Mary Shelley's overreacher is different. Frankenstein's exploration of the forbidden boundaries of human science does not cause the prolongation and extension of his own life, but the creation of a new one. He defies mortality not by living forever, but by giving birth. That this original twist to an old myth should have been the work of a young woman who was also a young mother seems to me, after all, not a very surprising answer to the question that, according to Mary Shelley herself, was asked from the start: "How I, then a young girl, came to think of, and to dilate upon, so very hideous an idea?"

Birth is a hideous thing in *Frankenstein*, even before there is a monster. For Frankenstein's procedure, once he has determined to create new life, is to frequent the vaults and charnel houses and study the human corpse in all its loathsome stages of decay and decomposition. "To examine the causes of life," he says, "we must first have recourse to death." His purpose is to "bestow animation upon lifeless matter," so that he might "in process of time renew life where death had apparently devoted the body to corruption." Frankenstein collects bones and other human parts from the slaughterhouse and the dissecting room, and through long months of feverish activity sticks them together in a frame of gigantic size in what he calls "my workshop of filthy creation."

SHELLEY'S OWN PREGNANCIES

It is in her journal and her letters that Mary Shelley reveals the workshop of her own creation, where she pieced together the materials for a new species of romantic mythology. They record a horror story of maternity such as literary biography hardly provides again until Sylvia Plath.

As far as I can figure out, she was pregnant, barely pregnant but aware of the fact, when at the age of sixteen she ran off with Shelley in July, 1814. Also pregnant at the same time was Shelley's legal wife Harriet, who gave birth in November to a "son and heir," as Mary noted in her journal. In February, 1815, Mary gave birth to a daughter, illegitimate, premature, and sickly. There is nothing in the journal about domestic help or a nurse in attendance. Mary notes that she breast fed the baby; that Fanny, her half-sister, came to call; that Mrs. Godwin, her stepmother, sent over some linen; that Claire Clairmont, Mrs. Godwin's daughter who had run off with Mary, kept Shelley amused. Bonaparte invaded France, the journal tells us, and Mary took up her incessant reading program: this time, Mme. de Staël's *Corinne*. The baby died in March. "Find my baby dead," Mary wrote. "A miserable day."

In April, 1815, she was pregnant again, about eight weeks after the birth of her first child. In January, 1816, she gave birth to a son: more breast feeding, more reading. In March,

Claire Clairmont sought out Lord Byron and managed to get herself pregnant by him within a couple of weeks. This pregnancy would be a subject of embarrassment and strain to Mary and Shelley, and it immediately changed their lives, for Byron left England in April, and Claire, Shelley, Mary, and her infant pursued him to Switzerland in May. There is nothing yet in Mary's journal about a servant, but a good deal about mule travel in the mountains. In June they all settled near Byron on the shores of Lake Geneva.

In June, 1816, also, Mary began *Frankenstein.* And during the year of its writing the following events ran their swift and sinister course: In October, Fanny Imlay, Mary's half-sister, committed suicide after discovering that she was not Godwin's daughter but Mary Wollstonecraft's daughter by her American lover. . . . In early December Mary was pregnant again, which she seems to have sensed almost the day it happened. . . . In mid-December, Harriet Shelley drowned herself in the Serpentine, she was pregnant by someone other than Shelley. In late December Mary married Shelley. In January, 1817, Mary wrote Byron that Claire had borne him a daughter. In May she finished *Frankenstein,* published the following year.

Death and birth were thus as hideously mixed in the life of Mary Shelley as in Frankenstein's "workshop of filthy creation." Who can read without shuddering, and without remembering her myth of the birth of a nameless monster, Mary's journal entry of March 19, 1815, which records the trauma of her loss, when she was seventeen, of her first baby, the little girl who did not live long enough to be given a name. "Dream that my little baby came to life again," Mary wrote; "that it had only been cold, and that we rubbed it before the fire and it lived. Awake and find no baby. I think about the little thing all day. Not in good spirits." *("I thought, that if I could bestow animation upon lifeless matter, I might in process of time renew life where death had apparently devoted the body to corruption.")*

So little use has been made of this material by writers about *Frankenstein* that it may be worth emphasizing how important, because how unusual, was Mary Shelley's experience as a woman. The harum-scarum circumstances surrounding her maternity have no parallel until our own time, which in its naïve cerebrations upon family life (and in much else, except genius) resembles the generation of the Shelleys.

Mary Godwin sailed into teenage motherhood without any of the financial or social or familial supports that made bearing and rearing children a relaxed experience for the normal middle-class woman of her day (as Jane Austen, for example, described her). She was an unwed mother, responsible for breaking up the marriage of a young woman just as much a mother as she. The father whom she adored broke furiously with her when she eloped and Mary Wollstonecraft, the mother whose memory she revered and whose books she was rereading throughout her teenage years, had died in childbirth—died giving birth to Mary herself.

Surely no outside influence need be sought to explain Mary Shelley's fantasy of the newborn as at once monstrous agent of destruction and piteous victim of parental abandonment. "I, the miserable and the abandoned," cries the monster at the end of *Frankenstein,* "I am an abortion to be spurned at, and kicked, and trampled on. . . . I have murdered the lovely and the helpless. . . . I have devoted my creator to misery; I have pursued him even to that irremediable ruin."

THE LEGACY OF *FRANKENSTEIN*

In the century and a half since its publication, *Frankenstein* has spawned innumerable interpretations among the critics, and among the novelists, playwrights, and filmmakers who have felt its influence. The idea, though not the name, of the robot originated with Mary Shelley's novel, and her title character became a byword for the dangers of scientific knowledge. But the work has also been read as an existential fable; as a commentary on the split between reason and feeling, in both philosophical thought and educational theory; as a parable of the excesses of idealism and genius; as a dramatization of the divided self; as an attack on the stultifying force of social convention.

The versatility of Mary Shelley's myth is due to the brilliance of her mind and the range of her learning, as well as to the influence of the circle in which she moved as a young writer. But *Frankenstein* was most original in its dramatization of dangerous oppositions through the struggle of a creator with monstrous creation. The sources of this Gothic conception, which still has power to "curdle the blood, and quicken the beatings of the heart," were surely the anxieties of a woman who, as daughter, mistress, and mother, was a bearer of death.

Analyzing *Dracula*'s Enduring Popularity

James B. Twitchell

A professor of English at the University of Florida, James B. Twitchell is the author of two studies of horror literature, *Dreadful Pleasures* and *The Living Dead*. Here, in an excerpt from *The Living Dead*, Twitchell confronts the issue of *Dracula*'s continuing popularity and seeks to explain that popularity primarily in terms of Bram Stoker's success at fashioning a "consummate retelling" of the traditional vampire myth. Since Twitchell dismisses the faulty technical aspects of the novel as lackluster, he turns to Sigmund Freud's psychoanalytic theory to explain the attraction readers have to the vampire tale. Employing Freud's ideas, Twitchell believes Dracula is a sexually charged figure who violates social taboos through his vampirism, and that these transgressions are part of the reader's fascination.

Ironically, *Dracula*, the greatest vampire novel, is the work of fiction that takes the vampire out of literature and returns him to folklore. As a literary work *Dracula* has suffered from this achievement, for although the novel has been exceedingly popular, there have been few critical commentaries about it. This is certainly because the vampire and Dracula have become synonymous, and the vampire is hardly considered a scholarly subject, but it is also because the book appeared in 1897, at the height of literary Realism and Naturalism. Had it been written in 1820, I suspect that it would have been hailed, as *Frankenstein* is, as a Romantic milestone. As Royce MacGillivray says, "Had *Dracula* come to literary life in the age of Romanticism and the Gothic novel, one imagines it would have been received rapturously into the literary tradition of western Europe instead of being sternly restricted, as it has been to the popular imagination.". . .

UNDERSTANDING *DRACULA*'S POPULARITY

It is rare that an almost century-old book can achieve such commercial success without scholarly approbation. Most books that "earn their keep" on publishers' lists do so because they are continually being revived in classrooms. *Dracula* is an exception; any publisher can make money with it. Why has this misplaced Gothic novel lasted in the popular marketplace while the works of Walpole or Lewis or Radcliffe or Maturin have gathered dust, to be opened only in classrooms and then primarily for purposes of literary history? Part of the reason must be that *Dracula* is, first of all, a good story, complete with a lusty villain, damsels in distress, and haunted castles. The earlier Gothics . . . had all this as well, yet they had something else—they made everything sensible. Unlike its early predecessors, *Dracula* seems to depend on its very inexplicableness, its nonsensibleness, to generate a kind of tension that is unrelieved and ultimately unexplained.

What sets *Dracula* apart then, is that it is primarily a story of psychological terror, not physical violence. True, the earlier Gothics were not exactly action-packed, at least by our kinetic standards, but in *Dracula* there is hardly any action at all. Partly this lack of immediate and close-up action is because of the epistolary method, and partly because Bram Stoker knew that action itself is always explainable. Dracula, unlike his literary brother the Frankenstein monster, simply cannot be explained. There is no calculating scientist who created him—he just is. Where does he come from? What does he do? And more important, why does he choose these specific victims? All this is never sufficiently answered to give us a sense of causality and predictability. In the earlier Gothic novels precisely the opposite happened: everything was finally explained, whether it needed to be or not—the creaking door, the misplaced baby, the recognition scenes. These occurrences are simply nowhere to be found in *Dracula*. Dracula is just a monster who attacks people. . . .

And so to what, if *Dracula* does not operate like the traditional Gothic novel, may we attribute its phenomenal success? Again, it is easier to answer in the negative. *Dracula*'s success is certainly not due to its organization and style. The book is cumbersomely plotted around five central events: (1) the "initiation" of Jonathan Harker into Dracula's world; (2) Dracula's pursuit of Lucy; (3) the staking of Lucy; (4) the staining of Mina; and (5) the pursuit of Dracula. The middle three of these sections are overlong and detract from the work's rising tension, while other parts, such as the correspondence between Mina and Lucy, are unnecessarily tedious. The style, too, is redundant and occasionally absurd—for instance, Van Helsing's annoying accent. Admittedly some of this awkwardness is a result of Stoker's working in a structure, the epistolary novel, that depends on the author's ability to vary styles, making each one fit a specific character. Stoker is not Wilkie Collins—he is best, I think, with the initial Jonathan Harker episodes and understandably less successful with Mina and Lucy. Because he is not a master of style, the secondary characters are often stilted or even superfluous. The central characters, Van Helsing, Renfield, Lucy, Mina, and of course Dracula himself, do indeed have distinct and memorable personalities (although one wonders about the credibility of Renfield), but the "boys"—Jonathan Harker, Quincey Morris, Lord Godalming, and John Seward—all seem fitted to the same pattern. They are stout, honest, loyal, brave—in short, good scouts all, and, unfortunately, dull.

If *Dracula*'s claim on our attention is not its historical importance or its artistic merit, then its power is derived from something below the surface, something carried within the myth itself. *Dracula* is the consummate retelling of the vampire story; all the pieces are used and all the pieces fit. Stoker had no artistic pretensions, no deep truth to plumb; the vampire is there to frighten and shock, to make us jealous, not to enlighten. If the book is poetic and powerful, it is because Stoker was wise enough never to dilute the psychological content of the legend; in fact, if anything, he made it more potent. Dracula is terrifically alluring; he has everything we want: he has money and power without responsibilities; he parties all night with the best people, yet he doesn't need friends; he can be violent and aggressive without guilt or punishment; he has life without death; but most attractive of all, he has sex without confusion (i.e., genitalia, pregnancy . . . love). It's all take, no give. If only he didn't have those appetites!

The story of Stoker's *Dracula* is this: a band of boys, a

gang if you will, under the direction of a wise father-figure/priest/doctor must destroy a demon who has been ravaging their women. It is more than a dragon-destroying quest, however; for this demon is articulate, shrewd, decidedly upper-class, intelligent, and sexually potent. There is no mention of this sexual potency, no mention of his incredible erotic power, but in every instance we are aware it is there. Dracula is evil, yes, but he knows how the world is put together and he knows how to get what he wants. What he wants is exactly what the "boys" want as well—women.

As an ancillary theory to the Oedipus complex, Freud, in *Totem and Taboo*, postulated that far in our cultural past the dominant male of the family, the father-figure, subjugated the weaker males by hoarding the women. In Freud's psycho-biological scheme the sons had to overthrow the father to continue their own genetic lines, as well as to express themselves sexually, and so they "displaced" the older male, perhaps even killing him. It is this removal (whether actual or imaginative makes no difference) that caused the sons to feel first exultation and then grief and then guilt, for they had destroyed their own progenitor. For this act they did penance by creating certain totems to alleviate guilt, while at the same time protecting themselves from being likewise displaced by the next generation of young men. The latter part of Freud's "primal horde" hypothesis need not concern us; rather, it is the gang killing of the father that seems to form the psychic core of the story of *Dracula*. . . .

It has also been pointed out that Dracula is as much a father-figure as Van Helsing, and that the central action of the book concerns the young boy's acceptance of the good father (Van Helsing) in order to destroy the evil father (Dracula). Dracula does exert an almost patriarchal influence: he is older than the boys, living eternally at a dignified retirement age; he is the lord of the castle; he is wealthy; he has his own women, to whom Jonathan Harker, at least, is attracted; and he is about to add new women (Lucy and Mina) to what he refers to as "my family." Van Helsing, on the other hand, has a wife (she is now institutionalized) and can promise the boys nothing except knowledge. It is this knowledge, however, that is power, for it will allow the boys to destroy the father/demon to achieve "justice" (read "women") at last.

Lest there be any doubt as to the sublimated sexuality of the story, let me briefly point to a few central events. First, it must be noted that all the central characters, with the exception of the evil totem, Dracula, appear to be models of chastity and Victorian virtue. Appearances are deceiving, however, as early in the story Jonathan Harker . . . falls to the blandishments of Dracula's women. In Dracula's castle we see the young married male hesitatingly respond to wondrous temptation:

> In the moonlight opposite me were three young women, ladies by their dress and manner. I thought at the time that I must be dreaming when I saw them, for, though the moonlight was behind them, they threw no shadow on the floor. They came close to me, and looked at me for some time, and then whispered together. Two were dark and had high aquiline noses, like the Count, and great dark piercing eyes, that seemed to be almost red when contrasted with the pale yellow moon. The other was fair, as fair as can be, with great wavy masses of golden hair and eyes like pale sapphires. I seemed somehow to know her face, and to know it in connection with some dreamy fear, but I could not recollect at the moment how or where. All three had brilliant white teeth that shone like pearls against the ruby of their voluptuous lips. There was something about them that made me uneasy, some longing and at the same time some deadly fear. I felt in my heart a wicked, burning desire that they would kiss me with those red lips. It is not good to note this down, lest some day it should meet Mina's eyes and cause her pain; but it is the truth.

> The fair girl advanced and bent over me till I could feel the movement of her breath upon me. Sweet it was in one sense, honey-sweet, and sent the same tingling through the nerves as her voice, but with a bitter underlying the sweet, a bitter offensiveness, as one smells in blood.

> I was afraid to raise my eyelids, but looked out and saw perfectly under the lashes. The girl went on her knees, and bent over me, simply gloating. There was a deliberate voluptuousness which was both thrilling and repulsive, and as she arched her neck she actually licked her lips like an animal, till I could see in the moonlight the moisture shining on the scarlet lips and on the red tongue as it lapped the white sharp teeth. Lower and lower went her head as the lips went below the range of my mouth and chin and seemed to fasten on my throat. Then she paused, and I could hear the churning sound of her tongue as it licked her teeth and lips, and I could feel the hot breath on my neck. Then the skin of my throat began to tingle as one's flesh does when the hand that is to tickle it approaches nearer—nearer. I could feel the soft, shivering touch of the lips on the super-sensitive skin of my throat, and the hard dents of two sharp teeth, just touching and pausing there. I closed my eyes in languorous ecstasy and waited—waited with beating heart.

If there ever was an example of Coleridge's "desire with loathing strangely mix'd," this is it, for Jonathan Harker is a willing/unwilling co-conspirator. The count, who is somehow related to these women, arrives like a good parent to stop the scene, but even so, as Professor C.F. Bentley has pointed out in "The Monster in the Bedroom: Sexual Symbolism in *Dracula*," the damage has been done. Bentley claims that to understand the extent of this damage we should treat the incident as "the masturbatory fantasy of an erotic dream," recalling Ernest Jones's words:

> The explanation of these phantasies is surely not hard. A nightly visit from a beautiful or frightful being, who first exhausts the sleeper with passionate embraces and then withdraws from him a vital fluid; all this can point only to a natural and common process, namely to nocturnal emissions accompanied with dreams of a more or less erotic nature. In the unconscious mind blood is commonly an equivalent for semen.

LUCY AS DRACULA'S "QUEEN"

If this is true, it sheds important light on other more central actions, especially the transfusion of blood from the young boys into the body of Lucy. Lucy herself is as extraordinary a character as Dracula. At first she is the giggly and silly ingenue, but after her encounter with the father/demon, Dracula, she is transformed into a highly erotic and captivating woman. Her "new life" is maintained, however, only by repeated infusions of the blood of Arthur, Quincey, and Drs. Seward and Van Helsing. She is the queen maintained by the boys—a queen to King Dracula. Hence it may be of more than passing interest that John Seward and Quincey Morris were previously her rejected suitors, and that in a sense through these transfusions they married her by the mingling of blood. Van Helsing even admits as much when he tells Seward not to mention to Arthur, Lucy's present fiancé, that he, Seward, has participated in one of the transfusions. After Lucy's death, in which Arthur has to drive a stake through his love's body (the phallic symbolism here, claims Bentley, is too obvious to miss), we are told that because of the transfusions "he felt as if the two had been really married, and that she was his wife in the sight of God."

If Professor Bentley is correct in believing, along with Ernest Jones, that blood is a metaphor for semen and that then these transfusions are, in a sense, analogies for the sexual act, it is possible to explain how the "boys" may partici-

pate without guilt. But what of Van Helsing? He should know
better, for as the father-protector, the most perceptive of the
Western males, he is aware of the psychological consequences. And indeed he seems to be, for when Van Helsing
recalls his own participation in the transfusions, he suddenly changes from a most rational and controlled man into
a hysterical maniac. This realization and transformation occurs in the puzzling "King Laugh" episode of chapter 13. All
of a sudden Van Helsing, after thinking about what has happened, starts babbling about how in times of stress "King
Laugh" starts shouting "Here I am! Here I am!" in his ear.
Van Helsing's decompensation makes no sense at all until he
later explains that when things are the most psychologically
traumatic "King Laugh" comes to break them apart with
comedy, i.e., in times of greatest pressure we laugh instead
of cry. Dr. Seward understandably asks precisely what kind
of situation needs this explosion, and in broken English Van
Helsing replies that since the transfusion represents "marriage," then Mina "is a polyandrist, and me, with my poor
wife dead to me, but alive by church's law, though no wits,
all gone—even I, who am faithful husband to this now-no-
wife, am bigamist." Worse still are the possible incestuous
overtones, as Lucy has been "almost a daughter" to him.

MINA'S ENCOUNTER WITH DRACULA

If such a symbolic link exists between transfusions and marriage, or blood and semen, it may be worthwhile to examine
the novel's other central scene, in which Dracula ravages
and "initiates" Mina Harker into his family. It is such a crucial scene that we are given a number of versions, the first
of which appears in Dr. Seward's diary. Seward recalls how
he and Van Helsing burst into the Harkers' room, finding the
count holding

> both Mrs. Harker's hands, keeping them away with her arms
> at full tension; his right hand gripping her by the back of the
> neck, forcing her face down on his bosom. Her white night-
> dress was smeared with blood, and a thick stream trickled
> down the man's bare chest which was shown by his torn-
> open dress. The attitude of the two had a terrible resem-
> blance to a child forcing a kitten's nose into a saucer of milk
> to compel it to drink.

We later have Mina's version:

> With that he pulled open his shirt, and with his long sharp
> nails opened a vein in his breast. When the blood began to

spurt out, he took my hands in one of his, holding them tight, and with the other seized my neck and pressed my mouth to the wound, so that I must either suffocate or swallow some of the—Oh, my God! my God! what have I done? What have I done to deserve such a fate, I who have tried to walk in meekness and righteousness all my days. God pity me!

Certain peculiarities of this scene are startling, the most striking of which is that Dracula is reversing the vampiric process by having Mina drink from his body as he presumably has drunk from hers. There is no precedent for this in vampiric folklore, although it seems a logical enough part of the story. The strain of sexual violation, which is already so prominent in the myth, is here given added hints of fellatio. That Stoker then compares this process to a kitten being forced to drink milk from a saucer may well reinforce the seminal imagery. So too does Mina's reaction, for she is horrified to admit to her spouse what she has done. . . .

While it would be a mistake to force the blood/semen analogy too far, it may account for the book's almost clairvoyant insight into the dynamics of the myth. It is our horror (and the Victorian horror) of such sexual activity that may well draw us to the sublimated reenactment of what is forbidden. It is our "desire with loathing strangely mix'd" that makes both the myth and the book so compelling.

Dracula's Antifeminism

Bram Dijkstra

Bram Dijkstra is a professor of Comparative Literature at the University of California, San Diego. His
most recent work is *Evil Sisters: The Threat of Female
Sexuality in Twentieth-Century Culture*, and he has
written books on Daniel Defoe, Georgia O'Keefe, and
William Carlos Williams. The following article comes
from *Idols of Perversity*, his 1986 study of representa-
tions of demonic women in late Victorian art and literature. According to Dijkstra *Dracula* is "a very
carefully constructed cautionary tale directed to men
of the modern temper, warning them not to yield to
the bloodlust of the feminist, the New Woman embodied by Lucy." Victorian male fears of modern
women who wanted political and intellectual freedom were based on a belief that such ambitions were
not proper and could lead heretofore chaste and
morally upright women to the seedier experiences in
life that only men were strong enough to overcome.
Fearing that a more-liberated woman would fall into
licentiousness and degradation, Stoker—in Dijkstra's
opinion—fashioned this cautionary tale to show how
a New Woman like Lucy could be seduced by dark
forces and become a vampire, sucking the life force
out of Victorian men—ultimately leading to an erosion of society as a whole. *Dracula* is thus one of the
many works from the period which exhibit Victorian
culture's "antifeminine obsession."

The cultural preoccupation around 1900 with the struggle of
evolutionary progress against the forces of bestiality and degeneration was dramatized most coherently and consistently
in what is certainly the masterpiece of vampire literature, the

ever-popular *Dracula* (1897) by Bram Stoker. In Stoker's novel virtually all elements of the dream of future evolutionary possibility and all aspects of the period's suspicions about the degenerative tendencies in women have been brought together in such an effortless fashion that it is clear that for the author these were not so much a part of the symbolic structures of fantasy as the conditions of universal truth. Stoker's work demonstrates how thoroughly the war waged by the nineteenth-century male culture against the dignity and self-respect of women had been fought, and how completely the ideological implications of the dualistic struggle between the angels of the future and the demons of the past had entered into that semiconscious world which nurtures the cultural commonplaces governing the average person's perceptual environment. Stoker clearly was a man of limited intelligence, typical of the fairly well-educated, fairly well-off, middle-minded middle class. But he had a remarkably coherent sociological imagination and a brilliant talent for fluid, natural-sounding, visually descriptive prose. Together these qualities made it possible for him to write, perhaps without ever completely realizing what he had done, a narrative destined to become the looming twentieth century's basic commonplace book of the antifeminine obsession.

GENDER CONFLICT IN *DRACULA*

It is certainly true that Dracula, the narrative's pivotal vampire, is a male, but the world in which he operates is a world of women, the world of Eve, a world in which reversion and acculturation are at war. Dracula himself is merely an updated version of the art world's vile, unevolved, grossly bestial satyr, whose inability to control his desires is only further illuminated by his effeminate aristocratic airs. Dracula may not officially have been one of those horrid inbred Jews everyone was worrying about at the time Stoker wrote his novel, but he came close, for he was very emphatically Eastern European. . . .

When Jonathan Harker crosses the Danube on his way to the Carpathian Mountains, he has the impression that "we were leaving the West and entering the East." He soon discovers the regressive ignorance and inefficiency of Eastern life: "The further east you go the more unpunctual are the trains. What ought they to be in China?" It is a hair-raising question for any efficient Britisher. To travel eastward is to travel into the past. The road to Castle Dracula is "hemmed in with trees, which in places arched right over the roadway till we passed as through a tunnel." Harker has to travel into the bowels of man's past to find Dracula, and when he finds him the count has all the phrenological characteristics of the sensuous satyr: "His face was a strong—a very strong—aquiline, with high bridge of the thin nose and peculiarly arched nostrils; with lofty domed forehead, and hair growing scantily round the temples but profusely elsewhere, his eyebrows were very massive, almost meeting over the nose, and with bushy hair that seemed to curl in its own confusion." If that weren't enough, he has the "peculiarly sharp white teeth" of an animal, ears "at the tops extremely pointed," and hands which, like a monkey's, "were rather coarse—broad, with squat fingers. Strange to say, there were hairs in the center of the palm." Centuries old, and therefore not surprisingly looking like an old man when Harker first meets him, Dracula, the personification of the past, feeds on the blood of young girls to grow young again, for the bestial past lives in the blood of woman.

Having had his fill of feminine coagulants, he becomes even more Semitic in appearance, "a tall thin man, with a beaky nose and black moustache and pointed beard.". . . Stoker felt called upon to show off his up-to-date knowledge of scientific fact in his characterization of the fiend of reversion. After he has his scholar-hero Van Helsing mumble in broken English that Dracula represents the regressive criminal type, is genetically "predestinate to crime," and has a "child-brain," he lets Mina Harker, for good measure, affirm that "Nordau and Lombroso would so classify him."

Once this devil of blood lust and regressive, effeminate sensuality has been transported to England, the predatory forces of atavistic bestiality symbolized by Dracula can begin their challenge to the evolutionary acculturation of British womanhood. For it is woman, after all, that the chilly count is after—a fact that soon becomes obvious. Of the truly "male" men in the novel, none, not even Harker himself, the man who ventured into the very lair of the beast, becomes a victim to the creature. Dracula, in this respect, demonstrates a very myopically heterosexual bent. The two women on whom the count sets his bloodshot eyes, Lucy Westenra and Mina Harker, represent the success and failure of modern man's arduous attempts to acculturate woman to the civilized world. They are the two faces of Eve.

LUCY'S "POLYANDROUS WOMAN"

Lucy, as any well-read Victorian reader would have guessed from the very start, does not stand a chance before the onslaught of the demon of bestial hunger, for Stoker makes it quite clear that in her the attempt at acculturation has failed. We soon learn that Lucy has all the immodest, aggressively eager, viraginous sensuality of "a horrid flirt," as she appropriately characterizes herself. Without even knowing it, she bears the degenerative stamp of the New Woman, for in rapid succession she is confronted with three different men—Arthur Holmwood, John Seward, and the American Quincy Morris—and horror of horrors, she falls in love with all three. In a shocking admission of her degenerate, bestial, polyandrous instincts, she exclaims, "Why can't they let a girl marry three men, or as many as want her, and save all this trouble?" Lucy admits that "this is heresy, and I must not say it," but the predatory cat is out of the bag, and it is no wonder that Dracula heads straight for Lucy upon his arrival in England.

On a symbolic level, Lucy is indeed to have her wish of marrying "as many as want her," for it is obvious that she was specifically created to demonstrate how the polyandrous woman becomes man's conduit to the primal beast. As Lucy, increasingly "languid and tired," becomes a true collapsing woman under the draining ministrations of the thirsty count, she receives, in rapid succession, blood transfusions from each of the three men she loves. Stoker leaves not the slightest doubt about the fact that these transfusions should be equated with a sexual union between Lucy and her donors. Van Helsing, the Dutch scientist and student of the occult who knows all about such rituals, calls upon each of Lucy's lovers to undergo this sacrifice of masculine essence as Dracula continues to drain Lucy's blood. Arthur is called upon first. "You are a man," says Van Helsing, "and it is a man we want"—for Stoker is determined to keep things heterosexual and "clean"—"to transfer from full veins of one to the empty veins which pine for him." After the transfusion has been completed, Van Helsing refers to the "much weakened" Arthur fondly as Lucy's "brave lover"—and Lucy contentedly notes in her diary: "Somehow Arthur feels very, very close to me. I seem to feel his presence warm about me."

Dracula continues to sip, and Doctor Seward is next to offer Lucy his blood. That done, Lucy's new conquest exclaims with all the ecstasy of a satisfied lover: "No man knows, till he experiences it, what it is to feel his own life-blood drawn away into the veins of the woman he loves." But Van Helsing has Seward swear to keep quiet to Arthur about his happy experience, for "it would at once frighten him and enjealous him, too." Given Lucy's fondness for the Dutch scientist ("I quite love that dear Dr. Van Helsing" she writes in her diary), it is no wonder that he, too, is drawn into the risqué ritual of transfusion. With Dracula continuing to do his thing, and Lucy sliding rapidly into the condition of the undead, Van Helsing cries out in desperation, "What are we to do now? Where are we to turn for help?" Nor does he fail to notice that there are robust, healthy women around who also hap-

---

DRACULA **REVIEWED**

Critics have long recognized, and filmmakers have long exploited, Dracula's rich and powerful latent sexuality. Stoker's novel, however, was initially treated much more as a Victorian adventure story along the lines of H. Rider Haggard's King Solomon's Mines *than as a steamy potboiler. Only occasionally did early reviews (like the one quoted below, from the December 17, 1899 edition of the* San Francisco Chronicle*) seem to acknowledge that something very interesting might be going on just below the surface.*

One of the most powerful novels of the day, and one set apart by its originality of plot and treatment, is "Dracula," by Bram Stoker. The author is well known in the dramatic world for his long connection with Sir Henry Irving as manager. Several years ago he wrote a weird story of Irish life, but this is his first long romance. It is a somber study of a human vampire, the Count Dracula, who uses beautiful women as his agents and compasses the death of many innocent people. Theophile Gautier [in "La mort amoureuse"(1836)] essayed the same subject, but his vampire, who was a priest by day and raven-ing wolf by night, was not half so terrible as this malignant Count with the three beautiful female devils who do his bid-ding. Nothing in fiction is more powerful than the scene at the killing of the vampire in Lucy's tomb or that other fearful scene at the extinction of the malign power of the Count. The story is told in such a realistic way that one actually accepts its wildest flights of fancy as real facts. It is a superb tour de force which stamps itself on the memory.

Bram Stoker, *Dracula*. New York: W.W. Norton and Company, 1997, pp. 366–67.

pen to have blood in their veins. But even with Lucy on the point of death, the decorum of heterosexual transfusion must be maintained, no matter how flimsy the excuse. "I fear to trust those women, even if they would have the courage to submit," the good doctor mutters.

Of course, Quincy Morris, the American suitor, appears just in time, and Van Helsing is pleased as punch. "A brave man's blood is the best thing on this earth when a woman is in trouble. You're a man, and no mistake. Well, the devil may work against us for all he's worth, but God sends us men when we want them." Thus Lucy gets her wish—the blood, the symbolic semen—of "as many men as want her.". . .

Lucy's Death

Fed by the seed of four men, Lucy turns into a wild woman, one of those horrible creatures who prey upon that central symbol of the future potential of mankind: the child. Woman's misplaced virginity, that masculinizing force which in real life encouraged feminists to renounce the holy duties of motherhood and, as it were, prey upon their as yet unconceived babies, manifests itself henceforth in Lucy in the form of a determined blood lust for children. As she dies, she slides back into a state of primal bestiality, and soon children begin having their throats torn open on Hampstead Heath.

To stop Lucy's viraginous evil, her depredation of future generations, her attempts to drag civilization back into the evil past, the four "husbands" who, in yielding to her blood lust, have contributed to the creation of this monstrous beast, must come together and, in a concerted effort, send her off forever into the arms of a permanent death. At night—under the light of the moon, naturally—the four see Lucy again. "The sweetness was turned to adamantine, heartless cruelty, and the purity to voluptuous wantonness." Becoming aware of her former lovers, "she drew back with an angry snarl, such as a cat gives when taken unawares," and "with a voluptuous smile" she "flung to the ground, callous as a devil, the child that up to now she had clutched strenuously to her breast, growling over it as a dog growls over a bone." Confronted with Van Helsing's crucifix, Lucy's "beautiful color became livid, the eyes seemed to throw out sparks of hell-fire, the brows were wrinkled as though the folds of the flesh were the coils of Medusa's snakes."

Arthur, the only man she should have married, the only

one whose gentle, fructifying gift of semen she should have wished for if she had been a decent British girl, becomes, in the presence of the other three men, the executioner of the vampire of degenerative polyandry. In punishment and revenge, he "rapes" the female beast whose evil desires had unlawfully siphoned off the manhood of all four. "He looked like the figure of Thor as his untrembling arm rose and fell, driving deeper and deeper the mercy-bearing stake, whilst the blood from the pierced heart welled and spurted up around it." Having forever "broken" Lucy's heart, her symbolic maidenhead, in his vigorously monogamous assertion of masculine right over woman's bestial inclinations, Arthur feels better right away. "A glad, strange light broke over his face and dispelled altogether the gloom of horror that lay upon it." Lucy, too, has now been brought under control:

> There, in the coffin lay no longer the foul Thing that we had so dreaded and grown to hate that the work of her destruction was yielded as a privilege to the one best entitled to it, but Lucy as we had seen her in her life, with her face of unequalled sweetness and purity. True that there were there, as we had seen them in life, the traces of care and pain and waste; but these were all dear to us, for they marked her truth to what we knew. One and all we felt that the holy calm that lay like sunshine over the wasted face and form was only an earthly token and symbol of the calm that was to reign for ever.

Thus, by means of a little show of monogamous masculine force, Lucy, the polyandrous virago, has been transformed into that ideal creature of feminine virtue of the mid-nineteenth century: the dead woman. Civilization and evolution have, in the nick of time, triumphed over the vampire of degeneration. . . .

MINA'S "NEW WOMAN"

But Dracula has another neck to bite: The far more virtuous jugular of Mina is still to be subjected to the temptation of bestial reversion. Mina's case is quite different, however, for she is truly the ideal modern woman: a virtuous footstool ready to do man's bidding in the world of scientific accomplishment and intellectual evolution.

It is important to keep in mind that the world of Stoker's novel was not the vaguely fantastic world of old-fashioned experience it has since come to seem in twentieth-century cinematic adaptations. On the contrary, Stoker's world was teeming with evidence of technological progress and scientific achievement. His characters always used the latest available scientific and technical equipment. Dr. Seward, for instance, uses a phonograph to record his diary. Van Helsing, as we have seen all too well, practices blood transfusions and travels back and forth between England and Holland at the drop of a hat. Last but certainly not least, Mina is a whiz at the typewriter and she takes great shorthand. Not only destined to be Jonathan Harker's determinedly monogamous wife, she is also his very convenient, practical, and willing personal secretary. She is thoroughly modern but also happy to be able to make fun of the New Woman, whose hilarious demands for what are masculine prerogatives she satirizes in her journal as she thinks about Lucy: "Some of the 'New Women' writers will someday start an idea that men and women should be allowed to see each other asleep before proposing or accepting. But I suppose the New Woman won't condescend in future to accept; she will do the proposing herself. And a nice job she will make of it, too! There's some consolation in that."

Bustling about industriously and making herself modestly useful, Mina has no use for viraginous nonsense. She is the perfect nurse and, as every male in the novel hastens to emphasize, a "wonderful woman," an updated household nun turned personal secretary in a changing world. But, being a woman, a daughter of Eve, and hence having by her own admission "some of the taste of the original apple that remains still in our mouths," she, too, is subject to the brutalizing, atavistic bite of the animal past, a potential victim for Dracula, who enters the room—and her body—through her woman's heart to try and awaken her bestial nature:

> With his left hand he held both Mrs. Harker's hands, keeping them away with her arms at full tension; his right hand gripped her by the back of the neck, forcing her face down on his bosom. Her white nightdress was smeared with blood, and a thin stream trickled down the man's bare breast which was shown by his torn-open dress. The attitude of the two had a terrible resemblance to a child forcing a kitten's nose into a saucer of milk to compel it to drink. . . .

DRACULA MUST DIE

It was considered a scientific fact by many turn-of-the-century intellectuals that for woman to taste blood was to taste the milk of desire, and that such a taste might turn an innocent, inexperienced woman into an insatiable nymphomaniac. To exorcise that hunger, to return Mina to her appointed role as man's efficient private secretary, Dracula must be hunted out, followed back into the distant past, destroyed at his point of origin. Just as Renfield, Dracula's degenerate male votary, tried to reach the condition of bestiality by swallowing, one after another, the creatures on the Darwinian food chain, thereby symbolically descending along the ladder of devolution, so Dracula must be forced to retreat from Mina and the hearts of all other British women by first being chased out of England and then back into the evil East from which he emanates. In the end, this creature of moonlight can only be executed in the daylight of modern science by technology and the righteous wrath of a virtuously monogamous husband.

Identity and Repression in *Dr. Jekyll and Mr. Hyde*

Mark Jancovich

Mark Jancovich is a lecturer in the Department of American Studies at England's University of Manchester. He is the editor of *Popular Approaches to Film* and the author of *Rational Fears: American Horror in the 1950s.* In the following article, taken from his 1992 work entitled *Horror*, Jancovich discusses the theme of dual identity in Robert Louis Stevenson's *Dr. Jekyll and Mr. Hyde* and concludes that, through the character of the publicly upright Dr. Jekyll—seemingly a paragon of middle-class Victorian values with a beast lurking within—Stevenson constructs a critique of the "bourgeois morality" of late-Victorian England.

If the Gothic novel went into decline in Britain after 1820, the horror genre did not die out. As David Punter and others have shown, the influence of horror can be identified in much of the canonical literature of the nineteenth century, but it was mainly in the form of popular theatrical productions and publications that the genre thrived. Productions of *Frankenstein* were rarely off the British stage in the nineteenth century.

In the late nineteenth century, there was a dramatic resurgence of horror fiction, and this period produced four of the classics of the genre—H.G. Wells's *The Island of Dr Moreau* (1896), Oscar Wilde's *The Picture of Dorian Gray* (1891), Robert Louis Stevenson's *The Strange Case of Dr Jekyll and Mr Hyde* (1886), and, of course, Bram Stoker's *Dracula* (1897). These novels were not solely produced for a mass readership, as their authors aspired to be writers of 'serious literature' and, in some cases, they have been accepted as canonical writers. However, the two most enduring and influential works—*Jekyll* and *Dracula*—were produced by the two writers with the most marginal relation to the canon. It is also ironic that while Stevenson aspired to be a 'serious writer', the novel which he tailored most closely to the demands of the popular market has come to be seen as his most important and serious work. . . .

[*Jekyll* and *Dracula*] deal with transformation and doubling, but they are not produced by the anxieties of a failed or failing aristocracy, but an anxious bourgeoisie. Both *Jekyll* and *Dracula* work in relation to crises in bourgeois distinctions between the public and private spheres of life. *Jekyll* is the story of a man who is leading a double life, and has both a public and a private face. *Dracula*, on the other hand, concerns an invasion which not only penetrates and threatens the bourgeois home, but the inner sanctum of bourgeois privacy, the bedchamber.

Both novels have been interpreted as conservative narratives. It is often claimed that *Jekyll* works in relation to a fear of 'a beast within' which must be kept repressed and never allowed expression; that unconscious desires are presented as primitive urges within the novel, urges which are associated with working-class corruption, sexuality and violence. *Dracula*, on the other hand, has been claimed to work in relation to fears concerning the New Woman. The narrative is said to endorse the repression of forms of sexuality defined as 'abnormal', the most problematic of which is presented as active, female sexuality. . . .

THE PROBLEM OF IDENTITY

Jekyll, like werewolf tales in general, examines the problem of identity through the transformation of physical and psychological states of being. Dr Jekyll appears to be a respectable member of bourgeois society, but he transforms himself into the monstrous figure of Mr Hyde. The novel was published in 1886, a period in which the British bourgeoisie was in turmoil over mass democracy and Irish Home Rule. They saw the working classes and the Irish as threatening forces which needed to be disciplined and pacified. Consequently, a series of electoral reforms and education bills were passed which culminated in the 1884 Education Act. For many, the justification for these bills was summed up by a remark made in relation to the 1867 Education Act that, given the electoral reforms 'we must learn to educate our masters'. The newly enfranchised working classes had to be educated to accept bourgeois concepts of discipline and order.

In this context, *Jekyll* is often read as the story of a bourgeois male who is destroyed by his failure to tame and discipline disruptive elements within his personality. However, the novel makes it quite clear that Jekyll and Hyde have a reciprocal relationship. They are the public and private faces of a bourgeois male. Neither character is a natural self, but both are products of a society which forces human beings to deny aspects of themselves. As Jekyll writes in his final statement:

> Though so profound a double dealer, I was in no sense a hypocrite; both sides of me were in dead earnest; I was no more myself when I laid aside restraint and plunged in shame, than when I laboured, in the eye of day, at the furtherance of knowledge or the relief of sorrow and suffering.

Jekyll is not a man who fails to repress his natural self, but quite the reverse. The novel suggests that bourgeois social life separates or divides the human subjectivity into two selves which are in conflict with one another, even as they act to protect each other. Jekyll uses Hyde to indulge his private pleasures, thereby clearing his conscience and enabling him to present a virtuous public face to the world. Hyde, on the other hand, uses Jekyll to mask his own activities. Hyde is not unconcerned with social convention; after knocking down the young girl at the start of the novel, he is threatened with scandal by two gentlemen, and uses the Jekyll persona to protect himself.

The novel does not suggest that Hyde must be kept repressed because he is monstrous, but that he is monstrous because he is kept repressed. The more Jekyll seeks to control and discipline Hyde, the more monstrous Hyde becomes. Rather than reassuring the bourgeois that it is morally justified in its mission to discipline and pacify the forces by which it felt threatened, the novel suggests that it is bourgeois discipline which had produced these threats. At the start of the novel, Hyde is not a recognizably monstrous figure, and he is not associated with working-class vice. Utterson does sense some 'deformity' and something 'extraordinary looking' about Hyde, but he 'can name nothing out of the way.' For Utterson, Hyde is indescribable because as the ultimate respecter of bourgeois moral and legal order in the novel, he can find no physical evidence to support his feelings that there was 'something wrong with [Hyde's] appearance; something displeasing, something downright detestable.' He lives according to social conventions and is disturbed when they are flaunted. He accepts things at face value. Unlike Jekyll, he does not indulge his pleasures but see[k]s to extinguish them. He even uses cheap spirits to extinguish a taste for fine wines.

Hyde is not a natural or unconscious beast within Jekyll which must be controlled. Both Jekyll and Hyde are masks and performances. They are both roles assumed by a divided and nameless personality in order to satisfy its desires for both social acceptance and pleasure, desires which are rendered contradictory and irreconcilable within the bourgeois society of the period. The presence of this nameless and divided personality can be identified in the language of the text. In Jekyll's final statement, it is neither the Jekyll persona nor the Hyde one who narrates the tale of these two, but a nameless personality who explains why he could neither 'cast my lot with Jekyll', or Hyde. . . .

A CRITIQUE OF VICTORIAN SOCIETY

Jekyll and Hyde are different aspects of the same structure of personality. They presuppose one another. The imagery of the doors within the novel makes this clear. The first chapter is titled 'Story of a Door', and it revolves around the realization that the door which Hyde uses is part of Jekyll's house. Doors are both entrances and exits; they are the threshold between the private world of the bourgeois home and the public world beyond. By using different doors on different sides of the house, Jekyll and Hyde are able to disguise the connection between themselves. But there is no interior where all aspects of the personality can be at home. The interior of the house is also structured around this division between the front rooms where Jekyll greets people, and the laboratory at the rear where he acts in secret.

As a result, the novel can be seen as critical of the bourgeois morality of the period. It does not present a case for restraint and discipline, but suggests that bourgeois morality is destructive, that it creates conflicts and contradictions within both the self and society. Both Hyde and Jekyll are products of a society which forces human beings to assume contradictory social roles. However, if the novel recognizes the necessity of an alternative form of morality, it fails to produce one. 'Jekyll' is destroyed by his own self division, and all the other characters are seen as incapable of dealing with the situation. Lanyon dies of shock on witnessing Hyde's transformation into Jekyll, and we are never told of Utterson's response to the situation. The last we see of him, he is heading for his office to read the accounts of Lanyon and Jekyll. What he will make of them is uncertain, especially as he has just told Jekyll's servant, Poole, that he will try to save Jekyll's reputation or 'credit'. (The use of the term 'credit' is a telling pun given that Utterson is responsible for Jekyll's finances and has been so concerned that Hyde should not inherit Jekyll's property.) He says he will shortly call the police but there is nothing practical that they can achieve. At the end of the novel, we are only left with the statements of two men who have been destroyed by their experiences. The final horror of the story is that, in the hands of Utterson, the episode will probably be repressed and hidden in silence for the sake of decorum: nothing will be learned and the errors of bourgeois culture will be repeated.

Tensions and Anxieties in *Dr. Jekyll and Mr. Hyde*

Susan J. Wolfson and Barry V. Qualls

Susan J. Wolfson is a professor of English at Princeton University. She has written two books on the Romantic movement in England, *The Questioning Presence: Wordsworth, Keats, and the Interrogative Mode in Romantic Poetry* and *Formal Charges*: *The Shaping of Poetry in British Romanticism*. Barry V. Qualls is Professor of English and Dean of Humanities at Rutgers University. He is the author of *The Secular Pilgrims of Victorian Literature*. Here, in an article excerpted from the Introduction to their 2000 Copley edition of *The Strange Case of Dr. Jekyll and Mr. Hyde*, Wolfson and Qualls discuss Stevenson's own lifelong fascination with the idea of a "double life" (expressed in the Jekyll/Hyde "split personality") and consider how that fascination helps illuminate the "cultural tensions and anxieties" at the heart of his most famous work.

Alternating between "the pattern of an idler" and the industry of writing, Robert Louis Stevenson embodied the dualities that animate his poems, essays, and fiction, from children's fantasies to complex studies of adult psychological "cases.". . .

In his essay "A Chapter on Dreams" (1892), he wrote, "I had long been trying to write a story on this subject, to find a body, a vehicle, for that strong sense of man's double being which must at times come in upon and overwhelm the mind of every thinking creature." The main incidents came to him in a dream, and he wrote this "fine bogy tale" in three feverish days. But his wife felt, according to her son (who later co-wrote some stories with Stevenson), that he had "missed the allegory"; it was "merely a story—a magnificent bit of sensationalism—when it should have been a masterpiece." Stevenson burned his draft and began again, and in three more days produced *The Strange Case of Dr. Jekyll and Mr. Hyde* as we know it.

Its immediate success in England and America made Stevenson one of the celebrated writers of the *fin de siècle* [end of the century]. The story became so famous that its title characters are now *the* cultural emblem of a divided doubled self. . . .

STEVENSON'S DOUBLE LIFE

We can see why critic Elaine Showalter crowned Stevenson "the fin-de-siècle laureate of the double life." He earned this title on the pulse of his own experience. "From his early days in Scotland till the last chapter of his life as enacted in Samoa," proposes Karl Miller *(New York Review,* 29 May 1975), "there were at least two Stevensons: the respectable and the bohemian, the successful and the delinquent, the man of letters and the prototypical hippie." In "A Chapter on Dreams," Stevenson recalls a dream of being able to lead "a double life—one of the day, one of the night." Like his author, Dr. Jekyll reports a childhood disciplined and constrained by paternal strictures and expectations and fortified against escapist fantasies: "the days of my childhood when I walked with my father's hand." But Stevenson knows that a child's imagination may slip loose, may turn with fascination to the night life, may even invent a second self to explore it. . . .

THE THEME OF THE SPLIT PERSONALITY

With this competition of two selves in one identity, Stevenson's novel has become the most famous fable in the English language on the theme of a split personality. Dr. Jekyll describes himself (and all of us, he implies) as "two natures" or "polar twins" contending in consciousness: one desires and labors for social approval; the other rebels and labors to avoid social apprehension. A "Jekyll-and-Hyde" personality is the term bequeathed us by this tale to describe someone given to opposite, unhomogenized personalities. Although Stevenson could not have known that his characters would enter our cultural language this way, it is clear that he grasped the cultural determinant. Mr. Hyde's name, echoing the novel's recurrent vocabulary of "hid," "hidden," "secret," and "concealed," is almost too obviously devised to pun on this theme: "You have not been mad enough to hide this fellow?" cries Dr. Jekyll's lawyer, Mr. Utterson, to him.

What are the social and psychological currents that produce this hidden fellow? The sensation of "man's dual nature" is not just a metaphysical and psychological configuration, as Dr. Jekyll's summary "Statement of the Case" proposes. It is also a socially impelled formation. Stevenson writes the novel with terms that suggest that Jekyll's experiment is less a strange case of one man's amoral and antisocial science than an uncannily familiar, representative product of society itself—or, more specifically, the social contradictions and conditions that, as Jekyll puts it, "committed [him] to a profound duplicity of life" well before the idea of creating a second self occurred to him. All the contradictions that Stevenson elaborates in the world of grim, gray, proper Victorian London—between the regime of law and order and the energies of spontaneity and violence, between the devotion to work and discipline and the desire for liberty and vitality, between the commitment to respectability and the appetite for sensation—all these contradictions remain insoluble in daylight social existence, where they define and permeate a culture of propriety.

To speculate, as Dr. Jekyll has, about the possibility of separating these contradictions into distinct, unwarring entities— one proper and respectable, the other wayward and hidden from public exposure—is to take the measure of how fully cultural values, practices, and beliefs regulate and inhibit certain kinds of human experience, driving it underground or into alienated forms such as "Mr. Hyde." That is, Stevenson is not just writing about the polarities of personality, but also linking these polarities to, and situating them in, cultural tensions and anxieties. The war of the "polar twins" that his fable locates dramatically in Henry Jekyll is also one that his novel maps conceptually onto a larger, encompassing social world of Victorian London, where respectable daylight streets, well-polished brasses, general cleanliness, and dull Sunday walks are haunted by a nether world of back alleys, secret entrances, and cellar doorways and shadowed by the imaginary geography of "Blackmail House" and "Queer Street.". . .

I was born in the year 18— to a large fortune, endowed besides with excellent parts, inclined by nature to industry, fond of the respect of the wise and good among my fellow-men, and thus, as might have been supposed, with every guarantee of an honourable and distinguished future. And indeed, the worst of my faults was a certain impatient gaiety of disposition, such as has made the happiness of many, but such as I found it hard to reconcile with my imperious desire to carry my head high, and wear a more than commonly grave countenance before the public. Hence it came about that I concealed my pleasures; and that when I reached years of reflection, and began to look round me and take stock of my progress and position in the world, I stood already committed to a profound duplicity of life.

This is not Mr. Utterson's story but the opening sentences of "Henry Jekyll's Full Statement of the Case," the last chapter of Stevenson's novel. By this point, such autobiography seems more familiar than strange. Here is another inventory of proper Victorian manhood: "large fortune," "excellent parts," a character of "industry," an ethos of "respect" and social reputation. At the same time, here are admissions to "concealed pleasures," judged improper and censurable from the perspective of respectability, not trusted, but evoking "a morbid sense of shame"; here, too, is a description of a self whose "impatient gaiety" of disposition is judged a fault by a more "imperious" self, given to a discipline of cultivating an "uncommonly grave," anti-vital social persona. No wonder that puns and figures of doubleness pervade the language of Dr. Jekyll's statement, even before he comes to the reification of this doubleness in a second self: a "profound duplicity of life" is a life conducted in two worlds, each of which belies and refuses the other; "reflection" (with a primary meaning of intellectual maturity) also names the perceived doubling of the self—the sense of mirroring becoming more obvious when Dr. Jekyll says that when he looked at Mr. Hyde "in the glass, I was conscious of no repugnance, rather of a leap of welcome. This, too, was myself. In my eyes it bore a livelier image of the spirit."

This, too, is Mr. Utterson's fascination with Hyde, who stirs an intuition of this dual nature in himself. Aware of his delicate poise on the threshold between blameless and ill conduct, Utterson sometimes wonders, "almost with envy, at the high pressure of spirits" in the misdeeds of his friends and, as though they were phantoms of his own "Mr. Hyde". . . , he takes vicarious pleasure in their forbidden life. He does not censure their actions but develops a compromise "character" to witness their border-land and their fall into the other side: "In this character it was frequently his fortune to be the last reputable acquaintance and the last good influence in the lives of down-going men." Indeed, Utterson is the one man in the novel whose imagination is more intrigued than revolted by the presence of Mr. Hyde in his world. More than intrigued, he is "enslaved" and "haunted," as if doubling his friend Jekyll's "strange preference or bondage" to Mr. Hyde. In this fascination with Mr. Hyde, Utterson extends his vicarious pleasure (or envy) of his friends' misdeeds to recall some of his own misdeeds from "the corners of memory." And the best he can say of these ghosts is that they are "fairly blameless," yet blameworthy enough that he hopes his overall record of sobriety might balance "the many ill things he had done." Hyde has pulled something uncomfortable from the corners of consciousness, and Utterson finds himself shaping a private identity—a more extreme and proactive form of the "character" in which he maintains his acquaintance with down-going men—to accommodate this haunting: "'If he be Mr. Hyde,' he had thought, 'I shall be Mr. Seek.'"

What is Mr. Seek really seeking? Like *Frankenstein,* the novel is structured so that the reader's attention does not just move forward through the pages as we pursue a mystery (for most of us now, the suspense is not what it was for Stevenson's first readers: we know the secret of Mr. Hyde). The fictional structure of this tale is repetitive as well as linear, moving our attention back and forth—from Mr. Utterson to Mr. Hyde to Dr. Jekyll to Dr. Lanyon, and always to the city itself—as we begin to see parallels, hear echoes, and discern patterns of repetition in this world of stolid, professional, bachelor gentlemen. None of these men seeks happiness in love; none has a family or even a pet; their liberations, whether cautious or full-throttle, are not in the direction of personal intimacy or sexual pleasure. In this pattern, Dr. Jekyll's experiment comes to seem less a case of individual madness than a mirror of general social pathology. Stevenson's novel presents a vivid, fragmented, and ultimately inconclusive exploration of this pathology from several perspectives, drawing cumulative power from an intensifying, expanding panorama of the contradictions that mark late nineteenth-century social and psychological experience. Mr. Hyde cuts a shadow march through and across these contradictions, exposing the comprehensive duplicity of Victorian London.

VICTORIAN LONDON'S SPLIT PERSONALITY

This city itself seems both the cause of the double life of Jekyll and Hyde and an extended figure of a split self. In its world of sober professional gentlemen, the worst that one can bring upon oneself is not unhappiness but "scandal," the death of a socially viable self: name, reputation, and public credit. When Mr. Hyde is apprehended in a citizens' arrest after trampling a little girl, this is what he is threatened with, the end of his good name and connections: "We told the man we could and would make such a scandal out of this, as should make his name stink from one end of London to the other. If he had any friends or any credit, we undertook that he should lose them." Just as a "name" is a social exterior, and a good name the badge of respectability, so all the town-houses inhabited by these respectable men have proper front-door appearances. It is within this symbolic cultural grammar that we "read" the syntax of Mr. Hyde's residence, which in every detail spells a retreat from public scrutiny, denoting a region where things are hidden, are socially unacceptable. Without windows to the world and repelling all invitation (the door has neither bell nor knocker), Hyde's house bears "in every feature the marks of prolonged and sordid negligence." Its doorway hosts figures outside the patriarchal (adult, male, respectable, and professional) social order: "Tramps slouched into the recess"; children play on its steps, and schoolboys commit minor vandalism on the moldings; his street is a place of ragged children and foreign domestics seeking a morning glass of gin.

Just as these details spell what is opposite to and repressed (or kept in the back streets) by establishment proprieties, so Mr. Hyde's actions, hidden from public scrutiny, suggest repressed and alienated energies. His victims are cultural icons—an angelic girl, a benign patriarch of Parliament. The fate of the last victim, moreover, suggests another world in hiding in Victorian London, a homoerotic culture: the scene faintly suggests a horrible turn of events in a respectable MP's concealed nightlife, a miscalculated proposition turned violent, from which Utterson is quick to sense "the eddy of a scandal." When Mr. Enfield first reports to him the strange affiliation of Mr. Hyde and Dr. Jekyll, whereby Hyde is able to buy his way out of the novel's first crime, the trampling of the angel-girl, he uses darkly suggestive terms to describe Hyde's hold: "Blackmail, I suppose;

an honest man paying through the nose for some of the capers of his youth. Blackmail House . . . the more it looks like Queer Street, the less I ask." "Queer" was a new word in English slang for homosexual, and blackmail was a frequent peril for its discovery (when the word "blackmail" first arose in Scotland in the sixteenth century, it was linked to such accusations). Stevenson keeps the suggestion of homosexuality as the "Mr. Hyde" of this culture implicit at best. We get no account of anyone's sex life; that much remains closeted. But the novel does present a markedly male homosocial world, in which the figure of Hyde repeatedly evokes revulsion, panic, a sense of scandal, of unnameable sins. As if mirroring a universal repressed, he produces a "loathing" and "repulsion" in those who behold him. All his witnesses agree on "the haunting sense of unexpressed deformity with which the fugitive impressed his beholders." Dr. Jekyll, speaking of himself clinically in his full statement, in the third person, writes that Hyde was an "insurgent horror . . . knit to him closer than a wife, . . . caged in his flesh.". . .

A CAUTIONARY TALE

In the horrors of Hyde's adventures, we might read a cautionary fable: that the "Hyde" within is always an "evil," "wicked," violent self, rigorously kept in control by normative social stricture and private conscience and is liberated only at peril. Jekyll thus deploys phrases such as "ape-like fury" to describe Hyde's violent rages, and even when Hyde is repressed, Jekyll feels his presence within as a caged devil or an animal licking his chops. Hyde is violent physical energy, the Satanic enemy of reason, morality, and "the spiritual side"; he is the worst nightmare of Darwinian theory, the primitive beast lurking within the most cultured, civilized, and rational of consciousnesses. Or, as Jekyll puts it in his "Statement," aware that his very identity is on the verge of extinction, "I was slowly losing hold of my original and better self, and becoming slowly incorporated with my second and worse." This paradigm of better and worse bodes a strong moral. Whatever the initial thrills, Jekyll ultimately finds no self-completion in Mr. Hyde but instead witnesses the gradual and unstoppable erosion of his self-possession and, finally, Hyde's usurpation of his "original" identity. . . .

The costs are not only personal but also social: Mr. Hyde is a public danger; his effect is not to humanize and rejuvenate those with whom he comes into contact but to imperil their lives—at the very least, to bring out their worst selves. Yet the structure of social repression that haunts all the reactions to Mr. Hyde suggests that he is not reducible to any simple or final moral analysis. As in *Frankenstein,* the moral horror of the tale does not encompass its psychological and sensational interest. The licensing of Mr. Hyde is a moral caution, to be sure, but Stevenson invests him with other vital qualities—youth, health, natural enthusiasm, and adolescent rebelliousness—that invite a socio-psychological speculation. The absence, loss, or repression of these energies, not only in Dr. Jekyll but in just about everybody in proper gray London, defines their social rectitude, but the absence also seems the symptom of emotional and spiritual disease. "Smaller, slighter, and younger" than Dr. Jekyll, Mr. Hyde reanimates Jekyll's lost youth; "He was wild when he was young; a long while ago, to be sure," Utterson remembers. Jekyll's profound commitment to respectability has necessarily kept under wraps everything that is released "in the disguise of Hyde"—"the liberty, the comparative youth, the light step, leaping pulses and secret pleasures."

In this perspective, Hyde seems less a monster than a more human, more lively self seeking liberation: "I was the first that could thus plod in the public eye with a load of genial respectability, and in a moment, like a schoolboy, strip off these lendings and spring headlong into the sea of liberty." Life in the public eye is a life of moral surveillance and supervision, with its boon of respectability feeling like a slow killing burden, one that turns the pace to dull plodding under a crushing load. Jekyll's life as Hyde is a liberation from what had come to seem a fundamentally false existence, composed only of artificial lendings. With a pointed pun, he sneers at Dr. Lanyon's fastidious disapproval of his "scientific heresies" as the reaction of a "*hide*-bound pedant," as if to say that men such as the good doctor were too unimaginative to sense, let alone liberate, their own Mr. Hydes. Indeed, when Dr. Lanyon finally witnesses Jekyll's transformation into Hyde, the revelation is too much for him; it is truly mortifying. Jekyll's statement of the case presents himself as the social (even, he suggests, the human) norm, from which Lanyon's fatal hysteria, and not Jekyll's impulse for finding Mr. Hyde, seems the aberration.

The complexity of this tension between polarized selves is

reflected in the overall moral irresolution of the novel. Although Dr. Jekyll renders a cautionary tale, *Dr. Jekyll and Mr. Hyde* is more than this final judgment. Stevenson presents four different points of view: Mr. Utterson's strange fascination with Hyde; Mr. Enfield's fear of probing into his mystery (his discomfort at being "surprised out of himself"—a telling phrase); Dr. Lanyon's moral disapproval of Dr. Jekyll and his inability to survive the revelation of Mr. Hyde; and finally, Dr. Jekyll's own statement of the case as his personality is on the verge of extinction by a Mr. Hyde who is no longer hidden, no longer able to be hid. Although Jekyll has the last word in the novel, its rhetorical axis leaves Mr. Utterson, like Mary Shelley's Robert Walton, in possession of the case and its several textual materials. Jekyll can refer only to a "nameless situation" and urge Utterson, the vehicle of future utterance, to "read the narrative" that Lanyon has written and then to read his own "confession." As privy to Jekyll's hidden history, Utterson becomes a second Hyde, a doubling suggested by Jekyll's rewriting of his will to name Utterson as his heir rather than Hyde. The syntax bearing this information glints with this superimposed doubling: "in the place of the name of Edward Hyde, the lawyer, with indescribable amazement, read the name of Gabriel John Utterson." As critic Garrett Stewart observes, Stevenson's word order briefly allows "Edward Hyde, the lawyer" to seem appositive, a false syntactic cue that nonetheless yields a truth about the linking of the two in Dr. Jekyll's willful secret.

As a reader of Hyde through these several narratives, Utterson is also the double of the novel's reader. Like Utterson, we are left with several texts to wonder over and assemble in our own moral self-reflection. Like Utterson, we may discover ourselves in Dr. Jekyll's strange case.

CHAPTER 4

Modern Masters of Horror

 Horror

H.P. Lovecraft's Life and Work

Robert Bloch

During his lifetime, H.P. Lovecraft wrote a huge number of letters, many of them to young "fans" of his work. One of Lovecraft's favorite correspondents was Robert Bloch, then only a teenager. Inspired by Lovecraft's example, Bloch went on to become an outstanding writer in the horror-suspense tradition. Bloch's most notable work is *Psycho*, made internationally famous by the Alfred Hitchcock film of the same title. In the following article, excerpted from his introduction to a collection of Lovecraft's short stories, Bloch discusses Lovecraft's work within both biographical and social contexts, highlighting central themes and artistic concerns and assessing Lovecraft's legacy—all the while arguing forcefully for the value of "fantastic" literature.

"The oldest and strongest emotion of mankind is fear, and the oldest and strongest kind of fear is fear of the unknown."

This is the opening sentence of "Supernatural Horror in Literature," one of the finest essays on horror fiction ever written. Its author, H.P. Lovecraft, is considered by many to be one of the finest writers of such fiction.

Howard Phillips Lovecraft was born in Providence, Rhode Island, on August 20, 1890. He was the last lineal descendant of an old New England family that had seen better days. His father died of paresis in 1898; his mother survived until 1921, but her own mental instability increased as the family fortunes declined.

Lovecraft wrote, "As a child I was very peculiar and sensitive, always preferring the society of grown persons to that of other children." Actually it was his neurotic mother who labelled him peculiar and "protected" him from contact with

Excerpted from "Introduction," by Robert Bloch in *Bloodcurdling Tales of Horror and the Macabre: The Best of H.P. Lovecraft* (New York: Ballantine Books, 1982) by H.P. Lovecraft. Copyright © 1982 by Robert Bloch. Reprinted with permission from Ralph Vincinaza Ltd., agent for the author.

other youngsters. A precocious child, he learned to read when he was four and soon experimented with writing. Poor health kept him from college and economic necessity eventually caused him to neglect amateur journalism in favor of ghostwriting or revising the work of others for professional publication. Gradually he began to produce poetry and fiction of his own.

After his mother's death he lived for a time in New York, married an older woman from whom he separated amicably two years later, then returned to Providence. Here he made his home with two elderly aunts. One of them died in 1932; he and his surviving relative resided together until his own death on March 15, 1937.

LOVECRAFT'S CAREER

Lovecraft's career as a professional writer was largely compressed into a span of about sixteen years. He remained virtually unknown except to the limited readership of pulp magazines such as *Weird Tales* in which his work appeared. It earned only a pitiful pittance to supplement the income from a meager inheritance, and he continued his anonymous chores for other writers. At the same time he brightened and broadened his uneventful existence with a widespread correspondence among fellow writers and readers of fantastic fiction. The most constant and devoted members of this group formed what would later be called "the Lovecraft Circle"; his lengthy letters of comment, criticism, and literary advice encouraged them to write or attempt writing in the genre. When a combination of cancer and Bright's disease claimed his life at the age of forty-six the loss was mourned by far-off friends, many of whom had known him only as a correspondent.

Lovecraft's literary style was distinctive and frequently imitated by protégés. With his approval, they and others borrowed the imaginary settings of his stories, together with the weird books and grotesque gods he created to heighten horror.

At the time of his death he had already become what would now be called a "cult figure." But the cult was comparatively small and had absolutely no influence on contemporary critics or publishers. It took long years to bring the man and his work to the attention of a larger audience.

Today Lovecraft is established as a major American fantasy writer, frequently ranked as the equal of Poe. His work is in print here and abroad and the mild-mannered, old-fashioned, conservative New England gentleman has become an acknowledged master of horror fiction. But certain critics disagree. Perhaps the earliest negative verdict was pronounced by Edmund Wilson, writing in *The New Yorker* in 1945 to accuse Lovecraft of "bad taste and bad art." Other nonadmirers broadened their attacks to include the man as well as his work. In recent years Ted White, former editor of *Amazing* and *Fantastic,* expressed the belief that this sort of "sick" writing is the product of a "sick" mind—and suggested that anyone attracted to it is also "sick."

The notion is interesting, but its revisionist attitude toward literature could have far-reaching implications. If safeguarding our mental health requires us to avoid the work of those whose life-styles depart from the accepted norm, then our bookshelves would soon be stripped bare. The literary efforts of chronic alcoholics, drug addicts, sexual deviants, and victims of psychosis with suicidal tendencies can indeed be dismissed, but we must be prepared to accept the consequences.

We will, of course, lose the efforts of Poe, Hawthorne, de Maupassant, and Kafka. But we will also be deprived of *Alice's Adventures in Wonderland, Huckleberry Finn, Moby-Dick, Crime and Punishment, A Farewell to Arms, The Great Gatsby, Remembrance of Things Past,* and hundreds of other titles that some regard as literary masterpieces. We must avoid O. Henry, Katherine Mansfield, Sherwood Anderson, Virginia Woolf, Jack London, André Gide, Thomas Wolfe, Somerset Maugham, Sinclair Lewis, Jean Cocteau, Christopher Isherwood, William Faulkner, and Oscar Wilde, to name only a few. The same applies to such diverse talents as Dashiell Hammett, Nietzsche, Brendan Behan, Raymond Chandler, Schopenhauer, and Hans Christian Andersen. Poets would vanish: Byron, Auden, Baudelaire, Rimbaud, Dylan Thomas, Edna St. Vincent Millay, Swinburne, Verlaine, Hart Crane, Walt Whitman. We would also cast into oblivion the plays of Marlowe, Genet, Tennessee Williams, Eugene O'Neill, Noel Coward and—according to some authorities—the complete works of William Shakespeare.

It seems a high price to pay for our mental hygiene, particularly in the case of Lovecraft. After all, the man didn't drink, smoke or do drugs. His sex life was apparently limited to a brief marriage but his wife pronounced him an "adequately excellent lover" and even his most ardent detractors have failed to find any evidence of homosexual activity. Although he admittedly suffered from psychological handicaps, his sedentary existence was unmarred by antisocial behavior.

"Sickness," like beauty, is often in the eye of the beholder. Sometimes it takes the form of personal convictions; Arthur Conan Doyle really believed in fairies and Emanuel Swedenborg had literal visions of heaven and hell. Both wrote earnestly about their unorthodox concepts but neither are generally regarded as "sick.". . .

"Sick" or healthy, all creative activity—including writing—is the product of individual imagination, colored by personal viewpoint, an attitude toward life. And it seems generated by an intense desire or need to communicate with others.

Most of us satisfy such urges in a simpler fashion. The physically attractive and the energetically aggressive seldom find a need to become "creative" in order to enjoy the rewards of our society. The losers and loners escape from competitive situations as "dropouts" or members of the counterculture; even the criminal element enjoys a shadowy status of its own. Rebellion and misbehavior become ways of attracting attention, even admiration.

Before society became so openly permissive the introvert had to find other solutions to his problems. If no one responded to a child's need for favorable attention—if no one answered the cry of "Look at me!"—then perhaps the pleas could be rephrased. "Look at my pictures—hear my music—listen to my story." In that context all writers can be called "sick," including those who assume the superior role of critic.

LOVECRAFT'S GENRES AND THEMES

Not all creative artists are physically unattractive or without charm and social graces. But for one reason or another most possess feelings of inadequacy or insecurity that they are impelled to overcome—and thus it must have been since time immemorial.

Hence the artists who decorated the walls of caves in our distant past, the singers who chanted and played upon primitive instruments in those echoing caverns, the tellers of tales who squatted beside the flickering campfires. And though means and methods changed, the impulse and conditions generating creativity remain constant; hence today's talent.

Hence Lovecraft, the child who was sickly and studious; the growing boy whose own mother inculcated a belief in his "ugliness"; the young man who found himself ill at ease and ill-equipped to compete socially or economically with his peer group. Like others not naturally endowed with qualities to make them easy winners but who are not satisfied to abandon the contest entirely, he had to find a vehicle for recognition. Writing solved the problem of communication, of gaining notice. If he found difficulty going out into the world he could send his writing out instead, and perhaps the world would come to him.

But what sort of writing? He tried his hand at many things—juvenile imitations of Poe, which he destroyed in his late teens; astronomy articles for local newspapers; scientific and literary essays self-published as a member of amateur journalism societies; poetry; criticism; then the ghostwriting and revision. None of this brought him the recognition he craved. He rationalized the lack by claiming to despise commercial success; a true gentleman wrote only as an amateur, free of all restrictions. Nevertheless he gradually resumed production of his own fiction.

Fiction, as we know, takes many forms, from gritty realism to farfetched fantasy. In recognizing categories we can also recognize the reasons why certain writers choose to work within them. Their efforts establish an image—often as wish-fulfillment—of the brawny he-man, the unshockable sophisticate, the romantic lover, the keen and objective analyst of human behavior, the cynical realist, the compassionate idealist, the wise philosopher, the sexual athlete, the poet, the carefree adventurer, and every possible persona in the Jungian pantheon of archetypes.

Writers are role players, but the role is not the man, even though it may incorporate certain of his beliefs and attitudes.

Lovecraft's work offers obvious examples of this. His lifelong aversion to cold is apparent in stories such as "Cool Air" and his short novel, "At the Mountains of Madness." An allergy to seafood is embodied in "The Shadow Over Innsmouth," and a tone-deaf distaste for music as dissonance echoes in "The Music of Erich Zann." A love of cats is obvious in many tales; so is a fondness for colonial architecture and outrage over its gradual destruction.

The literary detective will have no trouble finding clues

pointing to Lovecraft's lifelong Anglophilia; it surfaces even in his preference for English modes of spelling, as in "The Colour Out of Space." His style betrays a bias in favor—or favour, as he would put it—for the language, literary forms, and lifestyles of the eighteenth century that he professed to find superior to our own. Privately he often declared a longing to have lived as a loyal colonial subject of King George III in pre-Revolutionary days, and perhaps he truly believed this.

With tongue more obviously in cheek he began referring to himself as an "old gentleman" and signing his letters "Grand-

THE CALL OF CTHULHU

Lovecraft is most famous for his literature of "cosmic fear" developed around what came to be called the Cthulhu Mythos—a kind of artificial mythology which drastically minimizes the importance of the human race by placing it on the forgotten edges of a vast cosmos ruled by dark and fearsome forces. As the opening paragraphs of Lovecraft's famous short story "The Call of Cthulhu" suggest, in such a universe human ignorance is a blessing.

The most merciful thing in the world, I think, is the inability of the human mind to correlate all its contents. We live on a placid island of ignorance in the midst of black seas of infinity, and it was not meant that we should voyage far. The sciences, each straining in its own direction, have hitherto harmed us little; but some day the piecing together of dissociated knowledge will open up such terrifying vistas of reality, and of our frightful position therein, that we shall either go mad from the revelation or flee from the deadly light into the peace and safety of a new dark age.

Theosophists have guessed at the awesome grandeur of the cosmic cycle wherein our world and human race form transient incidents. They have hinted at strange survivals in terms which would freeze the blood if not masked by a bland optimism. But it is not from them that there came the single glimpse of forbidden aeons which chills me when I think of it and maddens me when I dream of it. That glimpse, like all dread glimpses of truth, flashed out from an accidental piecing together of separated things—in this case an old newspaper item and the notes of a dead professor. I hope that no one else will accomplish this piecing out; certainly, if I live, I shall never knowingly supply a link in so hideous a chain.

H.P. Lovecraft, *The Call of Cthulhu and Other Weird Stories.* Ed. S.T. Joshi. New York: Penguin Books, 1999.

pa" while still in his thirties. But the pose reveals a preoccupation with age and aging that is omnipresent in his work.
Old houses and old tombs are abundantly in evidence and often their presence is unpleasant, even unnatural. Ancient ed-
ifices hold monstrous secrets in "The Rats in the Walls," "The
Lurking Fear," "The Shadow Over Innsmouth," "The Shadow
Out of Time," "The Shunned House," "The Dreams in the
Witch-House" and a dozen other tales. Old people are often
equally evil; Wizard Whateley in "The Dunwich Horror" is
not exactly the sort of farmer the Department of Agriculture
would approve of, nor would nutritionists endorse the diet of
the elderly owner of "The Picture in the House." Other old-
sters in "He," "The Case of Charles Dexter Ward," and "The
Terrible Old Man" do not represent advances in geriatrics,
while both dwelling and dweller are equally disturbing in
"The Strange High House in the Mist." And the Elder Gods—
the "Great Old Ones" of his later stories—are hardly qualified
to bridge the generation gap. At best, Lovecraft's attitude toward age is ambivalent, but his obsession with the subject is
literally mirrored in "The Outsider."

SCIENTIFIC ELEMENTS

So is his interest in astronomy and the physical sciences; the
avowed antiquarian was also a lifelong student of developments in modern research. Generally regarded only as a
writer of fantasy, a good share of his output contains more of
a scientific element than much of what today is classified as
science fiction or—at higher word rates—"speculative fiction."

"The Colour Out of Space," "At the Mountains of Madness,"
and "The Shadow Out of Time" were first published in science
fiction magazines, and rightly so. But most of his work saw
print in *Weird Tales*, and its appearance there blinded readers
to its actual content. "Cool Air" anticipates cryogenic research;
"The Dreams in the Witch-House" suggests that advanced
physics will recapitulate the discoveries of powers used in
witchcraft. "The Whisperer in Darkness" is an outstanding
early example of one of science fiction's major motifs—the
"aliens among us" theme. "The Shadow Over Innsmouth" offers its own portraits of architectural decay and dirty old
men, together with a perverted worship of perverted beings,
but the main thrust of the story doesn't depend upon anything supernatural. Its grotesque monstrosities are the product of biological mutation rather than black magic. . . .

The one theme incontrovertibly constant in both his life and his work is a preoccupation with dreams.

From earliest childhood on, Lovecraft's sleep ushered him into a world filled with vivid visions of alien and exotic landscapes that at times formed a background for terrifying nightmares.

His earlier fiction often utilized the strange settings glimpsed in these dreamworlds; they were ideal for the prose poems he fashioned in the manner of Poe or Dunsany. Later, as his own style evolved, he confronted the nightmare elements as well and translated them into chilling, convincing realities. Many of the characters in his tales are dominated by their dreams. His alter ego in several stories, Randolph Carter, is a dreamer; "The Silver Key" and "Through the Gates of the Silver Key" (written in collaboration with E. Hoffman Price) both emphasize Carter's nocturnal fantasies. The novel-length *The Dream-Quest of Unknown Kadath* enters Carter's dreamworld and the first story in which he figures, "The Statement of Randolph Carter," derives directly from one of Lovecraft's nightmares. Dreams figure in "The Rats in the Walls," "The Dreams in the Witch-House" and many other tales. In "The Call of Cthulhu," the first story to deal fully with what later came to be known as the "Cthulhu Mythos," the dreams of a neurotic artist and his counterparts all over the world herald the resurrection of a hideous Elder God from his lair beneath the sea.

THE CTHULHU MYTHOS

The so-called "Cthulhu Mythos" represents Lovecraft's chief claim to fame and the stories in which it evolves bring together all of his major influences and interests.

An affinity for colonial New England and fears regarding its decadence both found embodiment in fictional settings for those tales. Kingsport and Innsmouth are ancient seaports; Arkham is an old city steeped in traditions of the witchcraft craze and now the site of Miskatonic University. In this milieu dwell the sensitive scholars who serve as narrators or protagonists of the stories. At Miskatonic some of them find access to one of six known remaining copies of a strange book containing the secrets of a race older than mankind—the Great Old Ones. Invaders from other dimensions and other worlds, they once ruled earth but were vanquished and expelled by other cosmic forces. In some cases they were merely imprisoned, like Cthulhu in the sunken city of R'lyeh, or in subterranea beneath deserts and polar ice caps. But their legend survives, as does their telepathic influence, and they are still worshiped by certain primitive people as well as more sophisticated members of cults dedicated to bringing about their return and reign.

"When the stars are right" the Great Old Ones could plunge from world to world through the sky or rise again from deathless sleep. And the blasphemous book, *The Necronomicon*, contained incantations that would aid their advent, as well as other spells and ceremonies designed to defeat them.

The original Arabic version had been lost, but the text was translated into Greek, then Latin, and the volume was sought after by both those who worshiped and those who opposed the Ancient Ones. It is these entities—creatures like Yog-Sothoth and Nyarlathotep—who haunt the "Cthulhu Mythos" tales.

Nyarlathotep emerged directly from Lovecraft's dreams, as did some of the weird locales he mentions—the plateau of Leng, and Kadath in the Cold Waste. Yuggoth, the dwelling place of certain terrifying extraterrestrial beings, was another name for the planet Pluto; in a poem cycle, "Fungi From Yuggoth," there are allusions to many more fantastic figures and places referred to in his prose.

Some of these were borrowed from the work of other writers and the basic concept of the "Cthulhu Mythos" probably owes a great deal to Arthur Machen, who wrote about a stunted and debased race of primitive beings still secretly existing beneath the lonely Welsh hills. Lovecraft was much impressed with this concept but he alone expanded the notion of a localized prehuman survival into a vast cosmology of his own creation.

Gradually he built up a rationale for both reality and dreams, nothing less than a history of the entire universe. As such, the "Cthulhu Mythos" is a literary creation far surpassing the word-worlds of Cabell, C.S. Lewis, or Tolkien in breadth and scope.

Lovecraft's Influence

While imaginary worlds abound in modern fantasy, few of today's writers set their sagas in Poictesme, Perelanda, or Middle-earth. But stories and novels based on the Mythos continue to proliferate. In terms of imitation and inspiration,

Lovecraft may well have had more influence on other writers than any contemporary except Ernest Hemingway.

It didn't happen overnight. As noted, he received scant critical attention during his lifetime. The annual "best" short-story collections list only two of his tales as "also-rans"; they printed none. And in *Weird Tales*, the lowly pulp magazine where most of his output appeared, he was never even granted a cover illustration for anything he wrote. Such honors were reserved for more popular authors and their creations—Seabury Quinn's French detective, Jules de Grandin, or Robert E. Howard's barbarian adventurer, Conan.

During the latter years of Lovecraft's life the most successful purveyors of short fiction found a hospitable and high-paying market in the weekly "slicks"—*Collier's, Liberty, The Saturday Evening Post*—and the big-circulation monthly magazines. Authors with "serious" aspirations often opted for *The Atlantic Monthly, The American Mercury, The New Yorker, Story*, or regional periodicals. The world's greatest short-story writer was William Saroyan; we knew, because he told us so.

Lovecraft made no such claims. At the time of his death glowing tributes graced the letter column of *Weird Tales* and some of the amateur "fanzines" privately circulated among a few devotees of fantasy or science fiction. But their readership was minimal and their influence nugatory.

Aside from a small Canadian edition of *Weird Tales*, Lovecraft's efforts had appeared abroad only in Christine Campbell Thompson's sleazily printed British "Not at Night" series. One story was reprinted in an American anthology but attempts to publish two of his novellas in hardcover had failed. There were no foreign translations at all. In the years that followed, a single tale was adapted for radio. Filmmakers weren't interested; television didn't exist, nor paperback books. Lovecraft was dead, and to all intents and purposes, so was his work.

But the "Lovecraft Circle" of correspondents remained. Two of them, fellow-writers August Derleth and Donald Wandrei, tried to interest publishers in putting out a collection of his stories. Meeting with no success, they then founded a company of their own called Arkham House and announced the publication of *The Outsider and Others*. This imposing volume of over three hundred thousand words would sell for $5, but could be purchased at a prepublication price of $3.50.

Despite wide advance publicity throughout the fantasy and science fiction field, only 150 orders were received, and the remaining 1,118 copies took more than four years to sell out.

Determined to overcome indifference, Arkham House went on to print a companion volume, *Beyond the Wall of Sleep*, then gradually extended its list to include the work of other contemporary fantasy authors. A series of complications subsequently arose, involving royalty bequests from Lovecraft's aunt who died in 1941, the suicide of his literary executor ten years later, plus legal disputes between Wandrei and Derleth.

Lovecraft's work survived it all. It even survived Derleth's imitations of his style and subject matter, which he began writing in the forties. . . .

It was Derleth who constantly used the term "Cthulhu Mythos" to describe Lovecraft's cosmic concepts. Unfortunately, his own writing involved a distortion of its meaning that may have derived from his own status as a lapsed or lax Catholic. In any case, he divided Lovecraft's Great Old Ones into what in effect were the Good Guys and the Bad Guys, fighting over possession of the earth instead of the ranch. Some later imitators picked up on this, straying far from Lovecraftian logic.

But when considering Derleth's influence, one single fact remains all-important—he championed the revival of interest in Lovecraft's work. After Donald Wandrei's service in World War II his Arkham House activity was largely limited to editing Lovecraft's letters, eventually published in five volumes. Derleth, however, continued to keep the stories in print, reissuing portions of the original collections under other titles. When fantasy anthologies began to flourish, he sold one-time reprint rights to various stories, including those in public domain, and until his death in 1961 he claimed control of the literary estate. As early as 1945 he compiled a paperback Lovecraft collection for an Armed Services edition. Its unexpected popularity with a wide readership encouraged later reprinting efforts by other paperback publishers here and abroad. Gradually this continued exposure led to the formation of a new fandom, enthusiasts interested in every aspect of the man and the work. Following recognition on the part of foreign critics, Lovecraft—like his predecessor, Edgar Allan Poe—finally came to the attention of the American literary establishment.

Stephen King's "Art of Darkness"

Douglas E. Winter

Douglas E. Winter is one of the more respected names
in contemporary horror literature. He has written a
horror novel (*Millenium*), edited several important
collections of horror fiction (including *Revelations*
and *Prime Evil*), and collected a series of interviews
with leading horror novelists under the title *Faces of
Fear*. In the following article, taken from the introduction to his study of Stephen King entitled *Stephen
King: The Art of Darkness*, Winter surveys and evalu-
ates the first dozen (and artistically the most important) years of King's prolific career, the years that produced *Carrie, Salem's Lot, The Stand, The Shining*,
and a handful of truly first-rate short stories.

"The Reach was wider in those days," says Stella Flanders,
the oldest resident of Goat Island, Maine. Ninety-five years
old and dying of cancer, Stella Flanders has decided to take
a walk. It is winter, the Reach has frozen over for the first
time in forty years, and Stella Flanders has begun to see
ghosts. And she has decided that, having never before left
Goat Island, it is time for a walk across the Reach. The in-
land coast of Maine is a mile and a half distant, and so far as
we know, neither the coast nor Goat Island has had occasion
to move. But Stella Flanders is nevertheless right—the Reach
was wider in those days.

The storyteller's name is Stephen King, and although he
asks "Do the Dead Sing?" his story is about a journey.
Stella Flanders, having left her home behind, sets forth on
an odyssey of discovery that, paradoxically, looks home-
ward with every step. The lonely crossing of the dark,
frozen waters of the Reach means death for Stella Flan-

ders; and the question "Do the dead sing?" asks what really lies upon the far side of the Reach.

What Lies Beyond

That question, asked and answered in different guises, resounds throughout the fiction of Stephen King. Not very far from Goat Island, but in another version of reality called *The Stand*, Fran Goldsmith waits in expectation on the mainland coast at Ogunquit, Maine. She is pregnant, alone, and one of the few people left alive in a world decimated by the flu. Further south, in the fictional hall of mirrors known as *The Talisman*, twelve-year-old Jack Sawyer stands at Arcadia Beach on the tiny seacoast of New Hampshire. His mother is dying, and he senses that her fate—and perhaps the fate of the world—may soon be held in his young hands. Both Fran Goldsmith and Jack Sawyer have also decided to take a walk, and although the distances they must travel are considerable in miles, their journeys cross a Reach no different in meaning than that facing Stella Flanders—although each of them will return, for a time, to the near side of the Reach.

That Stella Flanders' journey is westward may be a fluke of geography, but that west is the prevailing movement of the travelers of *The Stand* and *The Talisman* is not. These stories enact the recurrent American nightmare—the terror-trip experienced by Edgar Allan Poe's Arthur Gordon Pym, Herman Melville's Ishmael, and a host of fellow journeyers: the search for a utopia of meaning while glancing backward in idyllic reverie to lost innocence. It is a journey taken by Jack Torrance in *The Shining*, driving west to the promise of a new life at the Overlook Hotel; by Johnny Smith in *The Dead Zone*, who crosses time, if not space; by Louis Creed in *Pet Sematary*, carrying the body of his dead son along the uphill path to a secret burial ground; by character after character in Stephen King's fiction, all trapped between fear of the past's deadly embrace and fear of future progress in a world that placidly accepts the possibility of total war. It is a night journey, both literally and symbolically, and Stephen King is its foremost practitioner in contemporary fiction. . . .

The Literature of "What If?"

Asking whether the dead sing is much like offering Johnny Smith's rhetorical toast in *The Dead Zone:* "To the three Ds— death, destruction and destiny. Where would we be without them?" These questions have been asked since the first horror story was told by firelight, and they are as inevitable—and as unanswerable—as the question of why we tell and listen to horror stories. To suggest that the tale of terror is an inextricable element of the human condition—a guilty fascination with darkness and irrationality, with the potential for expanding human consciousness and perception, with the understanding of our mortality and our universe—would be true but insufficient. More pragmatic answers seem to be in order. Western society is obsessed with horror fiction and film—the past fifteen years have seen an eruption of interest in horror stories rivaled only by the halcyon days of the ghost story at the close of the nineteenth century.

To ask why we read horror fiction is to ask why Stella Flanders took that walk on that cold winter's day of the storyteller's imagination. Death stalks Stella Flanders, and her faltering steps onto the Reach are an adventure, an escape from a mundane life—and a mundane death. At a minimum, horror fiction is a means of escape, sublimating the very real and often overpowering horrors of everyday life in favor of surreal, exotic, and visionary realms. Escapism is not, of course, necessarily a rewarding experience; indeed, horror fiction's focus upon morbidity and mortality suggests a masochistic or exploitative experience, conjuring subjective fantasies in which our worst fears or darkest desires are brought into tangible existence. "It was the way things worked," says Officer Hunton in King's short story "The Mangler"—"the human animal had a built-in urge to view the remains." But conscientious fiction of escape provides something more—an art of mimesis, a counterfeiting of reality whose inducement to imagination gives the reader access to truths beyond the scope of reason. As D.H. Lawrence would write of Poe's horror fiction: "It is lurid and melodramatic, but it is true."

The escapist quality of horror stories and other popular fiction speaks in a conditional future voice. As King has observed: "Literature asks 'What next?' while popular fiction asks 'What if?'" Despite its intrinsic unreality, the horror story remains credible—or at least sufficiently credible to exert an influence that may last long beyond the act of reading. One does not easily forget the thing that waits inside "The Crate," or the grinning, cymbal-clashing toy of "The Monkey." This credibility is possible because horror's truths are judged not by the real fulfillment of its promises, but by the relevance of its fantasies to those of the reader or viewer. Although horror fiction appeals to the source of daydreams—and of nightmares—its context is waking reality.

THE WAKING DREAMS OF HORROR FICTION

The tensions between fantasy and reality, wanderlust and nostalgia, produce an intriguing paradox. Stella Flanders' escape across the Reach is a search for the ghosts of her past—the lives, and years, that have departed; it can lead only to her death. In the stories "The Ballad of the Flexible Bullet" and "The Jaunt," King even more forcefully portrays how the active pursuit of the uncanny leads, with whirlpool inevitability, to destruction. As in many of the stories of the early-twentieth-century master of horror, H.P. Lovecraft, the uncanny provokes a self-destructive impulse, reflecting the alternately repulsive and seductive nature of horror fiction. "[W]hat is sought after—the otherworldly—makes us realize how much we need the worldly," writes critic Jack Sullivan, "but the more we know of the world, the more we need to be rid of it."

The six o'clock news is sufficient to show our need to be rid of the world: assassination, rampant crime, political wrongdoing, social upheaval, and war are as much a part of our daily lives as the very air we breathe. And we can no longer trust that air—or the water that we drink, the food that we eat, our machines, or our neighbors. Just ask Richie Grenadine, who popped the top on a funky can of beer in "Gray Matter"; or Harold Parkette, who employed "The Lawnmower Man"; or the young woman who met "The Man Who Loved Flowers"; or the characters of *Cujo*, whose reality is, in the final trumps, as inescapable as our own. And we live in the shadow of the atomic bomb, harbinger of our total destruction and the ultimate proof that we can no longer trust even ourselves.

Psychoanalyst and sleep researcher Charles Fisher once observed that "Dreaming permits each and every one of us to be quietly and safely insane every night of our lives." His words apply as well to the waking dreams of horror fiction. In the tale of horror, we can breach our foremost taboos, allow ourselves to lose control, experience the same emotions—terror, revulsion, helplessness—that besiege us daily. If we fear heights, we can step out on "The Ledge"; or if rats are our phobia, we can work "The Graveyard Shift." The confinement of the action to the printed page or motion picture screen renders the irrationality safe, lending our fears the appearance of being controllable. The achievement of horror's conditional future is endlessly deferred; except within the closed environment of the fiction or film, the fantasy does not—and, perhaps more important, cannot—become reality. Our sensibilities are offered a simple escape from escapism: wanderlust fulfilled, we can leave horror's pages and shadowed theaters with the conviction that the horror was not true and cannot be true. Every horror novel, like every nightmare, has a happy ending, just so long as we can wake up, and we can say, with Herman Melville's *Pierre* (1852), that "It is all a dream—we dreamed that we dreamed we dream."

But horror fiction is not simply an unquiet place that we may visit in moments of need. Along with its obvious cathartic value, horror fiction has a cognitive value, helping us to understand ourselves and our existential situation. Its essential element is the clash between prosaic everyday life and a mysterious, irrational, and potentially supernatural universe. The mundane existence of Stella Flanders is never the same after she first sees the ghost of her long-dead husband. Her haunting is a traditional one, and Stephen King conjures an atmosphere of suspended disbelief by his very reliance upon the traditions of the supernatural tale. Just like settling into a comfortable chair, King's conscientious use of such traditions—both in terms of theme (as in the vampire lore of *Salem's Lot* and the Gothic castle/hotels of *The Shining* and *The Talisman)* and of narrative technique (as in the Lovecraftian epistolary tale of "Jerusalem's Lot" and the smoking room reminiscence of "The Man Who Would Not Shake Hands")—lends credibility to the otherwise unbelievable. The supernatural need not creep across the floorboards of each and every horror story, however; reality itself often is sufficiently frightening—and certainly credible—as short stories like King's "Strawberry Spring" and "Survivor Type" prove through themes of psychological distress and aberration.

THE PLACE OF REALISM IN KING'S FICTION

Then there are the stories that fall somewhere in between. Although Stella Flanders sees ghosts in "Do the Dead Sing?"

these ghosts are no more adequately proved than the aliens who schoolmarm Emily Sidley believes have replaced her third-graders in "Suffer the Little Children." To be sure, Stella Flanders follows the ghosts (just as Miss Sidley takes the little children, one by one, to the mimeograph room, where she kills them), but there is no extrinsic evidence of their reality. Do the dead sing? The question is not simply one of faith—how close does it come to reality?

The pursuit of realism suggests that horror fiction should follow a consequential pattern: that some semblance of reason, however vague, should underlie seemingly irrational or supernatural events. The leap of faith necessary to persuade the purblind skeptic that zombies can walk is made slightly easier by a springboard based in voodoo or—as in the classic zombie film, *Night of the Living Dead* (1968)—the strange radiation of a returning Venus probe, even if these explanations are themselves intrinsically illogical. And once that leap of faith is made, the reader may as well shout that the water's fine: if zombies can walk, then we have little additional trouble in accepting that they will feast upon the flesh of the living rather than serve as ideal elevator operators. The fact that the typical reader of horror fiction is willing to believe should render the author's task that much easier. There is a secret self— the eternal child, perhaps—lurking somewhere within each of us who yearns to be shown that the worst is true: that zombies can walk, that ghosts really beckon to Stella Flanders.

DOES HORROR FICTION REQUIRE EXPLANATION?

When the printed tale of terror was young—in those days of the "penny dreadfuls" and their more respectable kin, the Gothic novel—a rigid dichotomy was observed between fiction based in supernatural events and that based in rational explanation. The latter form, best exemplified by the novels of Ann Radcliffe—such as *The Mysteries of Udolpho* (1794)—and reprised briefly in the "shudder pulps" of the 1930s and the "Baby Jane" maniac films of the 1960s, proposed apparently supernatural events that were explained rationally at the story's end. As the modern horror story emerged in the late 1800s, however, neither a rational nor a supernatural explanation of events needed ultimately to be endorsed. Even formalist M.R. James would write: "It is not amiss sometimes to leave a loophole for a natural explanation, but I would say, let the loophole be so narrow as not to be quite practicable.". . .

Stephen King's most pervasive short story, "The Boogeyman," suggests that explanation, whether supernatural or rational, may simply not be the business of horror fiction—that the very fact that the question "Do the dead sing?" is unanswerable draws us inexorably to his night journeys.

"I came to you because I want to tell my story," says Lester Billings, comfortably enthroned on the psychiatric couch of Dr. Harper. "All I did was kill my kids. One at a time. Killed them all." So begins Lester Billings' journey through the retrospective corridors of psychoanalysis. He quickly explains that he did not actually kill his three children, but that he is "responsible" for their deaths because he has left certain closet doors open at night, and "the boogeyman" has come out. A rational mind must reject such a confessional, and Billings is an abrasive personality—cold, insensitive, filled with hatred for the human condition. Immediately, we doubt his credibility and his sanity. By the story's close, Billings has made it clear that it is he who fears "the boogeyman," and the reader can only conclude that he has murdered his children. Dr. Harper states that therapy will be necessary, but when Billings returns to the psychiatrist's office, he notices that the closet door is open—first, just by a crack, but it quickly swings wide: "'So nice,' the boogeyman said as it shambled out. It still held its Dr. Harper mask in one rotted, spade-claw hand."

On a metaphorical level, the boogeyman's appearance may be an affirmation of Billings' psychosis—this is the loophole for a rational explanation. Symbolically, we see psychiatry, the supposedly rational science of mind—and, indeed, the science that explained as disease what earlier beliefs had held to be the workings of supernatural forces—succumb to the slavering irrationality of a "boogeyman." The retrogression to childhood, so intrinsic to Freudian solution, ironically affirms the correctness of childhood fears. And this very image is revisited again and again in King's fiction. When Father Callahan confronts "Mr. Barlow," the king vampire of *Salem's Lot,* he recognizes the face: it is that of "Mr. Flip," the boogeyman who haunted the closets of his youth. The thing that haunts Tad Trenton's closet in *Cujo* prefigures that rabid dog, the nightmare unleashed in daylight. And the Overlook Hotel of *The Shining* is revealed in the end as the quintessential haunted closet, from which the boogeyman shambles. . . .

KING'S "RATIONAL SUPERNATURALISM"

On both the literal and symbolic levels, "The Boogeyman" shattered the distinction between the supernatural and the empirical, offering the chilling possibility that there is no difference. In its wake, King put forward a theme of "rational supernaturalism" in his novels—first seeded in *Carrie,* but brought to fruition in *The Stand, The Dead Zone,* and *Firestarter*—granting credence to unnatural phenomena through elaborate rationalizations not unlike those of science fiction, and simultaneously suggesting a dark truth that we all suspect: that rationality and order are facades, mere illusions of control imposed upon a reality of chaos.

Like the mask worn by the boogeyman, what Stella Flanders has left behind in the small community of Goat Island is deceptive. Surface appearances are not to be trusted, as two young men learn when they test the fledgling ice of the Reach on a snowmobile. The apparent serenity and pastoral simplicity of Goat Island are stripped away through Stella Flanders' memories of the town's complicity in the deaths of a mongoloid baby and a child molester. Artifice and masquerade are recurring themes in Stephen King's fiction, reminding us that evil works from within as well as from without—that, like the ravaged hulk of the 1958 Plymouth Fury that sits at the roadside at the beginning of *Christine,* we are clothed with the thin veneer of civilization, beneath which waits the beast, eager to emerge.

Horror fiction is thus an intrinsically subversive art, which seeks the true face of reality by striking through the pasteboard masks of appearance. That the lifting of the mask may reveal the face of the boogeyman, the new world of *The Stand,* or the nothingness of *Cujo* is our existential dilemma, the eternal tension between doubt and belief that will haunt us to our grave, when we surely must learn. But the lifting of the mask also strikes at the artifices of control that we erect against this dilemma—our science, religion, materialism, and civilization. That horror fiction evokes current events and religious and sociopolitical concerns should thus come as no surprise. The masterpieces of "yellow Gothic"—Robert Louis Stevenson's *Dr. Jekyll and Mr. Hyde* (1886), Oscar Wilde's *The Picture of Dorian Gray* (1891), H.G. Wells's *The Island of Dr. Moreau* (1896), and Bram Stoker's *Dracula* (1897)—reflected the fears of an age of imperial decline. More recently, the "technohorror" films of the 1950s were obvious analogs of the doomsday mentality created by the atomic bomb and the cold war. . . . The novels and stories of Stephen King exploit this subversive potential, consciously creating sociopolitical subtexts that add timely depth and meaning to their horrifying premises.

Stella Flanders does not read a horror story in "Do the Dead Sing?" but she does the next best thing—attend a funeral. Its ritual is not unlike a horror tale, organizing and packaging fears, giving meaning and value to death (and, in so doing, to life). And Stella Flanders helps us see something more; her attendance is compelled not so much by mere inquisitiveness, escape, catharsis, or the demands of society as by her memories of the past. Things were better then; after all, the Reach—indeed, the whole world—was wider in those days. When Stella Flanders embarks upon her journey, she understands what she is leaving behind in the "small world" on this side of the Reach: "a way of being and a way of living; a feeling.". . .

KING'S STORIES OF INNOCENCE AND EXPERIENCE

In an era of continuous social and technological revolution, however, contemporary horror fiction lacks a pretechnological culture to sentimentalize. Indeed, the horror lurking within certain of Stephen King's novels—particularly *The Stand*—is precisely the lack of an "earlier way of life" worthy of our sentiment. Rather than indulge in a spurious attempt to recapture a social milieu, King's fiction often looks to our youth as the earlier way of life whose "swan song" must be sung. His stories are songs of innocence and experience, juxtaposing childhood and adulthood—effectively completing the wheel whose turn began in childhood by re-experiencing those days from a mature perspective. Indeed, several of his novels suggest that horror fiction performs the role of the modern fairy tale—*Cujo* begins with the words "Once upon a time," while *Carrie* and *Firestarter* respectively evoke the traditions of "Cinderella" and "Beauty and the Beast."

This is a powerful motif; it may cause the reader to look to his or her life as well as that of the characters. In King's works, we experience again those occasions in our lives when it has seemed important to understand what a person really is—to perceive the genuine identity beneath the social exterior of manner, habits, clothes, and job. Such moments are most common in childhood, when no one's identity is certain and when any exterior is likely to be impermanent or false. Uncertainty in our own sense of self renders the processes of knowing and communicating with others difficult and intense. We live in a world of emotion and moral significance, in which the business of life is the process of social relation and social judgment; we constantly attempt to fix our view of others, to do justice to emotions and judgments, yet language always seems inadequate to express what we *know*. We leave this world behind as we mature. As King wryly notes, "the only cure is the eventual ossification of the imaginary faculties, and this is called adulthood." We lose our sense of the mysticism of life—of fear and fantasy, of unhindered and yet inexplicable vision, of unscalable heights and limitless possibilities. This lost world is sought by Ben Mears of *Salem's Lot* in his nostalgic journey to the haunted house of his childhood, and found by Stella Flanders on the far side of the Reach. It is the world that we recapture in the fiction of horror.

The Novels
of Anne Rice

Lynda Haas and Robert Haas

Next to Stephen King, Anne Rice was probably the
most important voice in horror fiction to emerge
during the last three decades of the twentieth century. Perhaps even more so than King, Rice has
tested and expanded the "outer limits" of horror,
particularly in the several novels comprising *The
Vampire Chronicles*. The first novel in the series,
1976's ground-breaking *Interview with the Vampire*,
is a richly textured, brooding meditation on vampirism in which Rice refused to shy away from exploring the homoerotic implications of her story. In
the following article, Lynda Haas and Robert Haas
(who both teach in the writing program at Ithaca
College) discuss Rice's fascination with "marginalized" characters—characters, like the vampire Lestat, who inhabit the boundary regions of human
society and the human imagination.

"I want a lot. I want to be immortal."
—Anne Rice, Bill Moyers's interview

Castrated opera singers. Spirits who desire fleshly existence.
Vampires and witches. The *gens de couleur*. Mummies who
become immortal. These are the characters who occupy the
margins of Anne Rice's fictional worlds. Boundary creatures, all. In her narratives that span time from the first
recorded literate culture—the Sumerians who told the tale
of Gilgamesh—to the present-day bustling with computers
and fax machines, Rice always chooses to write about fugi-
tives and nomads. And whether they are human or supernatural, they are characters who can never be part of the
normal or dominant society. Between the lines of their narratives, Western society reads about itself and its own philo-

Excerpted from "Living With(out) Boundaries: The Novels of Anne Rice," by Lynda and
Robert Haas. Copyright © 1996 by the University of South Carolina Press. Reprinted
with permission from University of South Carolina Press.

sophical and physical struggles to place itself within cultural boundaries. This sympathy of the marginalized, perhaps, is why so many readers are drawn to the fictional worlds of Anne Rice. Even beyond the boundaries of her American audience, Rice's characters have become known to readers of the Gothic in several cultures.

RICE'S LITERATURE OF THE MARGINALIZED

Although Rice has an increasing number of fans worldwide (and also some critical admirers), reviews of her work are usually filled with complaints that her writing is fetid, humid, overstuffed, baroque, pretentious, formulaic, and downright awful. By new critical standards, perhaps Rice's novels do not have what it takes to "stand the test of time." Her novels are, however, interesting and important as cultural commentary, and as an intriguing combination of Gothic literary conventions with a postmodern sensibility about identity formation, sensual/sexual embodiment, and historical perspective. Whether she is writing about Louis or Lestat (*The Vampire Chronicles*), Ramses (*The Mummy*), or Rowan and Lasher (the *Taltos* series), the struggle of Rice's characters to understand shifting cultural boundaries becomes a means of interrogating who we are and how we live—questions with no easy answers.

Additionally, there is no contemporary writer with stronger ties to the Gothic tradition than Anne Rice. Beginning in 1976 with *Interview with the Vampire* and continuing to *Taltos,* Rice has consistently and successfully combined many of the Gothic conventions initiated by Horace Walpole in *The Castle of Otranto* (1765) with her own unique style and with the concerns of postmodern philosophy. It is an enticing combination—a "witches' brew" of elements that millions of readers find difficult to resist. This essay concentrates on two texts, *The Vampire Lestat* and *The Mummy*, that include the supernatural. In addition, this essay analyzes postmodern elements of history and identity within all of Rice's novels and develops connections between these two contemporary issues and the Gothic tradition which spans two centuries.

HISTORY AND PERSPECTIVE IN *THE MUMMY*

Since the arrival of "new historicism" (a postmodern approach to examining narratives), the act of writing and interpreting history has been problematic for its parallel to creating fiction. From Plutarch's account of Roman history and Holinshed's chronicles of England to Ken Burns's documentary of the Civil War and E.L. Doctorow's ficto-historical worlds, writers have exercised the literary license of describing historical persons, incidents, and places in a subjective way that meets their own narrational and ideological purposes. Rice's novels are often described as historical, for she uses well-known fragments of history as she traces her stories throughout various epochs; often interweaving and rewriting narratives familiar to the reader, Rice retells them in such a way as to open new interpretations. Her historical revisioning is so often tied to religious perspective that one might hypothesize her purpose in revising is to interrogate and replace the influences of the Christian era with influences that are decidedly pre- or post-Christian.

The use of history within narratives has always been an integral part of the Gothic tradition. Dracula's relationship to Genghis Khan or the ancient and exotic horrors of [William Beckford's] *Vathek* and [Matthew Lewis's] *The Monk* rely on both natural and mythical history to advance the plot. These narratives' historical moments are related from a religious and highly moralistic perspective; conversely, Rice's approach to the historical conventions of the Gothic tradition is decidedly post-Christian. Specifically, Rice questions the validity of history and also removes the influence of Christian morality and its judgmental interpretation of historical figures and incidents that have greatly colored not only narratives, but culture and society in general.

In her 1989 novel, *The Mummy,* Ramses (a ficto-historical character himself—Ramses II of Egypt), the protagonist who has transcended death and walked the earth since the times of ancient Egypt, has an extended conversation with his twentieth-century counterparts in the novel. They offer their interpretations of history from ancient times to the industrial revolution; Ramses's perspectives—those of an ancient, pre-Christian king of Egypt—are quite different. Rice thus creates what could never exist outside the realm of fiction: a person who is from another time and place, but who now exists in the modern era. From his interpretations, the way he walks, the values he holds, and the way he reacts to the modern world around him, we are presented with a different kind of historical glimpse into the ancient past—one that historians cannot offer, but one that is presented within this fictional world as being every bit as historical as something in a textbook. Rice's narrative shows Ramses's perspective as having more information and as being untainted by later developments in Western culture.

To teach Ramses about history, Julie takes him to a twentieth-century diorama: Madame Tussaud's Wax Museum. He does not react well to the figures because he knew them when they were alive: "Cleopatra had been no Roman. Cleopatra had been a Greek and an Egyptian. And the horror was, Cleopatra meant something to these modern people of the twentieth century which was altogether wrong. She had become a symbol of licentiousness, when in fact she had possessed a multitude of amazing talents. They had punished her for her one flaw by forgetting everything else." Although Ramses has much to offer the early twentieth-century characters in the way of opening up the limitations of their particular perspective, he also gains knowledge of the boundaries of his own standpoint as he notices that what has survived in the modern culture is not his perspective, but the Christian appropriation of Rome's culture, values, and perspectives: "Roman numerals. Everywhere he looked he saw them; on cornerstones, in the pages of books; on the facades of buildings. In fact, the art, the language, the spirit of Rome ran through this entire culture, hooking it firmly to the past. Even the concept of justice . . . had come down not from the barbarians who once ruled this place with their crude ideas of revealed law and tribal vengeance, but from the courts and judges of Rome where reason had reigned."

As Rice's narrators question historical perspectives, she simultaneously interrogates cultural memory and how it, like identity, is constructed by language and ideology. When Ramses is first awakened (after having become tired of the world and sleeping through many centuries), he does not have his full memory—he regains it in flashes. The ways in which his memory is different than the memories inscribed by historians is often his starting point as he attempts to outline his narrative of history as a correction to what the twentieth century had forgotten. But then, to Ramses, Karl Marx and his philosophy are nothing more than "sheer nonsense, as far as he could see. A rich man, it seemed, writing about poor men when he did not know how their minds worked." The work of Marx, so influential to anything that followed his moment in history, means nothing to Ramses. In the advantages and disadvantages of each particular perspective, Rice shows that history and memory, in all their different versions, are not foundations, but fragments dependent upon the culture and language from which they come. . . .

HISTORY AND PERSPECTIVE IN *THE VAMPIRE CHRONICLES*

In *The Vampire Chronicles*, Rice introduces historical and cultural perspectives through the time in which each character is reborn or made as a vampire. The culture from which the characters originally come partially shapes their identity and philosophical perspective; for instance, Lestat is from the eighteenth-century "Age of Reason"—a time when "white-wigged Parisians tiptoed around in high-heeled satin slippers, pinched snuff, and dabbed at their noses with embroidered handkerchiefs" while "the poor hovered in doorways, shivering and hungry, and the crooked unpaved streets were thick with filthy slush." Louis, however, was made during the romanticism of the nineteenth century. Both are marked by the dominant philosophical schools and ethical mores of their original culture. Even older is Armand, a sixteenth-century Renaissance vampire, who looks like a da Vinci saint or "the little god from Caravaggio." Armand's perspectives are enigmatic because he was made at such a young age, but he has, like the other elders who have survived, learned to adapt to the changing cultural landscapes of Europe.

A crucial figure to Rice's revisionist history is Marius, an ancient Roman centurion who witnessed the great conquests of the empire, the conquering of the barbarians of western Europe, and the defeat of Rome at the hands of the barbarians of eastern Europe. More importantly, before he became a vampire, Marius was a historian. Marius was born to vampirism in the years of Augustus Caesar: "when Rome had just become an empire, when faith in the gods was, for all lofty purposes, dead." So Marius's philosophy is to live a life without need for illusions or systems of rationalization; he has instead "a love of and respect for what is right before your eyes."

Because of his status as an elder and the way Lestat presents him, the reader accepts the narrative reliability of Marius. However, even here, Rice subverts the reader's expectations. Marius, just like every other historian, has limited perspective and is subjective in his accuracy. Readers are first told the story of Akasha and Enkil (the original vampires) by Marius in *The Vampire Lestat.* Only in the next novel, *The Queen of the Damned,* does the reader realize that he has left many gaps in the story. The history is revised when Khayman and then Maharet (both primary actors at the birth of the first vampires) narrate; we find out other things that were left out of Marius's version, because Marius heard the story so many hundreds of years after the fact. As Rice's narratives unfold, we are constantly invited to question historical narratives and note how they change with cultures and with narrators.

Rice even questions her own narrative and narrators. Louis narrates the first book of the series, *Interview with the Vampire*; in the second book, *The Vampire Lestat,* Lestat (as narrator) questions the reliability of the first book and advises the reader to "read between the lines." This questioning, instead of creating cynicism or undecidability in the reader, serves to bind the books of the series together and lends more sympathy to Lestat as narrator. Unlike Louis, Lestat refers to himself as "I" and the reader as "you"—creating a symbiosis between them. He presents himself from many different angles: sometimes charming, fond, and delightfully nervy; at other times, he alters the lens just a little and crosses over into gloating, pettiness, defensiveness, score settling (which includes self-hate), and whining about his victimization. The trick is that somehow Lestat's personal style does cross the symbiotic bridge—elucidating widespread human traits and making his readers feel a little less lonely and freakish. . . .

RELIGIOUS BELIEF AND MYTHICAL EXPLANATION

As Rice weaves together historical and mythical narratives with her own history of the vampires, the boundaries between these genres are blurred. One could say that she attempts too much and ultimately fails to deliver a "good" novel (this was most said by critics of *The Queen of the Damned*). One could also say that as Rice blurs the boundaries of these genres that she questions, the placement of the boundaries becomes another postmodern methodology. Especially as the relationship between myth and religion becomes interrogated, Rice replaces foundational religious belief with mythical explanation. Rice's texts pose religion as a result of the need for ritual, and her character, Lestat, continues and transforms the ancient rites into a present-day context when he performs as a rock star: "Now I knew all that had been left out of the pages I had read about the rock singers—this mad marriage of the primitive and the scientific, this religious frenzy. We were in the ancient grove alright. We were all with the gods." Marius explains the connected boundary more directly:

> As the Roman Empire came to its close, all the old gods of the pagan world were seen as demons by the Christians who rose. It was useless to tell them as the centuries passed that their Christ was but another God of the Wood, dying and rising, as Dionysus or Osiris had done before him, and that the Virgin Mary was in fact the Good Mother again enshrined. Theirs was a new age of belief and conviction, and in it we became devils, detached from what they believed, as old knowledge was forgotten or misunderstood.

Here Marius provides not only a revisionist historical account of religion, but an analysis of language. He goes on to describe a point in time when the word "evil" was attributed a new value: "when the Children of Darkness came to believe they served the Christian devil . . . they tried to give value to evil, to believe in its power in the scheme of things, to give it a just place in the world." Marius then offers an astute philosophical interpretation of history: "Hearken to me when I say: There has never been a just place for evil in the Western world. There has never been an easy accommodation of death. . . . The value placed upon human life has only increased. . . . It is the belief in the value of human life that carries man now out of the monarchy into the republics of America and France." In passages such as these, Rice becomes much more than a writer producing entertaining Gothic tales; she addresses highly philosophical concepts while simultaneously blurring, questioning, and testing the boundaries between fact and fiction. . . .

IDENTITY IN RICE'S WORK

Rice's novel, *The Vampire Lestat*, is narrated by her most famous creation, Lestat de Lioncourt, who explains that his prose is a bit of a "cross between a flatboatman and detective Sam Spade" with a French accent. Lestat's struggles to accept himself as either evil or good, human or nonhuman, lover or monster, shape who he is. He has no identity of his own and does not know ethically what he is; he wishes he could believe that evil is a binary necessity because then he could just be happy about playing the monster—his best performance. Since he has no place in any culture (even the one he is from), Lestat must construct his "self." He has no transcendental identity and no spiritual afterlife awaits him—his only soul is the one he makes. In the case of Lestat, his identity is constructed in performance by his desire to communicate through his roles as writer, rock star, vampire, and lover. He fashions not only himself, but also his philosophy—reasons and purposes for continuing to live— just as the old ones constructed mythologies around their powers and rituals to give them a place while adding human meaning to their existence. . . .

As "an immortal being who must find his own reasons to exist," Lestat's eternal quest is to find an identity he can "live" with. The identity forged for him by Rice, although Gothic in feeling, is postmodern in form. Lestat's first identity as hunter, or "wolfkiller," is given to him by his mother, Gabrielle. After being forbidden by his family to enter the monastery where he thinks he will belong, Lestat is forlorn until his mother brings him the clothes and weapons of a hunter; from this moment on, Lestat performs the role of wolfkiller. Later, he is excited by the emotions created by the traveling actors' troupe and wishes to fashion a new identity as Lelio, young lover to Isabella, in Paris's *Commedia dell' arte*. The acting career he chooses (although his family forbids him to continue) makes up his identity throughout the rest of the chronicles. Lestat performs—that is who he is. He soon finds out that fooling mortals into thinking he is human is just as easy as performing Lelio.

Lestat is drawn to the actors because they create: "Actors and actresses make magic, they make things happen on stage; they invent; they create." Musicians, like Nicki, receive the same esteem in Lestat's economy. Although he takes pleasure in his creativity as an actor with many roles, his cultural encoding makes it impossible for him to be at peace with these vampiric creations, which he still sees as immoral. He, therefore, constructs a philosophy (eclectically drawn from the writers of the cultures he has experienced) that allows him to justify his "art": "I took up the theme again that music and acting were good because they drove back chaos. Chaos was the meaninglessness of day to day life, and if we were to die now, our lives would be nothing but meaninglessness. . . . We are going to die and not even know. We'll never know, and all this meaninglessness will just go on and on and on. . . . How do you live, how do you go on breathing and moving and doing things when you know there is no explanation?"

Lestat fills the void left by his question with art and materialism—the "art for art's sake" philosophy of the decadents. Therefore, any value ascribed to nature comes by way of its artistic value. When Lestat drinks innocent blood for the first time, he describes his vision as a garden of savage beauty: "[It] had been a true vision. There was meaning in the world, yes, and laws, and inevitability, but they had only to do with the aesthetic." The philosophies and justifications that Lestat develops, however, continue at odds with the ethical encoding of his primary culture. As he continues to question his purpose and meaning, his identity resists cultural boundaries and is reforged and changed. Only at the end of his last book does Lestat seem to grasp the idea that his is not a transcendental self, but a constructed self.

As he closes *The Tale of the Body Thief*, Lestat writes: "Yes, say something—for the love of heaven and the love of Claudia—to darken it and show it for what it is! Dear God, to lance it and show the horror at the core. But I could not. What more is there to say, really? The tale is told." Lestat's inability to go deeper—to find what is at the core—exists not because he is unable to dive deeply enough, but because there is no core. The telling of the tale, the performance of it, is his only meaning. Lestat struggles with this question of the interiority and exteriority of identity. Finally, at the end of his latest book, he seems to come to an understanding that his performances (whether vampire, monster, lover, son, rock star, master, friend, wolfkiller, or actor) are his self-definition. What he has been doing as he dons his many roles is the ritual of creating meaning and testing boundaries. . . .

Unlike her readers, Rice's characters have been forming an identity since the first days of recorded time. In this way, Rice's self-fashioned characters are caught up in redefining the manners of many cultures. Perhaps Rice will get her wish for immortality; her textual creatures have entered the *zeitgeist* of the twentieth century, and will live on—not only as vampires, mummies, spirits, and witches, but also as cultural philosophers, storytellers, critics, and historians.

Sex, Death, and Violence in the Early Works of Clive Barker

S.T. Joshi

Regarded as something of an *enfant terrible* when he first achieved notoriety in the 1980s with his *Books of Blood* series and *Hellraiser* films, Clive Barker quickly became a powerful driving force in horror and certainly served as one of the principal influences in the "splatterpunk" movement of the 1990s. Barker's stage background (in *Grand Guignol*–style productions) helps explain the frequently shocking and gruesome "theatricality" of his fiction, which delights in presenting scenes combining elements of sex, violence, death, and gore in horrific ways. Not surprisingly, Barker's "anything-goes" approach to horror has elicited both praise and criticism. In the following article, S.T. Joshi, a prominent scholar and editor of horror fiction and the author of a biography of H.P. Lovecraft, examines Barker's early work and concludes that, when it comes to sex, death, and violence in horror literature, less is often more.

When Clive Barker's *Books of Blood* were published by Sphere Books in London in 1984–85, the world took notice: hitherto known only as a dramatist whose plays had been performed but not published, Barker (b. 1952) accomplished a feat almost unheard of in publishing by having not one but six paperback volumes of his short stories issued by a major firm; at a time when even established authors in the field had difficulty in publishing collections of short fiction, Barker's achievement was more than singular. Barker then issued a novel, *The Damnation Game* (1985), a novella, "The Hellbound Heart", in the third volume of *Night Visions*

Excerpted from "Clive Barker: Sex, Death, and Fantasy," by S.T. Joshi, *Studies in Weird Fiction*, Spring 1991. Reprinted with permission from the author. A revised version of this essay will appear in S.T. Joshi's book, *The Modern Weird Tale* (Jefferson, NC: McFarland, 2001).

(1986), and two more novels, *Weaveworld* (1987) and *The Great and Secret Show* (1989), along with a short novel, *Cabal* (1988), and random other short stories. *The Great and Secret Show* was subtitled *The First Book of The Art*, a projected series of four or five novels.

A MIXED RECEPTION

Early in his career Barker was lauded by Stephen King with the now famous tag, "I have seen the future of horror . . . and it is named Clive Barker". Accordingly, Barker has not merely received generally more favourable reviews in the mainstream press but has, in consequence, generated higher expectations for his work than might be expected for a popular best-seller such as King: it is reasonable to demand greater literary substance from Barker, and Barker himself has not been shy in claiming such substance for himself. But whether Barker belongs in the class of [Algernon] Blackwood, [Lord] Dunsany, and [H.P.] Lovecraft—or even of Shirley Jackson and Ramsey Campbell—is far from clear.

The keynote of Barker's early work is a frenetic mix of gruesome physical horror, rather conventional supernaturalism, and explicit sex. It would be a little untrue to say that Barker is aiming purely at shock value in all this; but it is also untrue to believe that Barker has the literary skill to raise this subject-matter very much above the level of sensationalism. Barker is a writer of tremendous imagination but extraordinarily slipshod style, conception, and execution; like many writers, he has already written (or published) too much. It would not be an exaggeration to say that, of his voluminous work, only perhaps two or three stories from the *Books of Blood* and *The Damnation Game* are all that are worth reading.

What I find most interesting about Barker is his place in the history of weird fiction. Barker is in many ways a herald of the complete and possibly irremediable decadence of the field. In contrast to weird writers of a prior generation, Barker has no world-view to convey—or if he does, it is of the most trivial and superficial sort. He is not trying to "say" anything of consequence in his work; or, rather, he may be trying but he is not succeeding. More significantly, he evidently no longer feels the need to *account* for the supernatural phenomena he introduces so insouciantly in his work: everything in Barker is directed toward the level of pure sensation. . . .

MIXING SEX, DEATH, AND VIOLENCE

As it is, one of the most interesting features of Barker's work is a powerful mix of sex and death in such a way that the one leads to the other, and vice versa. It is true that Barker frequently depicts sex in his work, and it is also true that much of this sex (most of it heterosexual) is of a somewhat unwholesome sort; but I am not entirely convinced that all this is merely a product of Barker's own gay orientation: I do not believe that Barker is merely trying to exact a little vengeance on the straight community. Barker genuinely seems to envision an intimate connexion between sex, violence, and death; as he wrote with some cynicism in *The Damnation Game:* "It wasn't difficult to smudge sexuality into violence, turn sighs into screams, thrusts into convulsions. The grammar was the same; only the punctuation differed". I will confess that the most wholesome sexual passage in all Barker's work is toward the opening of "In the Hills, the Cities", where we are given a lengthy, explicit, and very powerful vignette of homosexual love between two male companions. The heterosexuals in Barker's tales rarely act with such honesty and purity.

"The Age of Desire" is perhaps Barker's most powerful story. Here a man is given a drug that so stimulates his sexual desire that everything becomes seductive:

> Aroused beyond control, he turned to the wall he had been leaning against. The sun had fallen upon it, and it was warm: the bricks smelt ambrosial. He laid kisses on their gritty faces, his hands exploring every nook and cranny. Murmuring sweet nothings, he unzipped himself, found an accommodating niche, and filled it. His mind was running with liquid pictures: mingled anatomies, female and male in one undistinguishable congress. Above him, even the clouds had caught fire; enthralled by their burning heads he felt the moment rise in his gristle. Breath was short now. But the ecstasy?; surely that would go on forever.

It becomes evident that Barker is intending a sociopolitical message here, a commentary on the complete sexualisation of our minds and our age; as one character remarks, "All our so-called higher concerns become secondary to the pursuit [of sex]. For a short time sex makes us obsessive; we can perform, or at least we *think* we can perform, what with hindsight may seem extraordinary feats". Later it is said of the drugged patient: "His back ached, his balls ached: but what was his body now?; just a plinth for that singular monument, his prick. Head was *nothing;* mind was *nothing*". It is clear what we have become:

> The world had seen so many Ages. The Age of Enlightenment; of Reformation; of Reason. Now, at last, the Age of Desire. And after this, an end to Ages; an end, perhaps, to everything. For the fires that were being stoked now were fiercer than the innocent world suspected. They were terrible fires, fires without end, which would illuminate the world in one last, fierce light.

Other stories on this theme are rather less successful. Two stories are feminist in their suggestion that men are useless encumbrances to the entire process of birth, life, and death. In "The Skins of the Fathers" we encounter bizarre monsters who have impregnated a woman in a small desert community. The intimation is that these creatures have created all earth-life:

> The creatures who were his fathers were also men's fathers; and the marriage of semen in Lucy's body was the same mix that made the first males. Women had always existed: they had lived, a species to themselves, with the demons. But they had wanted playmates: and together they had made men.

This transparent reversal of the myth of Eve's creation from Adam is simply presented too bluntly to be effective; and the story rapidly devolves into an exercise in bloodletting. Somewhat better is "The Madonna", in which a loathsome monster called the Madonna, the "Virgin Mother", is shown to give birth without the need of men. A male character who has had intercourse with her wakes up one day to find that he has become a woman. But what is the true point of the story? It is never made clear. "Jacqueline Ess: Her Will and Testament" may be mentioned in this connexion, as it deals with a woman who, purely through the power of her will, is capable of physically destroying human beings. If anything, the story hints at the superior strength of women, but beyond this the story seems to lack direction and focus.

"Dread" is less obviously sexual, but, as Barker's most effective non-supernatural story, it carries a clear message on men's habitual abuse of women. A philosophy professor decides to carry out an experiment on a bright young female student whom he finds perhaps excessively challenging to his intellect; he subjects her to hideous torture whereby she, a vegetarian, is locked in a room with only a gradually rotting piece of meat as her only means of sustenance. She eventually succumbs and eats the rancid meat. Powerful as this *conte cruel* is, it is ultimately no more than a tale of vengeance, as a man on whom the professor attempts a similar torture comes back to kill him. The story aims at profundity by means of pseudo-philosophical discussions of the nature of fear, but these in the end don't amount to much.

"The Hellbound Heart" also attempts a union of sex and death, but the result is clumsy and superficial. Frank, a jaded and unruly wastrel, stumbles upon a curious box . . . , a box that summons up mysterious creatures called Cenobites who promise him unheard-of pleasures. But Frank, in his limited way, conceives of these pleasures purely sexually:

> And yet . . . he had expected something different. Expected some sign of the numberless splendours they had access to. He had thought they would come with women, at least; oiled women, milked women; women shaved and muscled for the act of love; their lips perfumed, their thighs trembling to spread, their buttocks weighty, the way he liked them. He had expected sighs, and languid bodies spread on the floor underfoot like a living carpet; had expected virgin whores whose every crevice was his for the asking and whose skills would press him—*upward, upward*—to undreamed-of ecstasies. The world would be forgotten in their arms. He would be exalted by his lust, instead of despised for it.

Frank pays for his misconception, suffering a nameless fate that nearly obliterates his body; he survives, after a fashion, only because he had spilled his semen in the room he was occupying. "Dead sperm was a meager keepsake of his essential self, but enough". When Julia, married to Frank's brother Rory but secretly in love with Frank, moves into the house Frank had occupied, she eventually detects his presence, finds that he requires copious amounts of blood to reanimate himself, and promptly poses as a prostitute so as to lure unwitting johns into her house so that she can kill them and feed their blood to Frank, who gradually dons bone, flesh, and skin once more. All this is a perfectly entertaining mix of sex and death (rather more effective in the film version directed by Barker, *Hellraiser,* with its superb special effects), but ultimately no broader conclusions are drawn: Is sex our destroyer or our salvation? What significance does Julia's pseudo-prostitution have? Once again the tale lapses into a story of adventure and revenge, as the Cenobites exact punishment upon Frank for trying to escape their clutches.

A serious deficiency in Barker's work is a very naive good vs. evil moralism that renders many of his characters one-dimensional. Barker makes many pretensions toward main-

stream writing by elaborate character portrayal, and this occurs even in his *Books of Blood*: most of these tales are not
so much short stories as novellas, which might (at least in
theory) allow such characterisation. But both Barker's heroes and villains are simply flat and wooden. He has a pen-
chant for depicting vengeful small-town policemen ("The
Skins of the Fathers", *Cabal*), amoral criminals ("Cleve knew
in his heart he was a leopard born and bred. Crime was
easy, work was not"—"In the Flesh"), and diseased psy-
chopaths ("The Life of Death"). And those evil Europeans
who have come to disturb the peace-loving natives in the
Amazon in "How Spoilers Breed" are marked for destruction
from the beginning. [Critic] Les Daniels has rightly referred
to this sort of scenario not as tragedy but as melodrama: this
is not what adults want to read. In other cases, Barker's
attempts at fleshing out his characters in a short story or
novelette seriously disfigure the unity of the work: the me-
andering interludes depicting the sorry state of Jerry Colo-
qhoun's love life in "The Madonna" are wholly irrelevant to
the central plot of the story.

Miraculously, however, all this changes in *The Damnation
Game*. In some fashion or other, Barker has here produced a
sparklingly flawless weird novel that redeems all the absur-
dities of his earlier *Books of Blood* and all the verbosities of
his later novels. What is more, it fulfils the conditions of an
actual weird *novel*, or at least avoids Thomas Ligotti's criticism of the average weird novel as merely a mystery or suspense tale with horrific or supernatural interludes. *The
Damnation Game* has indeed been conceived as a weird
novel, and the supernatural manifestations are of such a sort
as to require novel length for their proper realisation.

The first thing that strikes us about the novel is the per-
vasiveness of the game motif. We have already seen indica-
tions of its fascination for Barker in "The Inhuman Condition" (the knots whose resolution releases the horror), and
we shall see it later in "The Hellbound Heart" with its mysterious box that must be decoded to unleash the Cenobites.
Here, however, it structures the whole novel. Joseph Whitehead, a petty thief and gambler preying upon the ruins of
postwar Warsaw, hears of a mysterious figure, Mamoulian,
who has never lost at cards. Moreover, those who play
against him and lose often meet hideous deaths. Whitehead,
his curiosity piqued (and also perhaps offended by this chal-

lenge to his own prowess at games of chance), seeks out
Mamoulian (or is perhaps led to him), challenges him to a
game of cards, and wins (or is perhaps allowed to win).
Years pass, and Whitehead returns to England; and it tran-
spires that, as a result of his victory over Mamoulian, he has
gained spectacular wealth, power, and prestige. But now he
increasingly senses that Mamoulian is after him, to exact
some sort of revenge, the purpose of which Whitehead cannot clearly ascertain.

The crucial point in the novel is the exact nature of the
"game" that Whitehead "won" from Mamoulian. Marty
Strauss, an ex-convict hired by Whitehead to be his body-
guard and who actually becomes the focal point of the novel,
first becomes aware of the means by which Whitehead ac-
cumulated his fortune:

> Life was a random business. Whitehead had learned that les-
> son years ago, at the hands of a master, and he had never for-
> gotten it. Whether you were rewarded for your good works or
> skinned alive, it was all down to chance. No use to cleave to
> some system of numbers or divinities; they all crumbled in
> the end. Fortune belonged to the man who was willing to risk
> everything on a single throw.

> He'd done that. Not once, but many times at the beginning of
> his career, when he was laying the foundations of his empire.
> And thanks to that extraordinary sixth sense he possessed,
> the ability to preempt the roll of the dice, the risks had almost
> always paid off. . . . When it came to knowing the *moment*, for
> sensing the collision of time and opportunity that made a
> good decision into a great one, a commonplace takeover into
> a coup, nobody was Old Man Whitehead's superior. . . .

The game Whitehead "won" from Mamoulian was the control of chance; as Mamoulian once told Whitehead, "All life
is chance. . . . The trick is learning how to use it".

But how did Mamoulian himself gain this quality? He is
merely a human being, albeit with superhuman powers. He
scoffs at Whitehead's query toward the end as to whether he
is the Devil: "You know I'm not. . . . Every man is his own
Mephistopheles". We finally learn of Mamoulian's past
through Whitehead's daughter Carys, a "sensitive" who can
probe people's minds; she ultimately summons up the
courage to enter Mamoulian's mind, and finds that, as a
sergeant in the army, he was nearly executed before a firing
squad when "Chance stepped in on your behalf", as a monk
who rescues him remarks. This monk teaches Mamoulian

all he knows—how to resurrect the dead, how to "take life from other people, and have it for yourself", and how to control chance. Mamoulian kills the monk, so that this knowledge is his alone; but later he realises that the monk really *wanted* to die once he had passed on his information (the influence of [Charles Maturin's] *Melmoth the Wanderer* is very obvious here). And what does Mamoulian himself want if not the same thing?

> "Don't you see how terrible it is to live when everything around you perishes? And the more the years pass the more the thought of death freezes your bowels, because the longer you avoid it the worse you imagine it must be? And you start to long—oh, *how* you long—for someone to take pity on you, someone to embrace you and share your terrors. And, at the end, someone to go into the dark with you.". . .

The portrait of Mamoulian is incredibly complex, and for the one and only time Barker has abandoned his naive good vs. evil dichotomy to present a rich and intricate conflict of wills. There is no flaw in *The Damnation Game;* its structure is perfect, its characters substantial and fully developed, its style pure and clean . . . and its denouement powerful and satisfying. Although it is part horror story, part historical novel, part mainstream novel, and part detective story, the supernatural premise structures the entire work, and is of such range and complexity as to require novel length for its exposition. . . .

THE POWER OF ART AND THE IMAGINATION

With *Weaveworld* and *The Great and Secret Show* Barker is attempting to do something entirely different. Perhaps irked by the charge that he writes only about gruesome physical horror, Barker in these two novels seeks a union between otherworld fantasy and modern horror. The union is reasonably successful in *Weaveworld,* rather less so in *The Great and Secret Show.* What is still more curious is that the fundamental theme of both works is really very much the same, and one wonders why Barker needs two very hefty novels (and the prospect of at least three more sequels to *The Great and Secret Show*) to expound a theme that is not intrinsically interesting—or, at any rate, one that Barker does not handle in a very interesting manner.

The theme is the power of art and the imagination: this is all that both these novels are about. In *Weaveworld* we encounter an elaborately woven carpet endowed with magical

powers: it contains an entire realm of entity within its substance. It becomes very clear very quickly that the Weaveworld is nothing but a symbol for art; the description of the
weave makes this evident:

> Every inch of the carpet was worked with motifs. Even the
> border brimmed with designs, each subtly different from its
> neighbor. The effect was not overbusy; every detail was clear
> to Cal's feasting eyes. In one place a dozen motifs congregated
> as if banded together; in another, they stood apart like rival
> siblings. Some kept their station along the border, others
> spilled into the main field, as if eager to join the teeming
> throng there.

And the Weaveworld itself, full of wondrous landscapes and
bizarre but enchanting creatures, is also a transparent symbol for the power of the imagination to transform the ordinary into the magical; as is stated toward the end, "Magic
might be bestowed upon the physical, but it didn't *reside*
there. It resided in the word, which was the mind spoken".

Once this symbolism is established, however, nothing in
particular is done with it; instead, we lapse again into a good
vs. evil paradigm where some cardboard villains—the oily
salesman Shadwell, the evil policeman Inspector Hobart—
attempt to gain control of the carpet either for personal gain
or in order to rule the Weaveworld. Two young people, Cal
and Suzanna, with assistance from various cute denizens
from the Weaveworld, come to the carpet's rescue and save
it from desecration. Indeed, the last two-thirds of the novel is
nothing more than an adventure story relating the battle for
the possession of the carpet—all symbolism pertaining to
the Weaveworld or its appurtenances is dropped. . . .

The remark in *Weaveworld* that the basic "story" of the
weave is "about being born, and being afraid of dying, and
how love saves us", however uninteresting and platitudinous
this is, seems to be the fundamental message of *The Great
and Secret Show*. Here we are involved with a mysterious
"dream-sea" called Quiddity; this appears to us at three critical junctures of our lives: "'It's a dream of what it means to
be born, and fall in love, and die. A dream that explains what
being is for'". The whole of this interminable and tiresome
novel involves the attempts by various good or evil persons
to gain control of Quiddity, which again is nothing more
than a symbol for our imaginations:

> He no longer cared what words were most appropriate for
> this reality [Quiddity]: whether it was another dimension or

a state of mind was not relevant. They were probably one and the same anyhow. What did matter was the *holiness* of this place. He didn't doubt for a moment that all that he'd gleaned about Quiddity and the Ephemeris was true. This was the place in which all his species knew of glory got their glimpses. A constant place; a place of comfort, where the body was forgotten (except for trespassers like himself) and the dreaming soul knew flight, and mystery.

And when we put together statements like this with other such remarks as "The real mystery—the only mystery—is inside our heads" and that one of the villains wants to "own the dreamlife of the world", there is little doubt what the nature of Quiddity is. But the brutal truth is that Barker has not made this entire concept interesting enough to sustain a novel of enormous length, much less the three or four projected sequels he has in mind. If Barker really carries through his threat of writing four or five books the size of this one on a theme that presents such a poverty of interest and complexity, then he may have made the most disastrous mistake of his career. . . .

THE VERDICT ON BARKER

A curious aspect of Barker's work is that the horror in his work revolves wholly around the physical harm that may come to human beings. There is no sign of Lovecraft's "cosmic" vision, where human events are seen against the vast backdrop of the uncaring universe, nor even much of an indication that harm to the physical body may not be the apex of horror. No doubt Barker, by consciously tailoring his work to "mainstream" criteria regarding the importance of human relationships, imagines that this limiting of perspective might render his work more acceptable to the general literary community; but the end result is simply a sense of narrowness in scope and conception. Note that even his most "cosmic" monster—the huge entities in "In the Hills, the Cities"—is made up of human beings; and even this impressive spectacle suffers from a pathetic anticlimax as Barker remarks at a key point in the narrative, "Was there ever a sight in Europe the equal of it?" "Rawhead Rex", although not human, is simply a giant somewhat larger and stronger than a human being; even in *The Damnation Game* all the characters are simply human or (as with Anthony Breer, a loathsome individual resurrected from the dead by Mamoulian) perversions of the human. In Barker's later work it is certainly suggested that the mind controls the body and that therefore the horrors of the mind surpass those of the body; but, firstly, we are still dealing with a human perspective and, secondly, there is still so much physical harm done to the characters that one cannot doubt that this represents Barker's view of the apex of horror.

What, in the end, is the verdict on Clive Barker? The honest truth is that, with the sole exceptions of *The Damnation Game* and a handful of stories, the entirety of his work is marred by poor conception and construction, slipshod writing, excessive violence that serves no aesthetic purpose, and, in general, simply a lack of depth and substance: his later novels make vast pretensions toward profundity but fail utterly to deliver on the promise. If *Weaveworld* effects a fairly convincing union of horror and fantasy, then Barker has seriously erred in embarking on what appears to be an interminable multi-novel series with *The Great and Secret Show*, which shows a complete lack of focus, direction, or purpose. If Barker truly is, as Stephen King claimed, the "future" of horror, then the field is in deep trouble.

Chronology

1764

Horace Walpole's *The Castle of Otranto*, the first Gothic novel, is published.

1787

William Beckford's *Vathek* is published.

1794

Anne Radcliffe's *The Mysteries of Udolpho* is published.

1796

Matthew G. Lewis's *The Monk* is published.

1798

Charles Brockden Brown's *Wieland* is published (the first American Gothic novel).

1816

In Switzerland, on the shores of Lake Geneva, the poets Byron and Shelley, together with Mary Godwin (soon to be Mary Shelley) and John Polidori (Byron's personal physician), engage in horror's most famous storytelling contest.

1818

Mary Shelley's *Frankenstein* is published.

1819

John Polidori's "The Vampyre" is published (the first English vampire story).

1840

Edgar Allan Poe's *Tales of the Grotesque and Arabesque* is published.

1872

J. Sheridan LeFanu's "Carmilla" is published (the first English story featuring a female vampire).

1886

R.L. Stevenson's *The Strange Case of Dr. Jekyll and Mr. Hyde* is published.

1897

Bram Stoker's *Dracula* is published.

1904

M.R. James's *Ghost Stories of an Antiquary* is published.

1921

The first film version of *Dracula* appears: F.W. Murnau's *Nosferatu* (in Germany).

1927

H.P. Lovecraft's *At the Mountains of Madness* is published.

1931

Tod Browning's *Dracula* and James Whale's *Frankenstein* appear.

1954

Jack Finney's *The Body Snatchers* and Richard Matheson's *I Am Legend* are published.

1959

Robert Bloch's *Psycho* is published.

1967

Ira Levin's *Rosemary's Baby* is published.

1971

William Peter Blatty's *The Exorcist* is published.

1974

Stephen King's *Carrie* is published.

1976

Anne Rice's *Interview with the Vampire* is published.

1978

Stephen King's *The Shining* is published.

1984–1985

Clive Barker's six-volume *Books of Blood* series is published.

1987

Thomas Harris's *The Silence of the Lambs* is published.

1999

Thomas Harris's *Hannibal* is published.

FOR FURTHER RESEARCH

GENERAL REFERENCE GUIDES

Neil Barron, *Fantasy and Horror: A Critical and Historical Guide to Literature, Illustration, Film, TV, Radio, and the Internet.* Lanham, MD: Scarecrow, 1999.

Don D'Ammassa, *D'Ammassa's Guide to Modern Horror Fiction.* San Bernardino, CA: Borgo, 1997.

Stephen Jones and Kim Newman, eds., *Horror: The One Hundred Best Books.* New York: Carroll and Graf, 1998.

Kim Newman, ed., *The BFI Companion to Horror.* London: Cassell, 1996.

Jack Sullivan, ed., *The Penguin Encyclopedia of Horror and the Supernatural.* New York: Viking Penguin, 1986.

Marshall B. Tymn, ed., *Horror Literature: A Core Collection and Reference Guide.* New York: Bowker, 1981.

Stanley Wiater, *Dark Thoughts on Writing: Advice and Commentary from Fifty Masters of Fear and Suspense.* Grass Valley, CA: Underwood Books, 1997.

Leonard Wolf, *Horror: A Connoisseur's Guide to Literature and Film.* New York: Facts On File, 1989.

GENERAL CRITICAL STUDIES

Terry Heller, *The Delights of Terror.* Urbana: University of Illinois Press, 1982.

Tony Magistrale and Michael A. Morrison, eds., *A Dark Night's Dreaming: Contemporary American Horror Fiction.* Columbia: University of South Carolina Press, 1996.

Martin Tropp, *Images of Fear: How Horror Stories Helped Shape Modern Culture.* Jefferson, NC: McFarland, 1990.

James B. Twitchell, *Dreadful Pleasures: An Anatomy of Modern Horror.* New York: Oxford University Press, 1985.

STUDIES OF INDIVIDUAL WRITERS

Suzanne J. Barbieri, *Clive Barker: Mythmaker for the Millennium.* London: British Fantasy Society, 1994.

George Beah, ed., *The Stephen King Companion.* Kansas City, MO: Andrews McMeel, 1989.

_____, *Stephen King: America's Best-Loved Boogeyman.* Kansas City, MO: Andrews McMeel, 1998.

Donald Burleson, *Lovecraft: Disturbing the Universe.* Lexington: University Press of Kentucky, 1990.

L. Sprague De Camp, *Lovecraft: A Biography.* Garden City, NY: Doubleday, 1975.

Gary Hoppenstand, *Clive Barker's Short Stories: Imagination as Metaphor in the "Books of Blood" and Other Works.* Jefferson, NC: McFarland, 1994.

Gary Hoppenstand and Ray B. Browne, eds., *The Gothic World of Anne Rice.* Bowling Green, OH: Bowling Green State University Press, 1996.

S.T. Joshi, *H.P. Lovecraft: The Decline of the West.* Gillette, NJ: Wildside, 1990.

Richard Matheson and Ricia Mainhardt, eds., *Robert Bloch: Appreciations of the Master.* New York: Tor Books, 1995.

Katherine Ramsland, *Prism of the Night: An Anne Rice Biography.* New York: Dutton, 1991.

Michael Riley, *Conversations with Anne Rice.* New York: Fawcett Books, 1996.

Kenneth Silverman, ed., *New Essays on Poe's Tales.* New York: Cambridge University Press, 1993.

Stephen J. Spignesi, *The Complete Stephen King Encyclopedia.* Chicago: Contemporary Books, 1991.

THE GOTHIC TRADITION

Valdine Clemens, *The Return of the Repressed: Gothic Horror from "The Castle of Otranto" to Stephen King.* Albany: State University of New York Press, 1999.

Juliann E. Fleenor, ed., *The Female Gothic.* Montreal: Eden, 1983.

Christoph Grunenberg, ed., *Gothic: Transmutations of Horror in Late Twentieth-Century Art.* Cambridge, MA: MIT Press, 1997.

Maggie Kilgour, *The Rise of the Gothic Novel.* New York: Routledge, 1995.

Anne Williams, *The Art of Darkness: A Poetics of Gothic.* Chicago: University of Chicago Press, 1995.

INDEX

primal horde theory of, 129

ghost stories, 21, 32
Godwin, Mary Wollestonecraft. *See*
  Shelley, Mary
Godwin, William, 111, 115–16, 125
Gothics, 17, 66–67
  characters, 66, 69–71, 74, 77
  contemporary, 71
  derivation of term, 63, 73–74
  development of, 74–75
  Dracula as, 127
  and dreams, 78–79
  emotional level of, 16–17
  fear in, 67, 71–72
  feminist criticism of, 70–71
  as feminist picaresques, 119
  grotesque in, 79–80
  horror as objective phenomenon in,
    107
  influence of, 16, 18–19
  natural laws in, 100
  popularity of, 16, 17, 64, 65–66
  prototypes of, 75
  and psychoanalytic theory, 71
  and realism, 75, 76
  repression in, 78
  as romances, 63–64
  and Romanticism, 18, 71, 74
  satire of, 18
  settings, 17, 74, 75
    castles, 62–63, 66, 76–78
    challenge three-dimensional
      space, 77
    decay in, 79
    transgression of boundaries in,
      81–82
  on television, 16
  terror in, 80–81, 102, 107
  themes of, 17, 81
  tone of
    anti-establishment, 82–83
    medieval, 78
  tradition of, in literature, 64–66
  transgression of boundaries in,
    81–82
  unconscious in, 78
  use of history in, 20, 181
  women in, 17, 69–71, 77, 119–20
  see also American Gothics; Female
    Gothics
Great and Secret Show, The (Barker),
  195–98
Griffith, Clark, 101, 104–105
grotesque
  appeal of, 84
    abnormal reaffirms normal, 43–45
  in art, 87, 88–90
  definition of, 85
  in modern literature, 90–92
  and natural laws, 88–89
  primitiveness of, 86–88, 89
  repression of, 86
  terror of, 85–86

as uncanny, 86–89

Haas, Lynda, 179
Haas, Robert, 179
Halloween (film), 38, 55–56
Hammer studios, 22
Hawthorne, Nathaniel, 19, 20, 95–96
"Hellbound Heart, The" (Barker), 192
horror
  appeal of, 42, 172
    catharsis, 24–25, 27, 173
    escapism, 171, 172
    fulfillment of expectations, 51
    psychoanalytic theory of, 25–27
    repulsiveness, 46–48
  Barker and decadence of, 189, 198
  as business, 15–16
  characteristics of, 34–35, 48–49, 53
  classics of, 15, 143
  comics, 39–41
  compared to terror, 81
  conclusions of, 43
  demonstrates power of nature, 69
  described, 11–12
  and dreams, 60, 172–73
  importance of disclosure within
    narrative
    and impossible
      existence of, 49–51, 53
      predictability of , 52, 53
    replusive nature of, 52–53
  influence of films on, 23
  levels of, 39–42
  and Lewis, 67–69
  as literature of extremes, 24
  mass-market novels, 23
  as modern fairy tales, 177
  as objective phenomenon in Gothics,
    107
  of physical harm, 197, 198
  physical reaction to, 39
  prototype, 37–39
  and rational supernaturalism, 174,
    175, 176
  realism in, 70, 171–72, 173–74
  resurgence of interest in, 171
  and shrinking of aesthetic distance,
    25
  as subversive, 176
  transgression of boundaries and
    repression in, 26
  union with fantasy, 195, 198
Hume, David, 48, 49, 50

identification
  primitive fears of, 90
  of reader, 13, 80
images
  blood as, 131–32, 137, 139
  carpets as, 196
  doors as, 146, 155, 175
  games as, 193–95
  sea as, 196–97
imagination

as reflection of imperial decline, 176
and repression of beast within, 144,
   154
as serious literature, 143–44
setting of, 155
structure of, 152
themes of, 21
   doubling/transformation, 144
   identity, 144–46, 149–52, 154–56
   public vs. private lives in Victorian
      England, 144, 145, 146
supernatural
   explanation for
      lack of, 189
      rational, 174–76
   and realism, 81
   in *The Damnation Game*, 193–95
"Supernatural Horror in Literature"
   (Lovecraft), 158
suspension of disbelief, 13, 173

Tales of the Grotesque and Arabesque
   (Poe), 97
Talisman, The (King), 170
"Tartarus of Maids, The" (Melville),
   96–97
terror
   compared to horror, 81
   demonstrates power of mind, 69
   of grotesque, 85–86
   and imagination, 39, 40, 70
   and natural laws, 60
   and Poe, 102–104, 107, 108
   psychological, 127
   and Radcliffe, 67–68, 69
   reader identification with, 80
   and Rice, 67
   in *The Monk*, 103–104
themes
   artifice and masquerade, 176
   birth/creation, 120, 121, 123, 191
   doppelgänger, 21
   doubling/transformation, 144
   identity, 21
      construction of, 186–87
      in *Dracula*, 144
      in *The Strange Case of Dr. Jekyll
         and Mr. Hyde*, 144–46, 149–52,
         154–56
   living dead, 81
   mad scientist, 21, 121
   power of art and imagination,
      195–96
   repression of beast within, 176
   search for meaningful future, 170
   transformation of beast, 21
Them! (film), 34, 59
Thing, The (1951 film), 22, 34, 55
Thing, The (1982 film), 55–56
Totem and Taboo (Freud), 129
Tudor, Andrew, 54, 55
Turn of the Screw (James), 20, 32, 98
Twitchell, James B., 126

unconscious, 25–26, 78

Vampire Chronicles, The (Rice),
   183–84
vampires
   and catharsis, 27
   in *Dracula*, 21, 128
   as enemies of repression, 26–27
   and feminism, 65
   and homoeroticism, 179
   and loss of identity, 14
   and natural laws, 58
   as rejections of time, 81
   of Rice, 183–84, 185–87
"Vampyre, The" (Polidori), 18
Victorian England
   polarities in, 150–51
   political changes in, 144–45
   taboos about sexuality in, 120–21
violence, 23

Walpole, Horace, 15–17
   background of, 63
   importance of, 74
   on origin of *Castle of Otranto*, 78–79
Wandering Jew, 18
Wandrei, Donald, 167, 168
Weaveworld (Barker), 195–96, 198
weird tales, 30, 33
   appeal of, 30
   characteristics of, 33
Weird Tales (magazine), 21, 159, 167
Wells, H.G., 21
werewolves, 14
Wharton, Edith, 98
Wieland, or The Transformation
   (Brown), 95
Williams, Anne, 62
Winter, Douglas E., 169
Wolfson, Susan J., 148
Wollestonecraft, Mary, 111, 114, 125
women
   authors as mothers, 120
   characters
      and gender conflict, 135, 136–37
      in Gothics, 17, 69–71, 77, 119–20
      identification with, by Melville,
         96–97
      and maternity, 69–70
      and misogyny, 69–70
      as monsters, 191
      as New Woman, 65, 134, 140
      as other, 69
      of Poe, 97
      as polyandrous, 136–39
      in postmodern horror films, 56
      as queen, 131–32
      of Rice, 70, 119–20
   feminism, 98, 191–92
   feminist criticism, 70–71

yellow Gothics, 176
"Yellow Wallpaper, The" (Gilman), 32,
   97